ISBN 0-8373-5090-5

90 ADMISSION TEST SERIES

New **RUDMAN'S QUESTIONS AND ANSWERS ON THE...**

CGFNS

COMMISSION ON GRADUATES OF FOREIGN NURSING SCHOOLS QUALIFYING EXAMINATION

D1717252

How to qualify for eligibility to practice Nursing in the United States!
Intensive preparation for the examination including...

- Medical-Surgical Nursing
- Obstetric Nursing
- Pediatric Nursing
- Psychiatric Nursing

- Listening Comprehension
- Vocabulary
- English Grammar

NLC
NATIONAL LEARNING CORPORATION

Copyright © 2004 by

National Learning Corporation

212 Michael Drive, Syosset, New York 11791

(516) 921-8888
Outside N.Y.: 1(800) 645-6337
ORDER FAX: 1(516) 921-8743
www.passbooks.com
email: passbooks @ aol.com
sales @ passbooks.com
info @ passbooks.com

PRINTED IN THE UNITED STATES OF AMERICA

PASSBOOK®
NOTICE

PASSBOOK SERIES®

THE *PASSBOOK SERIES*® has been created to prepare applicants and candidates for the ultimate academic battlefield—the examination room.

At some time in our lives, each and every one of us may be required to take an examination—for validation, matriculation, admission, qualification, registration, certification, or licensure.

Based on the assumption that every applicant or candidate has met the basic formal educational standards, has taken the required number of courses, and read the necessary texts, the *PASSBOOK SERIES*® furnishes the one special preparation which may assure passing with confidence, instead of failing with insecurity. Examination questions— together with answers—are furnished as the basic vehicle for study so that the mysteries of the examination and its compounding difficulties may be eliminated or diminished by a sure method.

This book is meant to help you pass your examination provided that you qualify and are serious in your objective.

The entire field is reviewed through the huge store of content information which is succinctly presented through a provocative and challenging approach—the question-and-answer method.

A climate of success is established by furnishing the correct answers at the end of each test.

You soon learn to recognize types of questions, forms of questions, and patterns of questioning. You may even begin to anticipate expected outcomes.

You perceive that many questions are repeated or adapted so that you gain acute insights, which may enable you to score many sure points.

You learn how to confront new questions, or types of questions, and to attack them confidently and work out the correct answers.

You note objectives and emphases, and recognize pitfalls and dangers, so that you may make positive educational adjustments.

Moreover, you are kept fully informed in relation to new concepts, methods, practices, and directions in the field.

You discover that you are actually taking the examination all the time: you are preparing for the examination by "taking" an examination, not by reading extraneous and/or supererogatory textbooks.

In short, this PASSBOOK®, used directedly, should be an important factor in helping you to pass your test.

COMMISSION ON GRADUATES OF

FOREIGN NURSING SCHOOLS

QUALIFYING EXAMINATION (CGFNS)

The Commission on Graduates of Foreign Nursing Schools-an independent, non-profit organization- screens and examines foreign nursing school graduates while they are still in their own countries to determine their probable eligibility for professional practice in the United States.

The need for CGFNS certification is vital for the would-be nurse:

1. In order to practice professional nursing in the U.S. , an applicant must pass a licensing examination in one of the 50 states, the District of Columbia, Guam, or the Virgin Islands.

2. CGFNS tries to help foreign nursing school graduates to determine their probable qualification as full-fledged professional nurses in the U.S.A. *before* they leave their own countries. CGFNS test sites have been set up in the U.S.A. for foreign nurses *already* in the U.S. who need the CGFNS certificate for visa status.

3. The CGFNS Examination is *not* to be considered a substitute for the state board licensing examination. Even after passing the CGFNS Examination, applicants will still be required to sit for the state board examinations in the United States.

4. Obtaining a CGFNS Certificate, signifying a passing grade, *is* a requirement to obtain a non-immigrant occupational preference visa (H-1) from the U.S. Immigration and Naturalization Service. In addition, the CGFNS Certificate is a requirement in order to obtain an immigrant occupational preference visa and a labor certificate (work permit) from a U.S. Labor Department regional office.

5. Passing the CGFNS Examination is the first step to be taken by a foreign nursing school graduate who wishes to practice nursing in the U.S.

6. In most states, the CGFNS Certificate is also a requirement in order to take the state board licensing exam.

The CGFNS Qualifying Examination is sponsored by the two leading nursing organizations in the United States, namely, the American Nurses' Association and the National League for Nursing. It is given twice a year- in April and October- throughout the world on the same day.

While the CGFNS Examination contains two sections- Nursing Practice and English comprehension- both parts of the examination are given in the English (American) language and are required of all candidates. The examination takes up one full day.

CONTENTS OF THE EXAMINATION

In the Nursing area, the CGFNS covers medical and surgical, obstetric, pediatric, and psychiatric nursing, the fields of nursing which are required of registered nurses (first level) in the United States and which are included in state licensing examinations.

In the English area, the examination covers listening comprehension of English, vocabulary, and English grammar. All questions are of the multiple-choice type in English.

To obtain application forms for the examination, write:

Commission on Graduates of Foreign Nursing Schools (CGFNS)
3624 Market St.
Philadelphia, Pennsylvania   19104   U.S.A.

NURSING
CAREER DESCRIPTIONS

CONTENTS

NURSING

In the field of health, nursing plays a vital role in providing essential services to individuals and families in health-care facilities, schools, at play, and on-the-job. Caring for the sick is not the only function of contemporary nursing, however; nursing practice is equally concerned with the prevention of illness and the promotion of health in general.

The scientific aspects of modern nursing often provide the challenge desired by individuals, both male and female, who are making career choices. Today's nurse must understand patients' social and psychological needs; have a knowlege of complex drugs and their side effects; be familiar with modern techniques of treatment and rehabilitation; and be capable of using complex medical equipment. To meet these demands the individual must have a sound educational background in the humanities, the physical and social sciences, and the behavioral and biological sciences.

The nursing field offers a variety of careers, including such positions as registered nurse (RN), nurse anesthetist, nurse-midwife, nurse practitioner, and licensed practical or vocational nurse (LPN/LVN). Other jobs closely associated with this field are nurse's aide and homemaker-home health aide.

Registered nurses are an essential part of the health team and work primarily on hospital staffs, providing direct patient care. Some RN's engage in private duty, public health, industrial, or school nursing, while others work in physicians' offices and government agencies.

Nurse anesthetists are registered nurses (RN's) qualified by special training to administer anesthesia to patients. Working under the supervision of a physician, they are employed primarily by hospitals but also perform services in out-patient clinics, health-care facilities, dental clinics, and all branches of the military services.

Nurse-midwives are registered nurses (RN's) qualified by special training and experience in obstetrics to provide care for apparently normal expectant mothers and newborn infants.

Nurse practitioners are registered nurses (RN's) who have completed additional specialized medical training. They are middle-level health workers qualified to perform tasks usually performed by a physician, and work in physicians' offices, clinics, schools, homes, and hospital outpatient departments.

Licensed practical or vocational nurses (LPN/LVN's) provide basic nursing care to patients, under the direction of a licensed physician or registered nurse. They are important members of the health team and work in hospitals, nursing homes, extended-care facilities, physicians' offices, clinics, private homes, and schools.

Nurse's aides work under the supervision of nursing and medical staff while assisting in the care of patients in a health-care facility. Typical duties include serving meals, feeding patients, giving baths, responding to patient calls, and transporting patients to treatment units within the health facility.

Homemaker-home health aides are important members of a community agency's health and welfare team. Working in private homes, under the supervision of a nurse or social worker, they provide essential personal and homemaking services to ill, elderly, or disabled persons unable to care for themselves.

These positions are discussed in greater detail in the following section.

I. Homemaker-Home Health Aide

Homemaker-home health aides are paraprofessionals. As members of a community agency's health and welfare team they provide personal and homemaking services to ill, elderly, or disabled persons and to children of families unable to perform basic tasks for themselves. Their assistance enables the people served to remain in their own homes. The responsibilities of homemaker-home health aides include assisting with bathing or giving bed baths, helping patients with walking and prescribed exercises, and helping individuals with braces or artificial limbs. Aides check pulse and respiration rates, change surgical dressings, and assist patients with medications. They also change bed linens, do laundry, and clean patients' living quarters. Aides plan and prepare meals and special diets for the family and patient and do food shopping. They observe the patient's progress or lack of it, report findings to their supervisors, and help the professional health team to determine if services should be changed. Their supervisors are usually registered nurses but in some cases they are physical, speech, or occupational therapists, or social workers.

In addition to their regular duties, aides provide patients with instruction and emotional support. They teach, through practical demonstration, such things as preparation of nutritious meals on a limited income, proper care of children, and household management. Aides teach clients how to adapt to various limitations in their lifestyles caused by disability, frailty, or illness. During periods of stress or depression they provide emotional support which is often critical to the patient's recovery and mental attitude. Aides are employed by public-health and welfare departments, private health-care agencies, nonprofit community health and social service organizations, and some hospitals and nursing homes. Physical duties include lifting, moving, and supporting patients. Aides work alone in the patient's home and must be able to travel to and from work assignments. Aides work full or part-time, including weekends, and usually can obtain flexible work schedules from the employing agency.

Job Requirements

There are no formal educational requirements for this work except that the individual must be able to read and write. The employing agency usually provides a pre-service training program lasting a minimum of from 40 to 120 hours or more, which covers such subject areas as basic nutrition; meal planning and preparation; and techniques for bathing, turning, and lifting patients. Other subject areas include emotional problems associated with illness, the aging process and behavior of the elderly, supervision, and participation in case conferences. Some employing agencies require training and experience as a nursing aide.

There are no licensure, certification, or continuing education requirements for this job. A certificate indicating completion of a required training course does not constitute a license or certification as a private practitioner. As a paraprofessional, this worker functions only under professional supervision.

Opportunities

The number of jobs for homemaker-home health aides is expected to grow rapidly through the 1980's This estimate is based on growing public awareness of these services and increases in monies to pay for them, as States reconsider their expenditure of social-service funds. If new legislation permits public health plans, such as Medicare or national health insurance, to pay for long-term care, the increase in the number of jobs will be even greater. An aide with substantial experience in different types of cases may be promoted to an assistant supervisory position. The assistant supervisor assumes some of the supervisor's responsibility with regard to the more routine parts of supervision and case management.

For further information, contact:
National Council for Homemaker-Home Health Aide Services, Inc.

II.

Licensed Practical Nurse

Licensed vocational nurse

Licensed practical nurses (LPN's) or licensed vocational nurses (LVN's) work under the direction of a licensed physician or registered nurse or dentist. They provide bedside nursing care for the ill, injured, convalescent, and the handicapped in a medical facility or in the patient's home. In addition, LPN/LVN's assist the registered nurse with patients who are seriously ill. Typical duties include taking temperatures, blood pressure, and pulse and respiration rates and recording these data on the patient's chart. These nurses assist patients with personal hygiene and prepare them for medical examinations. They give injections, apply compresses, change surgical dressings, administer prescribed medications, and record the time and dosage on patients' charts.

LPN/LVN's observe and record pertinent information and report significant symptoms, reactions, and changes in the patient's condition to the appropriate person. These nurses assist physicians in performing therapeutic and diagnostic procedures and participate in the planning, implementation, and evaluation of nursing care. They assist with patient and family rehabilitation by providing emotional support, teaching self-care techniques, and suggesting the use of community resources. They often work in specialized activities, such as pediatrics; obstetrics; coronary care; intensive care; hemodialysis; or operating, recovery, or emergency rooms. When necessary, they gain additional training through continuing education, special courses, in-service training, or on-the-job training.

Licensed practical nurses work in hospitals, nursing homes, extended care facilities, day-care centers, physicians' or dentists' offices, clinics, homes, schools, camps, industrial establishments, public and home-health agencies, and correctional institutions. They work closely with patients, patients' families, and other health-care personnel, and must be physically able to spend prolonged periods of time walking and standing. LPN/LVN's are required to lift and turn patients regularly. Working conditions include exposure to infection, communicable diseases, unpleasant odors and sights, and various types of patient behavior.

Job Requirements

Candidates for this career are required to complete a 12- to 18-month course in a State-approved training facility. Educational requirements for entry into these schools vary from State to State, but the preferred level of education is completion of high school. However, some States permit candidates with 10th grade education to enter these training schools. Most schools require applicants to pass a written entrance examination as well as a complete physical examination. Training programs are offered in community colleges, public and private schools, hospitals, and health agencies.

Training programs consist of classroom instruction and clinical practice in basic nursing, medical-surgical nursing, obstetrics, pediatrics, and geriatrics. Classroom training includes anatomy, physiology, nutrition, community health, and human relations.

All States have laws for the licensing of practical nurses as LPN's (or LVN, licensed vocational nurse in California and Texas). Most States require graduation from an approved school to qualify for the State board exam for licensure. It is therefore important that the student choose a State-approved school. Graduates from correspondence schools are not eligible to take the licensing examination.

In addition, schools may be accredited by the National League for Nursing (NLN) or by the National Association for Practical Nurse Education and Service (NAPNES). The standards set by these organizations for accreditation are generally higher than those required for State approval.

LPN's as well as students enrolled in practical nursing courses may become members of the National Federation of Licensed Practical Nurses and of the National Association for Practical Nurse Education and Service (NAPNES). Both work toward the professional development of LPN's and also work in cooperation with allied health career groups in providing health-care services.

Opportunities

The employment outlook for LPN/LVN's is good through the next decade. The LPN/LVN provides approximately 80 percent of the bedside nursing care in the United States. Population increases, greater emphasis on private and public insurance plans, plus expanded programs for the aged are expected to broaden opportunities for these workers, especially in geriatric and acute-care health facilities. An LPN/LVN may advance to registered nurse after completing studies in an accredited school of professional nursing and passing the State licensing examination. Most bachelor's degree nursing programs give the LPN little or no advanced credit for previous training and experience. Many associate degree programs, however, permit the LPN/LVN to take a special "challenge" examination. On successful completion of a challenge examination, the LPN/LVN receives advanced standing credit.

For further information, contact:
National Association for Practical Nurse Education and
    Service
American Nurses' Association
National League for Nursing
The National Federation of Licensed Practical Nurses,
    Inc.

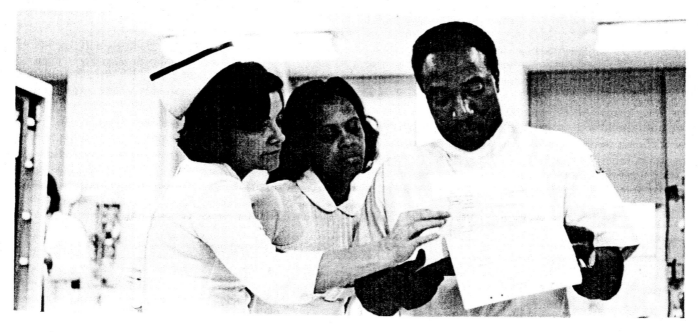

Nurse's Aide

Hospital attendant
Nursing assistant
Orderly

Nurse's aides, working under the direction of nursing and medical staff, assist in the care of patients in a health facility. They answer patients' signal lights or bell calls to determine service needed and bathe, dress, and undress patients. They serve food, feed patients requiring help, and collect food trays after meals. They transport patients to treatment units in wheelchairs or assist them in walking.

Aides drape patients prior to examinations or treatments and remain with patients, performing such duties as holding instruments and adjusting and positioning lights. They dust and clean patients' rooms, change bed linens, deliver messages, and direct visitors. Nurse's aides also take and record temperature, pulse, and respiration rates and food and liquid intake and output, as directed. They also give massages and apply compresses.

Most nurse's aides work in hospitals, but they are also employed in nursing or convalescent homes and other long-term care facilities. The average workweek is 40 hours with shift and weekend work usually required. This work involves extended periods of walking and standing and also requires lifting and moving patients and equipment. Working conditions are usually good, but nurse's aides, like other members of the nursing team, are often exposed to communicable diseases and unpleasant odors and sights.

Job Requirements

Candidates for this work must be at least 17 years old and have completed a minimum of 8 years of education, although some employers prefer persons with high school training. In addition, candidates must be tactful, neat, patient, emotionally stable, and have a genuine desire to help people. They should also be in good health and be able to pass a qualifying physical examination. Most employers conduct on-the-job training programs which last from several weeks to a few months.

Opportunities

Employment prospects for nurse's aides are expected to be good during the next decade. This is based on the public demand for expanded health services, increases in population, and a greater awareness of the medical needs of our country's elderly.

Opportunities for advancement are limited for nurse's aides unless further training is secured. With specialized training they may prepare for such jobs as licensed practical nurse (LPN) or respiratory therapy technician. Training for these positions is sometimes available through the employing health facility.

For further information, contact:
American Hospital Association
Your local hospitals or nursing homes

IV. Nurse Anesthetist

Certified registered nurse anesthetist

The nurse anesthetist is a registered nurse (RN) who is qualified, by virtue of special training, to administer anesthesia. Working under the direction of a physician, the nurse anesthetist administers intravenous, spinal, and other anesthetics which make the patient insensible to pain during surgical, obstetrical, and dental procedures. In conjunction with the physician, the nurse anesthetist evaluates the patient's condition and selects the proper anesthetic to be used. During the surgical procedure, the nurse anesthetist closely observes the patient's condition by checking vital signs and watches for significant changes in the patient's physical condition. The nurse anesthetist also provides patient care in the immediate post-operative period and submits a report to the physician when the anesthetic effects have subsided. In addition, nurse anesthetists frequently assist in the care of critically ill patients in intensive care, coronary units, and emergency rooms. Some nurse anesthetists work in the field of education or engage in research activities, while others do administrative work related to anesthesiology.

Nurse anesthetists work primarily in hospitals but also are employed in out-patient clinics, health-care facilities, dental clinics, and all branches of the military services. Nurse anesthetists work closely with physicians, patients, and other medical personnel, and the nature of this work requires that they be available to work irregular hours, including evenings, holidays, and weekends.

Job Requirements

Preparation for this career includes completion of high school and graduation from an approved school of professional nursing. Candidates must hold a current license as a registered nurse (RN) and are often required to have 2 years of nursing experience in the care of acutely ill patients.

Training for nurse anesthetists is offered in certain accredited hospitals and universities and lasts approximately 24 months. The curriculum is divided between academic and clinical areas. Academic studies include courses in anatomy, physiology, biochemistry, and pharmacology. The clinical studies center on techniques and procedures used in the administration of anesthesia. On satisfactory completion of this course of study, the individual is granted a certificate by the school.

All states and the District of Columbia require a registered nurse (RN) license to practice as a nurse anesthetist. This license is issued by the State board of nursing after the individual passes a State-administered examination. Persons who wish to receive certification as a Certified Registered Nurse Anesthetist (CRNA) must do so through the American Association of Nurse Anesthetists. To qualify, the individual must be a registered nurse, be a graduate of an accredited school for nurse anesthetists, and successfully pass a national qualifying examination. Certification is not required by law; however, the CRNA credential is generally recognized as proof of professional qualification. The AANA has a continuing education program which operates on a 2-year basis for continued certification.

Opportunities

Opportunities for nurse anesthetists are growing steadily as a result of increases in new hospital construction, expansion of existing health-care facilities, increases in population, and demands for greater medical services throughout the country. Opportunities for advancement in this field are numerous. For example, a nurse anesthetist who acquires sufficient experience, training, and advanced education may advance to chief of a department or section to a director's position in a school for nurse anesthetists or to a teaching position in an accredited university.

For further information, contact:
American Association of Nurse Anesthetists

V. Nurse-Midwife

Certified nurse-midwife

A nurse-midwife is a registered nurse (RN) who has successfully completed a recognized program of study and clinical experience in obstetrics and is qualified to provide care for apparently normal expectant mothers. Nurse-midwives furnish professional care during the pregnancy, labor, delivery, and after-birth phases for both the mother and newborn infant.

During prenatal care, nurse-midwives perform total physical examinations of expectant mothers, including breast examinations, abdominal and pelvic examinations and evaluations, and Pap-smear tests. They provide warmth and support to the woman in labor, encouraging her to participate in the birth process according to her wishes and ability. As long as the course of labor is normal, nurse-midwives manage the labor and perform the delivery. The obstetrician is consulted whenever there is any change from the normal. Treatments and medications such as sedatives and pain-relieving drugs are prescribed by nurse-midwives in accordance with the physician's and hospital's approved orders for nurse-midwifery service.

During delivery, nurse-midwives perform various technical procedures and assist mothers during the different stages of labor. After the birth, they provide immediate care for the newborn, perform simple resuscitation on the child if necessary, and are responsible for signing birth certificates. Nurse-midwives provide support and reassurance to mothers at times of infant feeding, emphasizing an early positive mother-newborn relationship. In addition, they provide examinations for mothers after they give birth and counsel and instruct those seeking birth control or family-planning information.

Nurse-midwives are never independent practitioners; they function as part of the obstetrical team. They manage and provide direct patient care, using delegated medical authority, in municipal and voluntary hospitals as well as with obstetrical groups for private patients. Many nurse-midwives have used their preparation in nurse-midwifery as background for employment in jobs as maternal and child-health consultants in Federal, State, and local health departments; as supervisors and administrators of maternity-care services; in parent education relating to childbirth; as professors and instructors of maternity nursing on all levels of nursing education; as teachers of nurse-midwifery; and in positions in the various branches of the armed forces.

The nature of nurse-midwifery practice requires these nurses to work closely with clients and their families, doctors, nurses and other health-care personnel. They frequently work long hours, sometimes on-call. Extra teaching and public-service activities, as well as the unpredictability of the obstetric specialty, often result in night, weekend, and holiday duties in addition to regularly scheduled clinic and patient rounds. Nurse-midwives must be in good physical condition to provide patient support during labor and birth, and must often lift, stoop, apply counter pressure, and do massages during the normal course of work.

Job Requirements

Preparation for this career is available at the post RN level and master's degree level. The post RN programs are of approximately 8 months' duration and provide an intensive program of theory and clinical experience leading to a certificate in nurse-midwifery. The master's degree programs are 12 to 24 months long and offer the graduate student an opportunity to earn a certificate in nurse-midwifery in conjunction with a master's degree. Most schools consider it advisable for applicants to have clinical experience in obstetrical nursing prior to entering an educational program of nurse-midwifery.

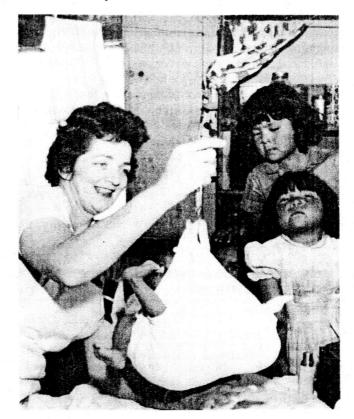

Eighteen schools of nurse-midwifery are approved by the American College of Nurse-Midwives, which means that their graduates are eligible to take the national certification examination administered by the American College of Nurse-Midwives (ACNM), and upon passing the examination, the graduates are then entitled to use the official CNM (Certified Nurse-Midwife) after their names.

The license to practice nurse-midwifery is determined by the jurisdiction or State in which the nurse-midwife is employed. Laws providing separate licensure for nurse-midwives are currently in effect in the following States: Arizona, Florida, Kentucky, Montana, New Jersey, New Mexico, New York, Ohio, Pennsylvania, Utah, Virginia, and West Virginia, plus Puerto Rico, Guam, and the Virgin Islands. In order to determine exact legal standards, individuals are urged to contact the local or State authorities responsible for professional licensure.

Opportunities

The employment prospects for qualified nurse-midwives, both male and female, are quite favorable. There is a shortage of trained personnel in obstetrics and gynecology, especially in rural areas, and the current consumer demand for quality health care should create increased demand. In addition, as obstetricians specialize to a greater degree and have less time for normal, uncomplicated pregnancy cases, maternity patients can be served efficiently by nurse-midwives acting as part of the medical team. Advancement in this field is based on experience, education, and skill level, and nurse-midwives with master's or doctoral degrees may advance to high-level administrative and academic positions.

For further information, contact:
American College of Nurse-Midwives
Maternity Center Association

VI. Nurse Practitioner

Nurse clinician

Nurse practitioners are registered nurses (RN's) with additional, specialized medical training, who are qualified to perform certain medical duties normally performed by a physician. They provide medical services to patients to maintain good health, prevent illness, or deal effectively with acute or chronic health problems. The majority of nurse practitioners are associated with individual physicians, medical groups, or hospital clinics and out-patient departments. In rural areas, where physicians are available only on a limited basis, practitioners must exercise independent judgment consistent with sound medical practice.

Nurse practitioners interview clients, record their health histories, and judge physical condition by conducting routine physical examinations. They perform diagnostic tests, examine patients for symptoms of disorders, and take appropriate action to treat common ailments. They give injections and recommend routine medications. Nurse practitioners evaluate medical information and develop treatment plans and carry them

out through health counseling, referrals to appropriate agencies, and collaboration with other health-care providers.

Nurse practitioners can enter private practice in some States. They offer skilled nursing care to the members of the community, make home visits, and have regular office hours. They perform such tasks as giving injections prescribed by the patient's physician, changing dressings, and counseling diabetics and persons with high blood pressure. In some States, nurse practitioners are permitted to take X-rays, set simple fractures, and suture minor cuts.

Nurse practitioners often work in specialty areas. Maternal-child nurse practitioners, for example, perform vaginal examinations, take Pap smears, and provide patients with counseling during pregnancy and after childbirth.

Pediatric nurse practitioners specialize in providing health care to children. They evaluate a child's health by judging growth, development, and physical condition, taking into account such factors as family makeup; physical environment; and social, economic, religious, and ethnic background. Using this information the practitioner determines the child's needs and problems and plans appropriate action such as medical consultation or referral to appropriate health care personnel.

The adult and family nurse practitioner specializes in providing health-care services to the total family unit, which can consist of adults with children, adults without children, and individual adults. The primary aim of this practitioner is to help the family attain good health through primary prevention techniques, health restoration activities, and practices aimed at maintaining good health.

The working conditions for nurse practitioners vary with the employment setting, but in general they are good. Most nurse practitioners work regular daytime hours. However, those employed in private homes are often called on to work irregular schedules, including weekends and evenings. Nurse practitioners work closely with their patients and must be able to develop good working relationships with other health professionals.

Job Requirements

Nurse practitioner training varies widely; it is provided in hospitals, colleges, and universities. Some bachelor's degree programs in registered nursing prepare students to assume roles as nurse practitioners on graduation. Other programs admit registered nurses and range from several months of formal education and clinical experience to a master's degree. In addition, some institutions require that the candidate be sponsored by a practicing physician, commonly known as a preceptor. The training program is composed of classroom work and clinical internship. Classroom work consists of programs of concentrated study in nursing theory and practice. The internship or preceptorship takes place in the clinical practice setting under the supervision of a licensed physician. The classroom and preceptorship portions of the training are usually coordinated so that the classroom instruction can take place under supervised clinical conditions, enabling the student to develop and demonstrate clinical competency.

Most training institutions grant a certificate on completion of the program. However, some schools offer students who qualify the opportunity to earn bachelor or master's degrees. The master's level program requires from 18 to 24 months of additional study beyond the bachelor's level. The school accrediting organization, in all cases, is the American Nurses' Association.

All nurse practitioners must be currently licensed as registered nurses (RN's), and since State laws govern services the practitioner can provide, it is suggested that the appropriate agency be contacted to determine current standards for practice.

Opportunities

The need for nurse practitioners qualified to provide primary care services is expected to grow; currently, the demand for nurse practitioners exceeds the supply available. Since this is a relatively new occupation in the health field, information on promotion or advancement prospects is not available. However, as this area of specialization grows, practitioners with substantial experience and higher levels of advanced education will find broader opportunities for advancement.

For further information, contact:
American Nurses Association, Inc.

VII.

Registered Nurse

Registered nurses (RN's) are an essential part of the health team and assist individuals with activities and patterns of behavior that promote recovery from illness. They help individuals to develop patterns of healthy living and to function independently. By means of a nursing diagnosis, nurses make a comprehensive assessment of the patient's total behavior, including psycho-social aspects, i.e., patient's interaction with family members. They also administer prescribed drugs, give injections, and provide treatments either when indicated or as directed by the physician. Nurses observe the patient's progress, record pertinent behavioral observations, and report reactions to drugs and treatments. They also assist the physician with treatments and examinations and prepare instruments and equipment for use. They are responsible for executing physician's orders and for supervising auxiliary nursing and other health personnel who perform routine care and treatment of patients.

Most nurses are employed as hospital staff nurses and provide direct patient care. Others are in private duty, public health, industrial or school nursing, or work in physicians' offices, community centers, nursing homes,

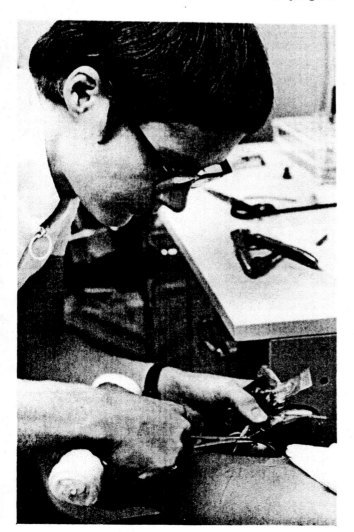

and rehabilitation centers. Areas of specialization require advanced education, as is demonstrated in the following examples: Gerontological nurses specialize in providing full nursing service to elderly patients in hospitals, nursing homes, clinics, and extended-care facilities. This specialty is relatively new, and greater emphasis is now being devoted to gerontological techniques in most nursing schools. Occupational health nurses, also known as industrial nurses, work in business, industry and government and provide for the overall health needs of employees. Duties include treating minor injuries and illnesses, assisting with physical examinations, and arranging for medical care. Intensive/critical-care nurses provide nursing services to acutely ill patients whose conditions require special attention. Nurses in this specialization are required to complete additional technical courses.

Medical-surgical nurses care for patients with acute and chronic medical problems and those recovering from surgery. Obstetrical nurses provide professional care to newborn infants and their mothers in the labor and delivery room, prenatal consultation, and care of mother and baby immediately after delivery. Operating room nurses are responsible for coordinating operating room nursing activities during surgical procedures. They also supervise other health workers in the operating room, such as scrub technicians and aides. Pediatric nurses specialize in providing care to children in hospitals, clinics, and schools. Psychiatric and mental health nurses, who have advanced training in mental health techniques, provide nursing care to patients with mental disorders. They usually work in private or government-operated psychiatric facilities and mental health clinics, although some have independent prac-

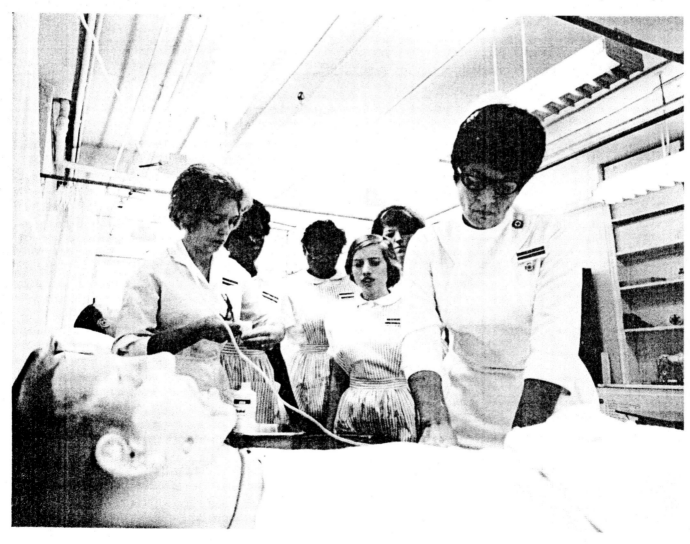

tices. Public health nurses assist nonhospitalized patients by providing nursing services and health counseling in private homes, clinics, community health centers, and schools. Restoring health, preventing illness, and carrying out good health practices are basic aims of this work. Duties include routine examinations, administering immunization shots, and recommending appropriate community resources to patients. The basic educational requirement for this work is graduation from a baccalaureate program in nursing. Rehabilitation nurses provide care and nursing services to patients in special hospital units or rehabilitation centers. The objective is assisting these patients to achieve their maximum level of health following serious illness or injury. School nurses plan and carry out, with the cooperation of school officials, the policies, standards, and objectives of the school health program. Most schools require such nurses to have at least a baccalaureate degree in nursing.

Registered nurses work closely with their patients and other health professionals and health workers, They must be able to communicate effectively with these individuals and be capable of dealing with changing or unexpected situations. The working hours of registered nurses are determined basically by the place of employment. The average workweek is 40 hours but nurses working in hospitals, nursing homes, or in private duty are usually required to work rotating shifts including weekends. Those working in schools, industry, and physicians' offices have more regular schedules. Nursing is demanding both mentally and physically and involves substantial amounts of standing and walking.

Job Requirements

Applicants for nursing programs must be 17 or 18 years of age. The maximum age limit depends on the individual applicant and the school. Most schools of professional nursing have strict admission requirements and will accept only applicants with excellent academic records.

Professional nursing schools fall into three general categories: junior or community-college schools offering a 2-year associate degree program; hospital schools of nursing offering a 2- to 3-year diploma program; and colleges offering a 4-year baccalaureate program. All three types require graduation from high school, pre-entrance examinations, and a physical

examination. Their programs cover the nursing arts and sciences, which form an essential background for nursing practice.

The associate degree program (2 years) includes general education courses, especially science at the junior or community-college level, in addition to nursing theory and practice, which includes supervised clinical experience working with patients in hospitals or other health facilities. The associate degree program is designed to stand alone and is not necessarily the first half of a 4-year bachelor's program. The diploma program is the only one conducted in a hospital. Training takes between 2 and 3 years and consists of general education courses, classroom instruction in nursing techniques and theory, and supervised clinical practice in hospitals or health facilities. The graduate of an associate degree or diploma program is known as a "technical nurse." Once licensed, a technical nurse is qualified to provide direct patient care requiring a high degree of technical nursing skill. Technical nurses are fully prepared to work with doctors and other health-team members to carry out treatment plans and meet the needs of patients.

Four-year baccalaureate programs leading to a bachelor's degree in nursing (BSN) are offered by colleges or universities. These programs consist of classroom studies in liberal arts, physical and social sciences, the humanities, and nursing. In addition, they include supervised clinical training working with patients in hospitals, clinics, community health centers, and nursing homes. A graduate of a 4-year program is a "professional nurse." In addition to providing traditional patient care, such nurses are prepared for assignments requiring independent judgment. These assignments may include health education, counseling, supervision, and administration.

It would be helpful to plan for a career in nursing as early as possible—even in the first or second years of high school. Since most nursing schools receive more applications than they can accept, it is advisable to apply by the end of the junior year. The National League for Nursing (NLN) maintains its own national accrediting program. Accredited programs must meet educational standards for faculty and curriculum above minimum standards set by State boards of nursing. Prospective students should try to select baccalaureate, diploma, or graduate programs accredited by NLN.

A license is required to practice professional nursing in all 50 States and the Districts of Columbis. In order to qualify for a license, the applicant must be a graduate of a State approved school of nursing and pass an examination administered by the State board of nursing. Students passing the State licensing examination are permitted to practice in the State and to identify themselves as registered nurses, using the initials RN after their names. Some nurses are licensed in more than one State, either by qualifying on an examination or through special agreements among States. Some States have begun to require evidence of continuing education as a condition for relicensing.

Registered nurses may become members of the American Nurses' Association. Along with friends of the nursing field, practical nurses, allied professional people, and others interested in health care, they may join the National League for Nursing, which provides them with an opportunity to work together with other people in their communities for the improvement of nursing education and nursing service. Professional nursing students have their own organization, the National Student Nurses Association.

Opportunities

Generally, employment opportunities for registered nurses are expected to be favorable in the next several years, and, at present, in most parts of the country nurses can obtain employment without difficulty. Employment prospects, however, are expected to be best for nurses with bachelor or graduate degrees.

Professional nurses with graduate degrees can advance to positions as administrators, teachers, clinical nurse specialists, nurse scientists, or independent practitioners. Clinical nurse specialists, for example, complete a master's program in a selected area of nursing and develop advanced technical and nursing skills. Nurse scientists have doctorate degrees in nursing combined with basic science and engage in research to improve the health of mankind and to promote nursing as a profession.

For further information, contact:
National League for Nursing
American Association of Occupational Health Nurses
Association of Operating Room Nurses
National Male Nurse Association
National Student Nurses Association

HOW TO TAKE A TEST

You have studied hard, long, and conscientiously.

With your official admission card in hand, and your heart pounding, you have been admitted to the examination room.

You note that there are several hundred other applicants in the examination room waiting to take the same test.

They all appear to be equally well prepared.

You know that nothing but your best effort will suffice. The "moment of truth" is at hand: you now have to demonstrate objectively, in writing, your knowledge of content and your understanding of subject matter.

You are fighting the most important battle of your life — to pass and/or score high on an examination which will determine your career and provide the economic basis for your livelihood.

What extra, special things should you know and should you do in taking the examination?

BEFORE THE TEST

YOUR PHYSICAL CONDITION IS IMPORTANT

If you are not well, you can't do your best work on tests. If you are half asleep, you can't do your best either. Here are some tips:

1. Get about the same amount of sleep you usually get. Don't stay up all night before the test, either partying or worrying — DON'T DO IT.

2. If you wear glasses, be sure to wear them when you go to take the test. This goes for hearing aids, too.

3. If you have any physical problems that may keep you from doing your best, be sure to tell the person giving the test. If you are sick or in poor health, you really cannot do your best on any test. You can always come back and take the test some other time.

AT THE TEST

EXAMINATION TECHNIQUES

1. Read the *general* instructions carefully. These are usually printed on the first page of the examination booklet. As a rule, these instructions refer to the timing of the examination; the fact that you should not start work until the signal and must stop work at a signal, etc. If there are any *special* instructions, such as a choice of questions to be answered, make sure that you note this instruction carefully.

2. When you are ready to start work on the examination, that is as soon as the signal has been given, read the instructions to each question booklet, underline any key words or phrases, such as *least, best, outline, describe,* and the like. In this way you will tend to answer as requested rather than discover on reviewing your paper that you *listed without describing,* that you selected the *worst* choice rather than the *best* choice, etc.

3. If the examination is of the objective or so-called multiple-choice type, that is, each question will also give a series of possible answers: A, B, C, or D, and you are called upon to select the best answer and write the letter next to that answer on your answer paper, it is advisable to start answering each question in turn. There may be anywhere from 50 to 100 such questions in the three or four hours allotted and you can see how much time would be taken if you read through all the questions before beginning to answer any. Furthermore, if you come across a question or a group of questions which you know would be difficult to answer, it would undoubtedly affect your handling of all the other questions.

4. If the examination is of the essay-type and contains but a few questions, it is a moot point as to whether you should read all the questions before starting to answer any one. Of course if you are given a choice, say five out of seven and the like, then it is essential to read all the questions so you can eliminate the two which are most difficult. If, however, you are asked to answer all the questions, there may be danger in trying to answer the easiest one first because you may find that you will spend too much time on it. The best technique is to answer the first question, then proceed to the second, etc.

5. Time your answers. Before the examination begins, write down the time it started, then add the time allowed for the examination and write down the time it must be completed, then divide the time available somewhat as follows:

   a. If 3½ hours are allowed, that would be 210 minutes. If you have 80 objective-type questions, that would be an average of about 2½ minutes per question. Allow yourself no more than 2 minutes per question, or a total of 160 minutes, which will permit about 50 minutes to review.

   b. If for the time allotment of 210 minutes, there are 7 essay questions to answer, that would average about 30 minutes a question. Give yourself only 25 minutes per question so that you have about 35 minutes to review.

6. **The most important instruction is** *to read each question* and make sure you know what is wanted. The second most important instruction is to *time yourself properly* so that you answer every question. The third most important instruction is to *answer every question.* Guess if you have to but include something for each question, Remember that you will receive no credit for a blank and will probably receive some credit if you write something in answer to an essay question. If you guess a letter, say "B" for a multiple-choice question, you may have guessed right. If you leave a blank as the answer to a multiple-choice question, the examiners may respect your feelings but it will not add a point to your score. Some exams may penalize you for wrong answers, so in such cases *only*, you may not want to guess unless you have some basis for your answer.

7. Suggestions

   a. Objective-Type Questions

      (1) Examine the question booklet for proper sequence of pages and questions.

      (2) Read all instructions carefully.

      (3) Skip any question which seems too difficult; return to it after all other questions have been answered.

      (4) Apportion your time properly; do not spend too much time on any single question or group of questions.

      (5) Note and underline key words — *all, most, fewest, least, best, worst, same, opposite.*

      (6) Pay particular attention to negatives.

      (7) Note unusual option, e.g., unduly long, short, complex, different or similar in content to the body of the question.

      (8) Observe the use of "hedging" words — *probably, may, most likely, etc.*

      (9) Make sure that your answer is put next to the same number as the question.

      (10) Do not second guess unless you have good reason to believe the second answer is definitely more correct.

      (11) Cross out original answer if you decide another answer is more accurate; do not erase, *until* you are ready to hand your paper in.

      (12) Answer all questions; guess unless instructed otherwise.

      (13) **Leave time for review.**

b. Essay-Type Questions

(1) Read each question carefully.

(2) Determine exactly what is wanted. Underline key words or phrases.

(3) Decide on outline or paragraph answer.

(4) Include many different points and elements unless asked to develop any one or two points or elements.

(5) Show impartiality by giving pros and cons unless directed to select one side only.

(6) Make and write down any assumptions you find necessary to answer the question.

(7) Watch your English, grammar, punctuation, choice of words.

(8) Time your answers; don't crowd material.

8. Answering the Essay Question

Most essay questions can be answered by framing the specific response around several key words or ideas. Here are a few such key words or ideas:

M's: manpower, materials, methods, money, management

P's: purpose, program, policy, plan, procedure, practice, problems, pitfalls, personnel, public relations

a. Six basic steps in handling problems:

(1) preliminary plan and background development

(2) collect information, data and facts

(3) analyze and interpret information, data and facts

(4) analyze and develop solutions as well as make recommendations

(5) prepare report and sell recommendations

(6) install recommendations and follow up effectiveness

b. Pitfalls to Avoid

(1) *Taking Things for Granted*
A statement of the situation does not necessarily imply that each of the elements is necessarily true; for example, a complaint may be invalid and biased so that all that can be taken for granted is that a complaint has been registered

(2) *Considering only one side of a situation*
Wherever possible, indicate several alternatives and then point out the reasons you selected the best one.

(3) *Failing to indicate follow up*
Whenever your answer indicates action on your part, make certain that you will take proper follow-up action to see how successful your recommendations, procedures, or actions turn out to be.

(4) *Taking too long in answering any single question*
Remember to time your answers properly.

EXAMINATION SECTION

EXAMINATION SECTION
TEST 1

DIRECTIONS: Each question or incomplete statement is followed by several suggested answers or completions. Select the one that BEST answers the question or completes the statement. *PRINT THE LETTER OF THE CORRECT ANSWER IN THE SPACE AT THE RIGHT.*

Questions 1-2.

DIRECTIONS: Questions 1 and 2 are to be answered on the basis of the following information.

Mrs. Smith, 34 years old, is admitted to the hospital after an automobile accident. She has a fractured hip and is taken to surgery for repair. On return from surgery, Mrs. Smith is very much concerned about her obesity.

1. Mrs. Smith asks the nurse how she should lose weight.   1.___
   The nurse's BEST reply would be to tell her that
   A. fats should be limited in her diet
   B. she needs to exercise vigorously no matter what she eats
   C. her eating pattern should be altered with all 4 basic groups and include light exercise
   D. only carbohydrates have to be completely stopped

2. The physician ordered non-weight bearing with crutches   2.___
   for Mrs. Smith.
   What should the nurse advise her regarding walking with crutches?
   A. To strengthen the muscles, exercise them, using triceps, finger flexors, and elbow extensors
   B. Sitting up in a chair strengthens back muscles
   C. The head and neck muscles should be exercised
   D. None of the above

Questions 3-7.

DIRECTIONS: Questions 3 through 7 are to be answered on the basis of the following information.

John, a factory worker, is admitted to the hospital for mild chest pain. A myocardial infarct is diagnosed. The physician orders morphine sulphate, diazepam, and lidocaine.

3. John asks the nurse why he is being given morphine   3.___
   sulphate.
   The nurse should tell him that morphine sulphate
   A. relieves pain associated with myocardial infarction

B. decreases apprehension
C. prevents cardiogenic shock
D. all of the above

4. The patient is also prescribed oxygen by nasal cannula.   4.___
The nurse takes safety precautions in the room because
oxygen
    A. converts to an alternate form of matter
    B. supports combustion
    C. has unstable properties
    D. is flammable

5. In a case of myocardial infarction, the finding on the   5.___
electrocardiogram should be
    A. disappearance of Q waves
    B. absent P wave
    C. elevated ST segments
    D. flattened T waves

6. Several days after admission, John develops pyrexia.   6.___
The nurse should monitor him for
    A. dyspnea   B. increased pulse rate
    C. chest pain   D. elevated blood pressure

7. John asks the nurse about the chances of his having   7.___
another heart attack if he watches his diet and stress
level.
The nurse should
    A. tell him he is at no risk
    B. suggest that he talk to a psychiatric nurse for his
       fear about this
    C. avoid giving him direct information
    D. none of the above

Questions 8-10.

DIRECTIONS: Questions 8 through 10 are to be answered on the basis
of the following information.

Mrs. Allbright is 65 years old and is suspected to have
pernicious anemia.

8. The first test ordered is a Schillings test.   8.___
The nurse should know that the purpose of this test is to
check the person's ability to _____ vitamin B_____.
    A. absorb; 12   B. digest; 12
    C. absorb; 6   D. store; 1

9. The nurse should explain the therapeutic regimen for   9.___
pernicious anemia to Mrs. Allbright as consisting of
    A. oral tablets of B_{12} daily
    B. IM injections daily
    C. IM injections once a month
    D. oral tablets every week

10. Mrs. Allbright wants to know how long she will need
    therapy.
    The nurse should reply that she will need therapy
    A. when she feels fatigued
    B. for the rest of her life
    C. until her symptoms subside
    D. during exacerbations of anemia

10.___

Questions 11-16.

DIRECTIONS: Questions 11 through 16 are to be answered on the
              basis of the following information.

    Mr. Roberts is 45 years old. He is brought to the emergency
room after a terrible motor vehicle accident in which he received
multiple crushing wounds of the chest, abdomen, and legs. His
right leg might have to be amputated.

11. Upon arrival, the nursing staff's FIRST priority should be
    to assess
    A. blood pressure
    B. pain
    C. quality of respiration and presence of pulse
    D. level of consciousness

11.___

12. Mr. Roberts' condition requires endotracheal intubation
    and positive pressure ventilation.
    The IMMEDIATE nursing intervention should be to
    A. facilitate verbal communication
    B. assess his response to the equipment
    C. maintain sterility of ventilation system
    D. prepare for emergency surgery

12.___

13. A chest tube with water seal drainage is inserted. The
    chest tube seems obstructed.
    The MOST appropriate nursing action at this time would
    be to
    A. clamp tube immediately
    B. remove chest tube
    C. milk the tube toward collection container
    D. take a chest x-ray

13.___

14. What is the function of the chest tube placed in Mr.
    Roberts?
    To
    A. normalize intrathoracic pressure
    B. drain fluid from pleural space
    C. drain air from pleural space
    D. all of the above

14.___

15. A response that would indicate that Mr. Roberts' condition   15.___
    was improving is
    A. increased breath sounds
    B. constant bubbling in drainage chamber
    C. increased respiratory rate
    D. crepitus on palpation of chest

16. In Mr. Roberts' case, adequate tissue perfusion to vital   16.___
    organs would be indicated by
    A. central venous pressure of 2 cm H_2O
    B. urinary output of 30 ml in an hour
    C. pulse rate of 120-110 in 15 minutes
    D. blood pressure of 50/30 and 70/40 in 30 minutes

17. A 47 year-old man is brought into the emergency room   17.___
    following an accident. He has severe abdominal pain in
    the left upper quadrant. Splenic rupture is diagnosed,
    and an emergency splenectomy is to be performed.
    The nurse should tell the patient
    A. about the presence of abdominal drains several days
       after surgery
    B. that splenectomy has a low mortality rate (5%),
       except with multiple injuries
    C. not to worry about bleeding as it occurs more fre-
       quently with repairs than removal
    D. all of the above

Questions 18-19.

DIRECTIONS: Questions 18 and 19 are to be answered on the basis
             of the following information.

     A 34 year-old woman was involved in an accident as a result of
which her left leg had to be amputated below the knee. After the
operation, the patient refused to talk, eat, or perform any
activities.

18. The BEST nursing approach in this case would be to   18.___
    A. appear cheerful, regardless of the patient's condition
    B. force her to do exercises
    C. accept and acknowledge that withdrawal is an initially
       normal and necessary part of grieving
    D. emphasize that nothing has changed in her life and she
       can and should resume normal life

19. The factors responsible for this change in this patient   19.___
    include the _____ of the change.
    A. client's perception   B. suddenness
    C. extent   D. all of the above

20. In dealing with a terminally ill patient who is in the
denial stage of grief, the BEST nursing approach is to
   A. encourage the patient's denial
   B. reassure the patient that everything will be okay
   C. allow denial but be available to discuss death
   D. leave the patient alone

20.___

Questions 21-25.

DIRECTIONS: Questions 21 through 25 are to be answered on the
basis of the following information.

A 62 year-old patient is admitted to the coronary care unit
with a diagnosis of left-sided congestive heart failure.

21. The findings in this case would MOST likely include
   A. dyspnea on exertion
   B. chest pain of the crushing type
   C. peripheral edema
   D. jugular vein distention

21.___

22. This patient was ordered a cardiac glycoside, a vaso-
dilator, and furosemide (lasix).
The site of effect of furosemide is the
   A. collecting tube   B. ascending loop of Henle
   C. distil tube   D. glomerulus

22.___

23. The distil tube is the site of action of
   A. thiazides   B. triamtere
   C. xanthines   D. spironolactone

23.___

24. Cardiac glycosides, such as digitalis, _____ the conduc-
tion speed in the myocardium and _____ the heart rate.
   A. increase; slow down   B. increase; speed up
   C. decrease; slow down   D. decrease; speed up

24.___

25. In cases of congestive heart failure, the nurse should
suggest a dietary restriction of
   A. potassium B. sodium   C. magnesium D. iron

25.___

KEY (CORRECT ANSWERS)

1. C	6. B	11. C	16. B	21. A
2. A	7. C	12. B	17. D	22. B
3. D	8. A	13. C	18. C	23. A
4. B	9. C	14. D	19. D	24. C
5. C	10. B	15. A	20. C	25. B

TEST 2

DIRECTIONS: Each question or incomplete statement is followed by
several suggested answers or completions. Select the
one that BEST answers the question or completes the
statement. *PRINT THE LETTER OF THE CORRECT ANSWER IN
THE SPACE AT THE RIGHT.*

1. While taking a history of a patient with G.I. bleeding,   1.____
the nurse should put the MOST emphasis on
    A. family history
    B. socioeconomic history
    C. history of any recent medications such as aspirin or
       prednisone
    D. travel of an endemic area

2. What kind of dietary management is APPROPRIATE for a   2.____
patient with gastric ulceration to prevent the mucosal
lining from the adverse effects of acids?
    A. Three meals a day
    B. Regular meals and snacks to relieve gastric discomfort
    C. One meal a day
    D. Eat whenever hungry

3. Precautions that should be taken by a nurse in order to   3.____
prevent infections from an indwelling catheter include
    A. changing the bag periodically and not emptying it
    B. maintaining the ordered hydration which flushes the
       bladder and prevents infection
    C. collecting specimens in order to check for infection
    D. all of the above

Questions 4-7.

DIRECTIONS: Questions 4 through 7 are to be answered on the
basis of the following information.

Mr. Connery, a 65 year-old patient, is scheduled for surgery
of transurethral resection of the prostate.

4. The nurse should let Mr. Connery know that after surgery   4.____
    A. his urinary control may be completely lost
    B. urinary drainage will be by a catheter for 24-48
       hours
    C. everything will be completely normal
    D. his ability to perform sexually will be completely
       impaired

5. In Mr. Connery's case, the MOST common complication   5.___
   following surgery is
   A. hemorrhage
   B. sepsis
   C. urinary retention with overflow
   D. none of the above

6. 24 hours after surgery, Mr. Connery, who is still on a   6.___
   catheter, complains of lower abdominal discomfort. The
   nurse notices that catheter drainage has stopped.
   The nurse's NEXT step should be to
   A. remove the catheter
   B. notify the physician
   C. irrigate with saline
   D. milk the catheter tubing

7. Which of the following discharge instructions given by   7.___
   the nurse is MOST important for Mr. Connery?
   A. Void at least every 3 hours
   B. Avoid exercise for 6 months after surgery
   C. Call the physician if urinary stream decreases
   D. Get 18 hours of sleep every 24 hours

Questions 8-10.

DIRECTIONS: Questions 8 through 10 are to be answered on the
             basis of the following information.

   Mrs. Ford is admitted to the hospital for a subtotal thyroidectomy. She has a history of Grave's disease.

8. It is important that the nurse know that in a subtotal   8.___
   thyroidectomy
   A. the entire thyroid gland is removed
   B. a small part is left intact
   C. part of the parathyroid is also removed
   D. only parathyroids are removed

9. Classical signs of hyperthyroidism include   9.___
   A. weight loss   B. exopthalmos
   C. restlessness   D. all of the above

10. Signs of postsurgical hypothyroidism of which Mrs. Ford   10.___
    should be aware include
    A. intolerance to heat   B. weight loss
    C. dry skin and fatigue   D. insomnia

Questions 11-13.

DIRECTIONS: Questions 11 through 13 are to be answered on the
basis of the following information.

Lisa, a 32 year-old woman, is admitted for treatment of partial
and full thickness burns on the lower half of her body. She is in
pain.

11.   The nurse applies sulphamylon cream to Lisa's burns.   11.___
This will
A. relieve the pain
B. inhibit bacterial growth
C. provide debridement
D. prevent scar tissue formation

12.   Pig skin temporary grafts are used for Lisa's burns.   12.___
The grafts will
A. relieve the pain
B. promote rapid epethelialization
C. provide a framework for granulation
D. all of the above

13.   Lisa suffers from periodic episodes of dyspnea.   13.___
The BEST position for her is the _____ position.
A. orthopheic   B. sims
C. semi-fowler's   D. supine

Questions 14-17.

DIRECTIONS: Questions 14 through 17 are to be answered on the
basis of the following information.

Mrs. Hunt is 61 years old. She has a history of hypertension
over the past 15 years. She complains of dyspnea and pedal edema.

14.   The dyspnea is PROBABLY due to   14.___
A. asthma
B. left ventricular failure
C. wheezing and coughing
D. none of the above

15.   Mrs. Hunt has been prescribed hydrochlorothiazide.   15.___
A COMMON side effect of this drug is
A. insomnia
B. increased thirst
C. generalized weakness due to hypokalemia
D. increased muscle strength as a result of hypercalcemia

16. Mrs. Hunt has also been prescribed a potassium supplement   16.___
    because of the diuretic she is taking.
    Potassium supplements
    A. are completely harmless
    B. should not be taken on an empty stomach as they cause
       GI ulceration and bleeding
    C. possess no side effects at all
    D. all of the above

17. The nurse should tell Mrs. Hunt to   17.___
    A. rest during the day to decrease the demand on her
       heart
    B. sleep with her head slightly elevated to facilitate
       respiration
    C. take her pulse just once daily
    D. all of the above

Questions 18-20.

DIRECTIONS: Questions 18 through 20 are to be answered on the
              basis of the following information.

    Mr. Edwards had a partial nephrectomy done and is admitted
with a nephrostomy tube in place.

18. The MOST common life-threatening complication in the early   18.___
    post-operative period is
    A. sepsis   B. hemorrhage
    C. renal failure   D. none of the above

19. The nurse's post-operative plan for Mr. Edwards should   19.___
    include
    A. turning him from back to operated site to facilitate
       drainage
    B. keeping him on clear fluid for 24-48 hours
    C. draining dressing frequently
    D. all of the above

20. Upon discharge, Mr. Edwards, who is being discharged   20.___
    with nephrostomy tube in place, should be instructed to
    A. change dressings frequently
    B. limit fluid intake
    C. maintain bedrest at home
    D. all of the above

21. Mrs. Beatty comes to the clinic with complaints of   21.___
    increased appetite, thirst, and weight loss despite
    more eating. She is diagnosed with diabetes mellitus,
    and the doctor prescribed her an oral hypoglycemic.
    The MOST common side effect of oral hypoglycemic agents is
    A. diabetic coma   B. weight loss
    C. hypoglycemia   D. all of the above

Questions 22-25.

DIRECTIONS: Questions 22 through 25 are to be answered on the
basis of the following information.

Mr. Mailer, a 34 year-old executive, is diagnosed with a
peptic ulcer.

22. The pain of a peptic ulcer is COMMONLY described as   22.___
    A. dull pain in the shoulder
    B. gnawing and boring in the epigastrium and back
    C. sharp pain in the abdomen
    D. heartburn upon lying down

23. The physician prescribes ranitidine for Mr. Mailer.   23.___
    Ranitidine
    A. can be given PO, IV, or IM
    B. is usually given with meals
    C. reduces gastric acid in the stomach
    D. all of the above

24. Mr. Mailer's condition worsens while in the hospital.   24.___
    He vomited and complained of severe epigastric pain.
    His pulse is 134, respiration is 32/minute, and there
    is an absence of bowel sounds. The nurse calls for the
    physician.
    The NEXT step should be to
    A. keep the client NPO in preparation for possible
       surgery
    B. start oxygen
    C. place the client in the Trendelenberg position
    D. all of the above

25. A subtotal gastrectomy (Billroth 1) is performed on Mr.   25.___
    Mailer. He starts eating more food, but he experiences
    cramping discomfort and rapid pulse with waves of weak-
    ness followed by nausea and vomiting.
    The nurse recognizes that Mr. Mailer is going through a
    dumping syndrome caused by the _____ into the small
    intestine.
    A. slow passage of food dumping
    B. rapid passage of food (hyperosmolar)
    C. rapid passage of dilute food
    D. none of the above

KEY (CORRECT ANSWERS)

1. C	6. D	11. B	16. B	21. C
2. B	7. C	12. D	17. D	22. B
3. D	8. B	13. A	18. B	23. D
4. B	9. D	14. B	19. D	24. A
5. A	10. C	15. C	20. A	25. B

EXAMINATION SECTION
TEST 1

DIRECTIONS: Each question or incomplete statement is followed by several suggested answers or completions. Select the one that BEST answers the question or completes the statement. *PRINT THE LETTER OF THE CORRECT ANSWER IN THE SPACE AT THE RIGHT.*

Questions 1-10.

DIRECTIONS: Questions 1 through 10 are to be answered on the basis of the following information.

Fifty year-old George Hoffman works in the basement of a garment factory. All of a sudden, he starts losing consciousness. An ambulance is called, and he is taken to the emergency room of the nearest hospital.

During the initial examination in the emergency room, he is found to have rapid, shallow breathing, non-palpable pulses over major vessels, and absent heart sounds.

1. Of the following, the MOST likely nursing diagnosis for this patient is   1.___
    A. arteriosclerosis
    B. cardiopulmonary arrest
    C. restrictive cardiomyopathy
    D. endocarditis

2. The nursing intervention of HIGHEST priority after receiving George in the emergency room would be   2.___
    A. to administer dopamine and norepinephrine to treat for shock
    B. to administer calcium chloride to help heartbeat
    C. defibrillation
    D. CPR

3. All of the following would be part of George's drug therapy EXCEPT   3.___
    A. lidocaine and procainamide
    B. epinephrine
    C. penicillin G
    D. sodium bicarbonate

4. While assessing George, the nurse probably does NOT expect to notice   4.___
    A. pallor   B. dilation of pupils
    C. ventricular fibrillation   D. petechiae and edema

5. George is unconscious. In an unconscious person, the
   relaxed tongue and neck muscles fail to lift the tongue
   from the posterior pharyngeal wall, blocking the hypo-
   pharyngeal airway. The nurse applies a basic head tilt
   maneuver to open the patient's airway, but does not
   receive a positive response.
   Additional measures which may then be used by the nurse
   to open the airway include
   A. head tilt-chin lift
   B. head tilt-neck lift
   C. mandibular jaw thrust
   D. all of the above

5.___

6. George is also found to have suffered cervical spine
   injury as a result of falling.
   The nurse should know that _____ is absolutely contra-
   indicated in the presence of cervical spine injury.
   A. direct current defibrillation
   B. external cardiac compression
   C. backward head tilt
   D. all of the above

6.___

7. In single-rescuer CPR, the nurse would give 2 breaths
   (1 to 1.5 sec. each) after each cycle of _____ cardiac
   compressions, delivered at a rate of 80 to 100/minute.
   A. 5   B. 10   C. 15   D. 20

7.___

8. All of the following would be important and appropriate
   nursing interventions to save George's life EXCEPT:
   A. Begin precordial thump and, if successful, administer
      calcium chloride
   B. If precordial thump is unsuccessful, perform
      defibrillation
   C. If defibrillation is unsuccessful, initiate CPR
      immediately
   D. Assist with administration of and monitor effects of
      additional emergency drugs

8.___

9. In 2-rescuer CPR, one ventilation (1.5 to 2 sec.) should
   be given after each cycle of _____ cardiac compressions,
   delivered at a rate of 80 to 100/minute.
   A. 5   B. 10   C. 15   D. 20

9.___

10. Which of the following drugs is used as the standard
    therapy for ventricular fibrillation (VF) or ventricular
    tachycardia (VT), and is used with countershock to
    convert VF?
    A. Procainamide   B. Bretylium tosylate
    C. Lidocaine   D. Epinephrine

10.___

Questions 11-20.

DIRECTIONS: Questions 11 through 20 are to be answered on the
              basis of the following information.

    52 year-old John Goodman is brought to the emergency room by
his wife with complaints of fever, cough, upper quadrant pain,
and joint pain. Mrs. Goodman informs the health care team that
John has also been losing weight.

11. John has been diagnosed with infective endocarditis. Mrs.   11.___
     Goodman has no knowledge about this disease, so she
     anxiously asks the nurse about it.
     The nurse explains to Mrs. Goodman that infective endo-
     carditis is a(n)
         A. inflammation of the parietal pericardium caused by a
            viral infection
         B. accumulation of fluid in the pericardium that prevents
            adequate ventricular filling, caused by a fungal
            infection
         C. microbial infection of the endocardium which may
            result in valvular incompetence or obstruction,
            myocardial abscess, or mycotic aneurysm
         D. formation of platelet and fibrin thrombi on cardiac
            valves and the adjacent endocardium in response to
            bacterial infection

12. Which of the following bacterias is among the common   12.___
     causes of infection in endocarditis?
         A. S. aureus
         B. S. viridans
         C. B. hemolytic streptococcus and gonococcus
         D. All of the above

13. While assessing John, the nurse expects to find all of   13.___
     the following EXCEPT
         A. malaise and fatigue   B. edema
         C. elevated WBC and ESR   D. increased Hgb and Hct

14. As a clinical manifestation, the symptom found in John   14.___
     that is NOT secondary to emboli is _____ pain.
         A. upper left quadrant   B. flank
         C. joint   D. chest

15. All of the following medications will be part of John's   15.___
     drug therapy EXCEPT
         A. epinephrine, to enhance endocardial contractile force
         B. antibiotics specific to the sensitivity of the
            organism cultured
         C. penicillin G and streptomycin, if the organism is
            not known
         D. antipyretics

16. In order for John to maintain homeostasis and avoid   16.___
    complications over long-term hospitalization, the one
    of the following things a nurse does NOT have to do is
    A. administer antibiotics as ordered
    B. control temperature elevation by administration of
       antipyretics
    C. evaluate for complications of emboli and congestive
       heart failure
    D. record baseline blood pressure in three positions,
       i.e., lying, sitting, and standing, in both arms

17. To isolate the etiologic agent, the nurse would perform 17.___
    _____ blood cultures of _____ mL each within 24 hours.
    A. 1 to 3; 10 to 20   B. 3 to 5; 20 to 30
    C. 5 to 7; 10 to 20   D. 3 to 5; 15 to 20

18. All of the following factors are associated with poor   18.___
    prognosis of infective endocarditis EXCEPT
    A. heart failure
    B. delay in initiating therapy
    C. young age
    D. major embolic events

19. Even after successful antimicrobial therapy, John will   19.___
    be at risk of sterile emboli and valve rupture for
    A. 6 months   B. 1 year   C. 1½ years   D. 2 years

20. John has recovered and is now ready to be discharged from 20.___
    the hospital.
    While discussing discharge planning, the nurse would
    instruct John and his wife regarding all of the following
    EXCEPT
    A. types of procedures or treatments that increase the
       chances of recurrence
    B. antifungal therapy, including name, purpose, dose,
       frequency, and side effects
    C. signs and symptoms of recurrent endocarditis
    D. avoidance of individuals with known infections

Questions 21-30.

DIRECTIONS: Questions 21 through 30 are to be answered on the
             basis of the following information.

    54 year-old Donna Smith is brought to the hospital's emergency
room by her husband after having fever, malaise, and chest pain
aggravated by breathing and swallowing.

21. After being examined by the physician, Donna is diagnosed 21.___
    with pericarditis. Mr. Smith asks the nurse about the
    nature of this disease.
    The nurse tells him that pericarditis is

A. an accumulation of fluid or blood in the pericardium that prevents adequate ventricular filling, caused by a fungal infection
B. an inflammation of the visceral and parietal pericardium, caused by a bacterial, viral, or fungal infection
C. the formation of platelet and fibrin thrombi on cardiac valves and the adjacent pericardium in response to bacterial infection
D. none of the above

22. Acute pericarditis may be a manifestation of all of the following EXCEPT   22.___
    A. rheumatoid arthritis
    B. systemic lupus erythematosus
    C. hemochromatosis
    D. scleroderma

23. Commonly used drugs that may produce acute pericarditis do NOT include   23.___
    A. procainamide   B. hydralazine
    C. isoniazid   D. lidocaine

24. Common causes of pericarditis include   24.___
    A. tuberculosis
    B. streptococcal infections
    C. staphylococcal infection
    D. all of the above

25. A scratchy, leathery sound heard in both systole and diastole is the CLASSIC sign of acute pericarditis known as   25.___
    A. pericardial friction rub
    B. epicardial rub friction
    C. myocardial friction rub
    D. dip and plateau

26. During Donna's assessment, the nurse does NOT expect to notice   26.___
    A. cough and hemoptysis
    B. tachycardia and pulsus paradoxus
    C. cyanosis or pallor
    D. decreased WBC and ESR

27. Which of the following is INCORRECT regarding Donna's drug therapy?   27.___
    It
    A. is medication for pain relief
    B. includes corticosteroids, salicylates, and indomethacin
    C. includes calcium chloride
    D. is specific antibiotic therapy against the causative organism

28. The FALSE statement regarding chronic pericarditis is: 28.___
    A. It may be serous, fibrous, adhesive, hemorrhagic, purulent, fibrinous, or calcific
    B. It is asymptomatic unless constrictive pericarditis is present
    C. Coagulants are usually contraindicated in pericardial disease
    D. As a general treatment, meperidine 50 to 100 mg orally or IM may be given q 4 hours for pain

29. All of the following are proper nursing interventions to 29.___
    control Donna's condition EXCEPT
    A. ensuring comfort: bedrest with semi or high-Fowler's position
    B. monitoring hemodynamic parameters carefully
    C. administering medications as ordered and monitoring effects
    D. assessing for vascular complications

30. Donna has recovered and is now ready to be discharged. 30.___
    During the discharge planning conference, the nurse would probably NOT advise Mr. and Mrs. Smith about
    A. signs and symptoms of pericarditis indicative of a recurrence
    B. medication regimen including name, purpose, dosage, frequency, and side effects
    C. keeping all the emergency medications available at all times
    D. none of the above

KEY (CORRECT ANSWERS)

1. B	11. C	21. B
2. D	12. D	22. C
3. C	13. D	23. D
4. D	14. C	24. D
5. D	15. A	25. A
6. C	16. D	26. D
7. C	17. B	27. C
8. A	18. C	28. C
9. A	19. B	29. D
10. C	20. B	30. A

TEST 2

DIRECTIONS: Each question or incomplete statement is followed by
several suggested answers or completions. Select the
one that BEST answers the question or completes the
statement. *PRINT THE LETTER OF THE CORRECT ANSWER IN
THE SPACE AT THE RIGHT.*

Questions 1-10.

DIRECTIONS: Questions 1 through 10 are to be answered on the
basis of the following information.

52 year-old Tim Brown visits his doctor after suffering for
the last 3 days from pain in his legs and feet and numbness and
tingling of the toes, and noticing shiny and taut skin with hair
loss on his lower legs.

1.   After being examined by the physician, Tim is diagnosed   1.___
with arteriosclerosis obliterans.
The nurse, after being asked by Tim about the disease,
explains to him that arteriosclerosis obliterans is a
chronic occlusive _____ disease that may affect the _____.
A. arterial; inferior vena cava or the extremities
B. venous; superior vena cava or the extremities
C. venous; pulmonary vessels or the extremities
D. arterial; abdominal aorta or the lower extremities

2.   The obstruction of blood flow with resultant ischemia   2.___
usually does NOT affect the _____ artery.
A. femoral   B. aortal
C. oesophageal   D. iliac

3.   Arteriosclerosis obliterans occurs MOST often in _____   3.___
ages _____.
A. men; 40-50   B. women; 40-50
C. men; 50-60   D. women; 50-60

4.   Which of the following is NOT a risk factor for arterio-   4.___
sclerosis obliterans?
A. Hypotension   B. Cigarette smoking
C. Hyperlipidemia   D. Diabetes mellitus

5.   While assessing Mr. Brown, the nurse expects to notice   5.___
all of the following EXCEPT
A. both intermittent claudication and rest pain
B. pallor after 1-2 minutes of elevating feet
C. diminished or absent radial pulse
D. diminished or absent dorsalis pedis pulse

6. The one of the following that is NOT a diagnostic test   6.___
   for arteriosclerosis obliterans is
      A. oscillometry   B. seriology
      C. angiography   D. doppler ultrasound

7. Mr. Brown is tired of staying in his bed and wants to   7.___
   walk around.
   The nurse's BEST advice for him would be that he can
      A. not do any physical activity until he is completely
         recovered and discharged from the hospital
      B. leave his bed not more than once a day
      C. leave his bed twice a day but not leave the room
      D. leave his bed 3-4 times a day and walk twice a day

8. All of the following would be appropriate nursing inter-   8.___
   ventions for Mr. Brown's recovery EXCEPT to
      A. assess for sensory function and trophic changes
      B. encourage slow, progressive physical activity
      C. order medications as required
      D. protect the patient from injury

9. Which of the following would NOT be appropriate teaching   9.___
   and discharge planning for the nurse to provide to Mr.
   Brown?
   The importance of
      A. a restricted kcal, high-saturated fat diet
      B. continuing with established exercise program
      C. avoiding constrictive clothing and standing in any
         position for a long time
      D. foot care, immediately taking care of cuts, wounds,
         and injuries

10. Doppler ultrasound is the most widely used method in   10.___
    arteriosclerosis obliterans.
    The SIMPLEST method for estimating blood flow to the
    lower extremities is to measure the _____ blood pressure
    at the level of the ankle and compare it to the _____
    pressure.
       A. systolic; brachial diastolic
       B. diastolic; brachial diastolic
       C. systolic; brachial systolic
       D. systolic; femoral systolic

Questions 11-19.

DIRECTIONS: Questions 11 through 19 are to be answered on the
              basis of the following information.

   32 year-old George Dawson visits the hospital after continuously
experiencing coldness, tingling, numbness, and burning in all his
extremities and, lately, getting an ulceration in one of his digits.
Mr. Dawson is also a cigarette smoker.

11. After being examined by the physician, Mr. Dawson is   11.___
    diagnosed with thromboangiitis obliterans.
    Thromboangiitis obliterans is BEST defined as an
       A. acute, inflammatory disorder affecting small size
          arteries of the lower extremities
       B. obliterative disease characterized by inflammatory
          changes in medium sized veins of the lower extremi-
          ties
       C. acute, inflammatory disorder affecting large sized
          arteries of the lower extremities
       D. obliterative disease characterized by inflammatory
          changes in small and medium sized arteries and veins

12. The symptoms and signs of thromboangiitis obliterans are   12.___
    those of arterial ischemia and of superficial phlebitis.
    A history of migratory phlebitis, usually in the veins
    of the foot or leg, is present in _____% of cases.
       A. 20   B. 30   C. 40   D. 50

13. Thromboangiitis obliterans occurs MOST often in _____   13.___
    ages _____.
       A. men; 35-50   B. women; 35-50
       C. men; 25-40   D. women; 25-40

14. While assessing Mr. Dawson, the nurse expects to find all   14.___
    of the following EXCEPT
       A. intermittent claudication
       B. an increased posterior tibial pulse
       C. trophic changes
       D. ulceration and gangrene

15. _____ is NOT a diagnostic test for thromboangiitis   15.___
    obliterans.
       A. Angiography   B. Contrast venography
       C. Oscillometry   D. Doppler ultrasound

16. Which of the following would NOT be included among the   16.___
    appropriate nursing interventions to control Mr. Dawson's
    disease?
       A. Prepare the patient for surgery when required
       B. Provide vasodilators and analgesics as ordered
       C. Administer coagulants not more than once a day
       D. All of the above

17. All of the following are appropriate teaching and dis-   17.___
    charge information which should be provided by the nurse
    to Mr. Dawson EXCEPT the
       A. drug regimen, including names, dosages, frequency,
          and side effects
       B. need to avoid trauma to the affected extremity
       C. need to avoid heat and have a good airconditioner
          in the bedroom
       D. importance of stopping smoking

18. The only REALLY effective treatment for thromboangiitis   18.___
    obliterans is
       A. antibiotics   B. corticosteroids
       C. anticoagulants   D. cessation of smoking

19. In thromboangiitis obliterans, since the adventitia is   19.___
    usually more extensively infiltrated with fibroblasts,
    older lesions show periarterial fibrosis, which may
    involve the adjacent
       A. artery   B. vein
       C. nerve   D. all of the above

Questions 20-30.

DIRECTIONS: Questions 20 through 30 are to be answered on the
             basis of the following information.

    30 year-old Sara Johnson got married six years ago. She never
became pregnant, having used oral contraceptives. Now she visits
the hospital after experiencing anxiety, fever, and chest pain.

20. After being examined by the physician, she is diagnosed   20.___
    with pulmonary embolism, which is BEST described as a(n)
       A. embolic obstruction to blood flow increasing venous
          pressure in the pulmonary artery and pulmonary
          hypotension
       B. embolic obstruction to blood flow involving the upper
          lobes of the lung because of higher blood flow
       C. lodgement of a blood clot in a pulmonary artery with
          subsequent obstruction of blood supply to the lung
          parenchyma
       D. lodgement of a blood clot in a pulmonary vein with
          subsequent obstruction of blood supply to the lung
          parenchyma

21. MOST pulmonary emboli arise as detached portions of venous   21.___
    thrombi formed in the
       A. deep veins of the legs   B. right side of the heart
       C. pelvic area   D. all of the above

22. Once released into the venous circulation, emboli are   22.___
    distributed to both lungs in about _____% of cases, to
    the right lung in _____% of cases, and to the left lung
    in _____% of cases.
       A. 45; 40; 30   B. 55; 30; 20
       C. 65; 20; 10   D. 75; 10; 5

23. _____ lobes are involved in pulmonary embolism _____   23.___
    times more often than _____ lobes.
       A. lower; 2; upper   B. upper; 2; lower
       C. lower; 4; upper   D. upper; 4; lower

24. Which of the following is NOT a risk factor for Mrs.   24.___
    Johnson?
    A. Trauma
    B. Pregnancy
    C. Oral contraceptives
    D. Intrauterine contraceptive devices

25. While assessing Mrs. Johnson, the nurse expects to   25.___
    notice all of the following EXCEPT
    A. severe dyspnea and a feeling of impending doom
    B. tachypnea and bradycardia
    C. increased pH due to hyperventilation
    D. crackles due to intensified pulmonic S_2

26. Concerning the diagnosis of pulmonary embolism, it is NOT   26.___
    correct that
    A. pulmonary arteriography reveals location and/or extent
       of embolism
    B. lung scan reveals adequacy or inadequacy of pulmonary
       circulation
    C. clinical symptoms and signs should suggest the
       diagnosis
    D. none of the above

27. All of the following drugs would be used in drug therapy   27.___
    for Mrs. Johnson EXCEPT
    A. anticoagulants
    B. dextran 70 to decrease viscosity and aggregation of
       blood cells
    C. narcotics for pain relief
    D. vasodepressors in the presence of shock

28. The surgical procedure used for the correction of   28.___
    pulmonary embolism is known as
    A. pulmonary thrombolectomy
    B. cardiac embolectomy
    C. pulmonary embolectomy
    D. cardiac thrombolectomy

29. It would be appropriate for the nurse attending to Mrs.   29.___
    Johnson to do all of the following EXCEPT
    A. administer oxygen therapy to correct hypoxemia
    B. provide adequate hydration to prevent hypocoagulability
    C. elevate the head of the bed to relieve dyspnea
    D. assist with turning, coughing, deep breathing, and
       passive ROM exercises

30. Which of the following is NOT considered among the appro-   30.___
    priate teaching and discharge planning provided by the
    nurse to Mrs. Johnson?
    A. Use of plastic stockings when ambulatory
    B. Need to avoid sitting or standing for long periods of
       time
    C. Drug regimen
    D. Gradually increase walking distance

KEY (CORRECT ANSWERS)

1. D	11. D	21. D
2. C	12. C	22. C
3. C	13. C	23. C
4. A	14. B	24. D
5. C	15. B	25. B
6. B	16. C	26. D
7. D	17. C	27. D
8. C	18. D	28. C
9. A	19. D	29. B
10. C	20. C	30. A

CARDIOVASCULAR SYSTEMS
EXAMINATION SECTION
TEST 1

DIRECTIONS: Each question or incomplete statement is followed by several suggested answers or completions. Select the one that BEST answers the question or completes the statement. *PRINT THE LETTER OF THE CORRECT ANSWER IN THE SPACE AT THE RIGHT.*

1. The wall of the heart is made up of all of the following EXCEPT the   1.___
   A. pericardium   B. epicardium
   C. myocardium   D. endocardium

2. Among the following statements, the one which is TRUE   2.___
   regarding the pericardium is:
   A. It contains about 30 ml of serous fluid
   B. It is tough and fibrous and does not readily stretch
   C. If more than 100 ml of fluid accumulates within the pericardium, it may compromise heart contractility
   D. All of the above

3. The MAIN function of the heart is to   3.___
   A. transport the waste products of metabolism to the cells
   B. deliver oxygenated blood and nutrients to every cell in the body
   C. deliver non-oxygenated blood to the cells in the body
   D. deliver chemical messages to the cells

4. Of the following, the structure which collects non-   4.___
   oxygenated blood returning from the body is the
   A. left atrium   B. right ventricle
   C. right atrium   D. left ventricle

5. The vessels that carry blood to the heart are   5.___
   A. arteries   B. arterioles
   C. capillaries   D. veins

6. It is NOT true that the heart   6.___
   A. weighs about 300 grams in males and 250 grams in females
   B. is usually 10-12 cm long
   C. is usually located in the right mediastinum
   D. is usually 9 cm wide and 6 cm thick

7. The MOST common location of atria is in the _____ portion   7.___
   of the heart.
   A. superior   B. inferior
   C. middle   D. all of the above

8. The MOST common location and function of the superior   8.___
vena cava are that it is located _____ and drains _____.
    A. at the right side of the heart; unoxygenated blood
       from the upper body
    B. at the left side of the heart; oxygenated blood from
       the lower body
    C. on the right side; unoxygenated blood from the
       lower part of the body
    D. in the right atrium; blood from the heart itself

9. The high-pressure pump that drives blood OUT of the   9.___
heart against the relatively high resistance of the
systemic arteries is called the
    A. right atrium   B. left atrium
    C. left ventricle   D. right ventricle

10. Oxygenated blood is usually supplied to the heart via   10.___
the _____ artery(arteries).
    A. carotid   B. coronary   C. pulmonary   D. subclavian

11. The MOST accurate definition of cardiac output is: 11.___
    A. The amount of blood pumped out by either ventricle,
       measured in liters per minute
    B. The amount of blood pumped out by either ventricle
       in a single contraction
    C. The number of cardiac contractions per minute
    D. None of the above

12. The MOST frequent location of the sino atrial node is   12.___
the _____ near the _____.
    A. right atrium; inlet of the inferior vena cava
    B. right atrium; inlet of the superior vena cava
    C. left atrium; inlet of the pulmonary vein
    D. left ventricle; aortic valve

13. The sinoatrial (SA) node is the fastest pacemaker in the   13.___
heart, normally firing at the rate of _____ to _____
times per minute.
    A. 20; 40   B. 40; 60   C. 60; 100   D. 100; 300

14. _____ is the process by which muscle fibers are   14.___
stimulated to contract.
    A. Depolarization   B. Repolarization
    C. Dyastole   D. Refractory period

15. The electrolyte that flows into the cell to initiate   15.___
depolarization is
    A. magnesium   B. potassium   C. sodium   D. phosphate

16. Of the following electrolytes, the one which flows out   16.___
of the cell to initiate repolarization is
    A. sodium   B. potassium   C. calcium   D. magnesium

17. Depolarization of the atria produces which of the follow-   17.___
    ing waves on the ECG?
    A(n)
       A. P wave   B. T wave
       C. QRS complex   D. N wave

18. Of the following waves, repolarization of the atria and   18.___
    ventricles produces _____ on the ECG.
       A. QRS complex   B. P waves
       C. T waves   D. none of the above

19. The coronary arteries   19.___
       A. originate from the base of the ascending aorta
       B. are above the leaflets of the aortic valve
       C. provide blood supply to the cardiac muscles
       D. all of the above

20. All of the following are caused by the stimulation of   20.___
    beta receptors EXCEPT
       A. bronchoconstriction
       B. increased heart rate
       C. increased heart contractability
       D. vasodilation

21. Alpha receptor stimulation does NOT cause   21.___
       A. vasoconstriction   B. bronchoconstriction
       C. no effect on the heart   D. increased heart rate

22. Which of the following is pure beta agonist?   22.___
       A. Isoproterenol   B. Metaraminol
       C. Norepinephrine   D. Dopamine

23. The agent of choice to treat increased blood pressure   23.___
    when hypotension has been caused by neurogenic shock
    (vasodilation) is
       A. isoproterenol   B. atropin
       C. norepinephrine   D. propranolol

24. Of the following sympathetic agents, the one usually   24.___
    indicated for asystole and anaphylactic shock is
       A. dopamine   B. epinephrine
       C. metaraminol   D. isoproterenol

25. When used in low doses, this sympathetic agent increases   25.___
    the force of cardiac contraction and helps to maintain
    urine flow and good perfusion to abdominal organs.
    This is a description of
       A. dopamine   B. norepinephrine
       C. metaraminol   D. isoproterenol

KEY (CORRECT ANSWERS)

1. A		11. A
2. D		12. B
3. B		13. C
4. C		14. A
5. D		15. C
6. C		16. B
7. A		17. A
8. A		18. C
9. C		19. D
10. B		20. A

21. D
22. A
23. C
24. B
25. A

TEST 2

DIRECTIONS: Each question or incomplete statement is followed by several suggested answers or completions. Select the one that BEST answers the question or completes the statement. *PRINT THE LETTER OF THE CORRECT ANSWER IN THE SPACE AT THE RIGHT.*

1. Propranolol is used clinically to 1.___
   A. slow the heart rate in certain tachyarrythmias
   B. decrease the pain of chronic angina
   C. decrease irritability in the heart
   D. all of the above

2. All of the following are functions of the parasympathetic 2.___
   nervous system EXCEPT
   A. increasing salivation   B. constricting pupils
   C. slowing the gut   D. slowing the heart

3. Which of the following is NOT a function of the sympathetic 3.___
   nervous system?
   A. Dilate pupils   B. Increase gut motility
   C. Speed the heart   D. Constrict blood vessels

4. Chest pain is often the presenting sign of acute myocar- 4.___
   dial infarction.
   When treating a patient with chest pain, the MOST
   important question for you to ask him is:
   A. What provoked the pain?
   B. What is the quality and severity of the pain?
   C. Does the pain radiate?
   D. All of the above

5. Paroxymal nocturnal dyspnea is one of the classic signs 5.___
   of
   A. pericarditis   B. right heart failure
   C. left heart failure   D. asthmatic bronchitis

6. The MOST prevalent preventable cause of death in the 6.___
   United States is
   A. diabetes   B. hypertension
   C. cigarette smoking   D. high serum cholesterol

7. Common sources of risk to the coronary artery include 7.___
   A. birth control pills   B. lack of exercise
   C. male sex   D. all of the above

8. Among the MOST common symptoms of angina pectoris are 8.___
   included
   A. sensations of tightness or pressure
   B. pain induced by anything that increases oxygen
      requirements

C. pain radiating to the lower jaw, upper neck, and
   left shoulder
D. all of the above

9. The difference(s) between the pain of angina pectoris and   9.___
   the pain from acute myocardial infarction is(are) that
   the pain of acute myocardial infarction
   A. may occur at rest
   B. may last for hours
   C. is not relieved by rest
   D. all of the above

10. All of the following are characteristic of angina pectoris 10.___
    EXCEPT that the pain usually
    A. occurs after exercise, stress and/or cold weather
    B. is relieved by rest
    C. is unresponsive to nitroglycerine
    D. lasts 3 to 5 minutes

11. Among the following, the classic symptoms of acute   11.___
    myocardial infarction include
    A. squeezing or crushing chest pain which is not
       relieved by rest
    B. a feeling of impending death
    C. diaphoresis, dyspnea, and dizziness
    D. all of the above

12. An elderly patient suffers a sudden onset of dyspnea,   12.___
    hypotension, and confusion.
    The MOST likely diagnosis is
    A. acute myocardial infarction
    B. angina pectoris
    C. pericarditis
    D. congestive heart failure

13. What is the treatment of choice for angina pectoris?   13.___
    A. Propranolol   B. Nitroglycerin
    C. Epinephrine   D. Metaraminol

14. The MAIN goal of treatment for acute myocardial infarction 14.___
    is to
    A. alleviate the patient's fear and pain
    B. prevent the development of serious cardiac dysrhyth-
       mias
    C. limit the size of the infarct
    D. all of the above

15. Cardiac work is minimal in the _____ position.   15.___
    A. standing   B. sitting
    C. semi-recumbent   D. none of the above

16. _____ therapy is the mainstay of emergency cardiac care. 16.___
    A. Epinephrine   B. Oxygen
    C. Propranolol   D. Norepinephrine

17. The proper treatment of uncomplicated acute myocardial   17.___
    infarction en route to the hospital should include all
    of the following EXCEPT
    A. administering oxygen by mask or nasal cannula
    B. D5W using a 250 ml bag and the infusion rate should
       be just enough to keep the vein open
    C. giving normal saline bolus
    D. taking blood pressure and repeating at least every
       5 minutes

18. In which of the following conditions should the patient   18.___
    be transported before he is stabilized?
    Cardiac
    A. arrest due to uncontrollable hemorrhaging
    B. arrest secondary to cold exposure
    C. rhythms that require immediate pacemaker insertion
    D. all of the above

19. The preferred pain medication for treating a hypotensive   19.___
    patient with acute myocardial infarction is
    A. morphine sulphate   B. nitrous oxide
    C. codeine   D. acetominophen

20. Of the following medications, the one you should draw   20.___
    BEFORE administering morphine to a patient with an
    acute myocardial infarction is
    A. atropine sulphate   B. nitroglycerine
    C. propranolol   D. digoxin

21. It would be acceptable to administer morphine to a   21.___
    patient suffering from
    A. low blood pressure
    B. bronchial asthma
    C. AMI involving the inferior wall of the heart
    D. hypertension and pulmonary edema

22. Criteria for thrombolytic therapy for acute myocardial   22.___
    infarction includes all of the following EXCEPT
    A. recent CPR
    B. alert patient who is able to give informed consent
    C. age between 30 and 75 years
    D. chest pain lasting more than 20 minutes but less
       than 6 hours

23. Common signs and symptoms of left heart failure include   23.___
    A. extreme restlessness and agitation
    B. severe dyspnea and tachypnea
    C. frothy pink sputum
    D. all of the above

24. Which of the following heart chambers is MOST commonly   24.___
    damaged by acute myocardial infarction?
    A. Right ventricle   B. Left ventricle
    C. Left atrium   D. Right atrium

25. Of the following medications, the one(s) which should be   25.__
    drawn up ready, pending the physician's order for
    administration, for the treatment of left heart failure
    is(are)
        A. morphine sulphate   B. furosemide
        C. digoxin   D. all of the above

Questions 26-30.

DIRECTIONS: In Questions 26 through 30, match the numbered descrip-
              tion with the lettered part of the circulatory system,
              as listed in Column I, to which it is most closely
              related. Place the letter of the CORRECT answer in the
              appropriate space at the right.

                          COLUMN I

                    A. Epicardium
                    B. Endocardium
                    C. Myocardium
                    D. Pericardium
                    E. Coronary sinus

26. The tough fibrous sac which surrounds the heart.   26.__

27. The outermost layer of the heart wall.   27.__

28. The innermost layer of the heart wall.   28.__

29. The middle layer of the heart wall.   29.__

30. A large vessel in the posterior part of the coronary   30.__
    sulcus into which venous blood empties.

KEY (CORRECT ANSWERS)

1. D	11. D	21. D
2. C	12. A	22. A
3. B	13. B	23. D
4. D	14. D	24. B
5. C	15. C	25. D
6. C	16. B	26. D
7. D	17. C	27. A
8. D	18. D	28. B
9. D	19. B	29. C
10. C	20. A	30. E

TEST 3

DIRECTIONS: Each question or incomplete statement is followed by
several suggested answers or completions. Select the
one that BEST answers the question or completes the
statement. *PRINT THE LETTER OF THE CORRECT ANSWER IN
THE SPACE AT THE RIGHT.*

1. Pre-hospital treatment of left heart failure would NOT   1.___
    include
        A. administration of beta blocker
        B. administration of 100% oxygen
        C. seating the patient with his feet dangling
        D. starting an intravenous line with D5W

2. The MOST common cause of right heart failure is   2.___
        A. cor pulmonale   B. tricuspid stenosis
        C. left heart failure   D. cardiac tamponade

3. All of the following can occur as a result of ventricle   3.___
    failure EXCEPT
        A. blood backs up into the vein
        B. back-up increases the venous pressure
        C. back-up decreases the venous pressure
        D. blood serum escapes into the tissue and produces
           edema

4. Signs and symptoms of right heart failure do NOT include   4.___
        A. collapsed jugular vein   B. hepatosplenomegaly
        C. peripheral edema   D. tachycardia

5. Common signs and symptoms of cardiogenic shock include   5.___
    all of the following EXCEPT
        A. pulse racing and thready
        B. severe hypertension
        C. respiration rapid and shallow
        D. confused or comatose state

6. The differentiating factor(s) between the pain of a   6.___
    dissecting aneurysm and an acute myocardial infarction
    is(are) that the pain of a dissecting aneurysm
        A. is maximal from the outset
        B. is often included in the back between the shoulder
           blades
        C. does not abate once it has started
        D. all of the above

7. A 60-year-old male has sudden back pain and a pulsatile   7.___
    abdominal mass. Ten minutes later, his blood pressure
    starts dropping.
    Pre-hospital management for this patient would include
    all of the following EXCEPT

    A. administering oxygen
    B. stabilizing the patient before transport
    C. applying (but not inflating) the mast
    D. starting an IV en route with normal saline or
       lactated ringer's

8. A 35-year-old comatose male has cold and clammy skin,   8.___
shallow breathing, and thready pulse.
The FIRST thing you should do to treat this patient is
    A. start an IV D5W
    B. apply monitoring electrodes
    C. secure an open airway
    D. administer epinephrine

9. The MOST common complications of hypertension include   9.___
    A. renal damage   B. stroke
    C. heart failure   D. all of the above

10. Acute hypertensive crisis is usually signaled by a sudden   10.___
marked rise in blood pressure to a level greater than
_____ mmHg.
    A. 120/80   B. 140/80
    C. 200/130   D. none of the above

11. Which of the following is the drug of choice for treat-   11.___
ment of hypertensive encephalopathy?
    A. Propranolol   B. Diazoxide
    C. Furosemide   D. Reserpin

12. The P wave represents depolarization of the atria.   12.___
When examining the ECG, you should look for the presence
of
    A. P waves in general
    B. a P wave before every QRS complex
    C. a QRS complex before every P wave
    D. all of the above

13. A P-R interval exceeding 0.2 second is called _____   13.___
degree AV block.
    A. first   B. second
    C. third   D. none of the above

14. Potential causes of sinus tachycardia include   14.___
    A. pain and fever
    B. shock and hypoxia
    C. hypotension and congestive heart failure
    D. all of the above

15. The treatment of choice for sinus tachycardia is   15.___
    A. atropin sulphate
    B. treatment of the underlying cause
    C. propranolol
    D. all of the above

3 (#3)

16. You should NOT treat patients with sinus bradycardia if   16.___
    they have
       A. unconsciousness
       B. a good or strong pulse
       C. cold and clammy skin
       D. systolic blood pressure of 80 mmHg or less

17. Which of the following drugs can be used to treat sinus   17.___
    bradycardia?
       A. Atropin sulphate   B. Propranolol
       C. Isoproterenol   D. A and C *only*

18. For premature atrial contraction,   18.___
       A. epinephrine is the best treatment
       B. dopamine is the best treatment
       C. no satisfactory treatment exists
       D. all of the above

19. A 40-year-old male has paroxymal supraventricular tachy-   19.___
    cardia and stable vital signs. The physician tells you
    to apply vagal maneuvers but, at the same time, the
    patient develops hypotension.
    The treatment of choice is
       A. to continue valsalva maneuver
       B. cardioversion
       C. verapamil
       D. digoxin

20. Some maneuvers that stimulate the vagus nerve will slow   20.___
    the heart rate and may convert some PSVT's back to normal
    sinus rhythm.
    These maneuvers include all of the following EXCEPT
       A. valsalva maneuver   B. ice water
       C. carotid sinus massage   D. hot water

21. You are taking a patient with PSVT to the hospital, which   21.___
    is 30 minutes away.
    The physician may tell you to administer
       A. verapamil   B. digoxin
       C. dopamine   D. all of the above

22. You are looking at the ECG of a patient who has regular   22.___
    rhythm, a rate of 50 per minute, absent P wave, and
    normal QRS complexes.
    The MOST likely diagnosis is
       A. sinus bradycardia
       B. junctional bradycardia
       C. third degree heart block
       D. none of the above

23. If the patient in the above question develops signs of   23.___
    poor perfusion, you should administer
       A. atropin sulphate   B. digoxin
       C. procainamide   D. all of the above

24. Propranolol is known by the trade name(s)   24.___
    A. pronestyle   B. inderal
    C. procardia   D. all of the above

Questions 25-30.

DIRECTIONS: In Questions 25 through 30, match the numbered descrip-
              tion or function with the appropriate lettered part of
              the cardiovascular system, as listed in Column I. Place
              the letter of the CORRECT answer in the space at the
              right.

COLUMN I

    A. Tricuspid valve
    B. Mitral valve
    C. Coronary sulcus
    D. Systole
    E. Diastole
    F. SA node

25. The groove which separates the atria and the ventricle, in   25.___
    which the arteries and the main coronary vein cross the
    heart.

26. Separates the right atrium from the right ventricle.   26.___

27. Separates the left atrium from the left ventricle.   27.___

28. Atrial and ventricular relaxation.   28.___

29. Atrial and ventricular contraction.   29.___

30. Located in the right atrium near the inlet of the   30.___
    superior vena cava.

KEY (CORRECT ANSWERS)

1. A	11. B	21. A
2. C	12. D	22. B
3. C	13. A	23. A
4. A	14. D	24. B
5. B	15. B	25. C
6. D	16. B	26. A
7. B	17. D	27. B
8. C	18. C	28. E
9. D	19. B	29. D
10. C	20. D	30. F

EXAMINATION SECTION

TEST 1

DIRECTIONS: Each question or incomplete statement is followed by
several suggested answers or completions. Select the
one that BEST answers the question or completes the
statement. *PRINT THE LETTER OF THE CORRECT ANSWER IN
THE SPACE AT THE RIGHT.*

Questions 1-10.

DIRECTIONS: Questions 1 through 10 are to be answered on the
basis of the following information.

Ms. Martha McCarthy, 32 years old, is brought to the emergency
unit on a stretcher. Ms. McCarthy was in an automobile accident
and is conscious upon admission. X-rays show that she has considerable vertebral damage at the level of T-6. The surgical unit is
notified that Ms. McCarthy will be brought directly from the x-ray
department.

1. Which of the facts about Ms. McCarthy, if obtained when   1.___
   she is admitted to the hospital, would MOST likely require
   early intervention?
   She
     A. is a vegetarian
     B. last voided 7 hours ago
     C. smokes 2 packs of cigarettes a day
     D. is menstruating

2. Twelve hours after admission, Ms. McCarthy begins to   2.___
   develop some difficulty in breathing.
   In addition to obtaining a respirator and calling the
   physician, the nurse would show the BEST judgment by
     A. turning Ms. McCarthy onto her abdomen to promote
        drainage from the mouth and throat
     B. encouraging Ms. McCarthy to exercise her upper
        extremities at intervals
     C. elevating the foot of Ms. McCarthy's bed
     D. bringing pharyngeal suction equipment to Ms. McCarthy's
        bedside

3. Considering the level of Ms. McCarthy's injury (T-6), it   3.___
   is MOST justifiable to assume that her respiratory difficulty is due to
     A. edema of the cord above the level of injury
     B. hemorrhage into the brain stem due to trauma
     C. movement of the parts of the fractured vertebrae
     D. severing of the nerves that activate the diaphragm

4. The nurse can prevent Ms. McCarthy's lower extremities   4.___
   from rotating externally by placing
       A. her feet against a footboard
       B. pillows against her calves
       C. trochanter rolls along the inner aspects of her knees
       D. sandbags against the outer aspects of her thighs

5. Ms. McCarthy is to have a laminectomy.   5.___
   The CHIEF purpose of a laminectomy for her is to
       A. realign the vertebral fragments
       B. relieve pressure on the cord
       C. repair spinal nerve damage
       D. reduce spinal fluid pressure

6. Ms. McCarthy is highly susceptible to the development of   6.___
   decubitus ulcers because
       A. an intact nervous system is necessary for maintenance
          of normal tone of blood vessels
       B. flexor muscles have a greater loss of tone than
          extensor muscles
       C. decreased permeability of the capillary walls results
          from central nervous system damage
       D. atonic muscles have an increased need for oxygen

7. Ms. McCarthy has a laminectomy and spinal fusion. The   7.___
   physician tells her that she will not be able to walk
   without the use of supportive devices.
   Before surgery, Ms. McCarthy should have been informed
   that the bone to be used as a graft for a spinal fusion
   is MOST likely to be obtained from the
       A. posterior iliac crest   B. adjacent sacral vertebrae
       C. humerus   D. sternum

8. The nursing staff notices a pronounced change in Ms.   8.___
   McCarthy's behavior after the physician discusses her
   prognosis with her. She is now overtly rebellious,
   responding negatively to personnel, to treatments, and
   to nursing measures.
   The interpretation of her behavior is that she is
       A. unable to face the prospect of a long rehabilitative
          program
       B. projecting her own unhappiness onto others
       C. reacting to the change in her body image
       D. seeking punishment for feelings of guilt about her
          injury

9. A rehabilitative program is started for Ms. McCarthy.   9.___
   She is to wear leg braces.
   When applying Ms. McCarthy's leg braces, it is ESSENTIAL
   for the nurse to consider that Ms. McCarthy
       A. cannot move her lower extremities
       B. has no sensation in her lower extremities
       C. can flex her knees to a 45-degree angle
       D. cannot fully extend her hip joints

10. To achieve success in a rehabilitation program for Ms.   10.___
    McCarthy, the MOST important information about Ms. McCarthy
    is her
       A. knowledge of services available to her
       B. personal goals
       C. being encouraged by her family
       D. relationship with members of the health team

Questions 11-16.

DIRECTIONS: Questions 11 through 16 are to be answered on the
              basis of the following information.

    Ms. Beth Marks, a 21-year-old college student, sustains a head
injury as a result of a fall down a flight of stairs. She is
brought to the emergency room with a pronounced swelling of the
forehead. She is admitted to the hospital for observation.

11. On admission, Ms. Marks' blood pressure was 110/80, her   11.___
    pulse rate was 88, and her respiratory rate was 20.
    It would be MOST indicative of increasing intracranial
    pressure if her blood pressure, pulse, and respirations
    were, respectively,
       A. 90/54; 50; 22   B. 100/66; 120; 32
       C. 120/90; 96; 16   D. 140/70; 60; 14

12. Ms. Marks' condition worsens. She has a craniotomy, and   12.___
    a hematoma is removed. Her postoperative orders include
    elevation of the head of her bed, and mannitol.
    When Ms. Marks reacts from anesthesia, she is put in a
    semi-reclining position to
       A. increase thoracic expansion and facilitate oxygena-
          tion of damaged tissue
       B. provide adequate drainage and prevent fluid accumula-
          tion in the cranial cavity
       C. decrease cardiac workload and prevent hemorrhage at
          the surgical site
       D. reduce pressure in the subarachnoid space and
          promote tissue granulation

13. It is CORRECT to say that in this case mannitol is   13.___
    expected to
       A. decrease body fluids
       B. elevate the filtration rate in the kidney
       C. control filtration of nitrogenous wastes
       D. increase the volume of urine

14. The PRIMARY purpose of administering mannitol to Ms.   14.___
    Marks is to
       A. promote kidney function
       B. prevent bladder distention
       C. reduce cerebral pressure
       D. diminish peripheral fluid retention

15. Eight hours after surgery, Ms. Marks' temperature rises   15.___
    to 104°F. (40°C.), and a hypothermia blanket is ordered
    for her.
    Ms. Marks' temperature elevation is MOST likely due to
    a(n)
    A. accumulation of respiratory secretions resulting
       from inadequate ventilation
    B. alteration of metabolism resulting from pressure
       on the hypothalamus
    C. increase in leukocytosis resulting from bacterial
       invasion
    D. constriction of the main artery in the circle of
       Willis resulting from a ventricular fluid shift

16. Following a craniotomy, a patient may be given caffeine   16.___
    and sodium benzoate to
    A. lessen cerebral irritation by depressing the cerebrum
    B. improve the sense of touch by blocking spinal nerve
       reflexes
    C. enable commands to be followed by activating the
       medullary cells
    D. increase mental alertness by stimulating the cerebral
       cortex

Questions 17-25.

DIRECTIONS: Questions 17 through 25 are to be answered on the
             basis of the following information.

    Mr. Paul Peters, 61 years old, is admitted to the hospital.
Vascular occlusion of his left leg is suspected, and he is scheduled
for an arteriogram.

17. The nurse is to assess the circulation in Mr. Peters'   17.___
    lower extremities.
    Which of these measures would be ESPECIALLY significant?
    A. Comparing the pulses in the lower extremities
    B. Comparing the temperatures of the lower extremities
    C. Noting the pulse in the left leg
    D. Noting the temperature of the left leg

18. Which of these symptoms manifested in Mr. Peters'   18.___
    affected left extremity would indicate that he has
    intermittent claudication?
    A. Extensive discoloration
    B. Dependent edema
    C. Pain associated with activity
    D. Petechiae

19. Following Mr. Peters' admission, an IMMEDIATE goal in   19.___
    his care should be to
    A. improve the muscular strength of his extremities
    B. achieve maximum rehabilitation for him
    C. prevent the extension of his disease process
    D. protect his extremities from injury

20. During the night following his admission, Mr. Peters says   20.___
    that he can't sleep because his feet are cold.
    The nurse should
    - A. offer Mr. Peters a warm drink
    - B. massage Mr. Peters' feet briskly for several minutes
    - C. ask Mr. Peters if he has any socks with him
    - D. place a heating pad under Mr. Peters' feet

21. Information given to Mr. Peters about the femoral arteri-   21.___
    ogram should include the fact that
    - A. a local anesthetic will be given to lessen discomfort
    - B. there are minimal risks associated with the procedure
    - C. the radioactive dye that is injected will be removed
      before he returns to his unit
    - D. a radiopaque substance will be injected directly
      into the small vessels of his feet

22. When Mr. Peters is brought back to his unit following   22.___
    the arteriogram, which of these actions would be appro-
    priate?
    - A. Encourage fluid intake and have him lie prone
    - B. Apply heat to the site used for introducing the
      intravenous catheter and passively exercise his
      involved extremity
    - C. Limit motion of his affected extremity and check
      the site used for the injection of the dye
    - D. Restrict his fluid intake and encourage him to
      ambulate

23. The results of Mr. Peters' arteriogram revealed a marked   23.___
    narrowing of the left femoral artery. He has a venous
    graft bypass performed. Following a stay in the recovery
    room, he is returned to his room.
    The postoperative care plan for Mr. Peters should include
    which of these notations?
    - A. Keep the affected extremity elevated
    - B. Check the pulse distal to the graft site
    - C. Check for color changes proximal to the proximal site
    - D. Check for fine movements of the toes

24. During the first postoperative day, Mr. Peters is kept   24.___
    on bed rest.
    Which of these exercises for Mr. Peters would it be
    APPROPRIATE for the nurse to initiate?
    - A. Straight leg raising of both lower extremities
    - B. Range of motion of both lower extremities
    - C. Abduction of the affected extremity
    - D. Dorsiflexion and extension of the foot of the
      affected extremity

25. When Mr. Peters returns to bed after ambulating, it   25.___
    would be MOST important for the nurse to check
    - A. his blood pressure
    - B. his radial pulse
    - C. the temperature of his affected extremity
    - D. the pedal pulse of his affected extremity

1. B		11. D	
2. D		12. B	
3. A		13. D	
4. D		14. C	
5. B		15. B	
6. A		16. D	
7. A		17. A	
8. C		18. C	
9. B		19. D	
10. B		20. C	

21. A
22. C
23. B
24. D
25. D

TEST 2

DIRECTIONS: Each question or incomplete statement is followed by
             several suggested answers or completions. Select the
             one that BEST answers the question or completes the
             statement. *PRINT THE LETTER OF THE CORRECT ANSWER IN
             THE SPACE AT THE RIGHT.*

Questions 1-8.

DIRECTIONS: Questions 1 through 8 are to be answered on the
             basis of the following information.

     Three days ago, Susan Cooper, 4 years old, was admitted to
the hospital with a diagnosis of heart failure. She was digitalized
the day of her admission and is now to receive a maintenance dose of
digoxin (Lanoxin) 0.08 mg. p.o.b.i.d. Susan has been under medical
supervision for cystic fibrosis and has severe pulmonary involvement.

1. The stock bottle of Lanoxin contains 0.05 mg. of the drug   1.___
    in 1 cc. of solution.
    How much solution will contain a single dose (0.08 mg.)
    of the drug for Susan?
    _____ cc.
        A. 0.06   B. 0.6   C. 1.6   D. 2.6

2. Prior to the administration of a dose of Lanoxin to Susan,   2.___
    the nurse should take her _____ pulse.
        A. femoral   B. apical
        C. radial   D. both apical and radial

3. The nurse would be CORRECT in withholding Susan's dose of   3.___
    Lanoxin without specific instructions from the doctor if
    Susan's pulse rate were below _____ beats per minute.
        A. 100   B. 115   C. 130   D. 145

4. Which of these measures is likely to be MOST helpful in   4.___
    providing for Susan's nutritional needs while she is
    acutely ill?
        A. Serving her food lukewarm
        B. Giving her only liquids that she can take through a
           straw
        C. Offering her small portions of favorite foods fre-
           quently
        D. Mixing her foods together so that they are not readily
           identifiable

5. Because Susan has symptoms of acute cardiac failure, her   5.___
    oral feedings will DIFFER from the feedings of a normal
    child the same age in the
        A. size of the feedings *only*
        B. rapidity and size of the feedings
        C. frequency and rapidity of the feedings
        D. size, rapidity, and frequency of the feedings

6. All of the following information is part of Susan's health   6.___
   history.
   Which fact relates MOST directly to a diagnosis of cystic
   fibrosis?
   A. Emergency surgery as a newborn for intestinal obstruc-
      tion
   B. Jaundice that lasted 4 days during the newborn period
   C. A temperature of 104°F. (40°C.) followed by a convul-
      sion when she was 6 months old
   D. A left otitis media treated with antibiotics when
      she was 12 months old

7. Susan is placed in a mist tent in order to   7.___
   A. increase the hydration of secretions
   B. prevent the loss of fluids through evaporation
   C. aid in maintaining a therapeutic environmental
      temperature
   D. improve the transport of oxygen and carbon dioxide

8. Susan is receiving pancreatin replacement therapy to   8.___
   promote the absorption of
   A. protein
   B. carbohydrate
   C. vitamin C (ascorbic acid)
   D. sodium

Questions 9-13.

DIRECTIONS: Questions 9 through 13 are to be answered on the
             basis of the following information.

Ms. Leslie Browne, a 21-year-old college student, is seen by a
physician because of fatigue and weight loss. Physical examination
reveals slight enlargement of her cervical lymph nodes. Ms. Browne
is admitted to the hospital for diagnostic studies.

9. Ms. Browne states that she has had a low-grade fever.   9.___
   Which of these questions pertaining to Ms. Browne's low-
   grade fever should the nurse ask INITIALLY?
   A. When did you first notice that your temperature had
      gone up?
   B. Has your temperature been over 102 degrees?
   C. Have you recently been exposed to anyone who has an
      infection?
   D. Do you have a sore throat?

10. Ms. Browne is to have a chest x-ray and is to be trans-   10.___
    ported to the x-ray department by stretcher.
    All of the following actions may be taken by the nurse
    when sending Ms. Browne for the x-ray.
    Which action is ESSENTIAL?
    A. Strap Ms. Browne securely to the stretcher.
    B. Place Ms. Browne's chart under the mattress of the
       stretcher.
    C. Ask Ms. Browne to remove her wristwatch.
    D. Assign a nurse's aide to accompany Ms. Browne.

11. The results of diagnostic tests establish that Ms. Browne   11.___
    has Hodgkin's disease with involvement of the cervical
    and mediastinal nodes. She is to have an initial course
    of intravenous chemotherapy with mechlorethamine (Mustar-
    gen) hydrochloride. The Mustargen that Ms. Browne receives
    is administered to her through the tubing of a rapidly
    flowing intravenous infusion.
    The purpose of this method of administration is to
       A. reduce the half-life of the medication
       B. minimize the side effects of the medication
       C. decrease irritation of the blood vessel by the
          medication
       D. control the rate of absorption of the medication

12. While Ms. Browne is receiving Mustargen therapy, she is   12.___
    MOST likely to develop
       A. alopecia   B. fecal impactions
       C. temporary neuropathy   D. transient nausea

13. The insertion site of Ms. Browne's intravenous infusion   13.___
    is edematous.
    Which of these actions should the nurse take?
       A. Lower the height of the infusion container
       B. Discontinue the infusion
       C. Flush the infusion tubing with 5 ml. of isotonic
          saline solution
       D. Reduce the rate of infusion

Questions 14-25.

DIRECTIONS: Questions 14 through 25 are to be answered on the
              basis of the following information.

    Mr. Robert Dine, a 66-year-old widower who has diabetes mellitus,
is admitted to the hospital in metabolic acidosis. He has gangrene
of the great toe of his left foot and ulceration of the heel.

14. Immediately after Mr. Dine's admission, the nurse places   14.___
    him on his side and then at frequent intervals turns him
    from side to side.
    The CHIEF purpose of these actions is to
       A. reduce the possibility of pulmonary embolism
       B. insure maximal circulation in the gangrenous extremity
       C. promote the exchange of oxygen and carbon dioxide
       D. facilitate the breakdown of lactic acid

15. Because Mr. Dine has a gangrenous toe and a heel ulcer,   15.___
    which of the following equipment is ESSENTIAL to his care?
       A. Sheepskin pad   B. Heat lamp
       C. Bed board   D. Cradle

16. The physician has ordered warm saline dressings to be   16.___
applied to Mr. Dine's heel ulcer for 20 minutes twice a
day. A nurse observes another staff nurse preparing a
clean basin and a washcloth to carry out the treatment.
Which of these approaches by the nurse who makes the
observation would be APPROPRIATE?
    A. Interrupt the nurse assembling supplies to discuss
       the procedure
    B. Present the situation for discussion at a team
       conference
    C. Do nothing, as the procedure is being done using
       correct technique
    D. Do nothing, as each nurse is accountable for her or
       his own actions

17. Mr. Dine's lesions have not responded to conservative   17.___
medical therapy. He is scheduled to have a below-the-
knee amputation of the affected extremity. Mr. Dine's
orders include administration of regular insulin on a
sliding scale. Mr. Dine, who received isophane (NPH)
insulin prior to his admission to the hospital, has been
on regular insulin since admission. Regular insulin is
to be continued for him until after his recovery from
surgery. Mr. Dine asks what the reason is for this order.
Which of the following information would give Mr. Dine
the BEST explanation?
    A. When complications are present, diabetes is more
       manageable with regular insulin.
    B. During the first week after a patient recovers from
       an episode of diabetic acidosis, the likelihood of a
       recurrence is greatest.
    C. Diminished activity intensifies the body's response
       to long-acting insulin.
    D. Diabetic acidosis causes a temporary increase in the
       rate of food absorption.

18. Mr. Dine asks why he cannot be given insulin by mouth.   18.___
He should be informed that insulin is NOT given by mouth
because it
    A. is destroyed by digestive enzymes
    B. is irritating to the gastrointestinal tract
    C. is detoxified by the liver
    D. cannot be regulated as it is absorbed

19. Mr. Dine is receiving an intravenous infusion of 5%   19.___
glucose in distilled water. Regular insulin is administered intravenously every two hours.
The purpose of the insulin is to
    A. enhance carbohydrate metabolism
    B. promote conversion of fat to glycogen
    C. stimulate gluconeogenesis
    D. assist in the regulation of fluid absorption

20. Regular insulin is given to Mr. Dine on a sliding scale   20.___
    to
    A. lengthen its peak action
    B. minimize the risk of hypoglycemia
    C. prolong glyconeogenesis
    D. prevent the rapid release of glucagon

21. Mr. Dine has a below-the-knee amputation. Following   21.___
    recovery from anesthesia, he is brought back to the
    surgical unit. Because Mr. Dine has diabetes mellitus,
    he is susceptible to the development of a wound infection
    postoperatively.
    Mr. Dine's care plan should include measures that will
    overcome the fact that patients with diabetes mellitus
    have
    A. ketone bodies excreted into their subcutaneous tissue
    B. a greater insensitivity to antibiotics
    C. decreased ability to combat pathogens
    D. a larger number of microscopic organisms on their
       skin

22. To prevent the deformities to which Mr. Dine is particu-   22.___
    larly susceptible, his affected limb should be placed
    with the hip
    A. flexed and the knee extended
    B. rotated outwardly and the knee flexed
    C. extended and the knee flexed
    D. and knee extended

23. Mr. Dine's condition improves. Physical therapy treat-   23.___
    ments are begun for him. He is to be taught crutch-
    walking. After returning from his first treatment, Mr.
    Dine begins to cry. The nurse's attempts to explore with
    Mr. Dine the reasons for his crying have been unsuccessful.
    Under these circumstances, it would be justifiable for
    the nurse to proceed on the assumption that Mr. Dine's
    behavior is PROBABLY related to a
    A. fear of becoming dependent
    B. feeling of loss
    C. reaction to physical pain
    D. response to muscle reconditioning

24. Mr. Dine is now receiving a daily dose of a long-acting   24.___
    insulin preparation that he will continue to take at
    home.
    Which of these bedtime snacks would be BEST for him?
    A. Cheese and crackers   B. An apple and diet cola
    C. Orange juice and toast   D. Canned peaches and tea

25. Before Mr. Dine is discharged, he should have which of   25.___
    these understandings about his own care?
    A. Less insulin will be required since the diseased
       tissue has been removed.
    B. Social activities must be limited to conserve energy.
    C. The stump should be examined daily.
    D. Tissue breakdown will be prevented if foods high in
       vitamin C are taken daily.

KEY (CORRECT ANSWERS)

1. C			11. C	
2. B			12. D	
3. A			13. B	
4. C			14. C	
5. D			15. D	
6. A			16. A	
7. A			17. A	
8. A			18. A	
9. A			19. A	
10. A			20. B	

21. C
22. D
23. B
24. A
25. C

———

TEST 3

DIRECTIONS: Each question or incomplete statement is followed by several suggested answers or completions. Select the one that BEST answers the question or completes the statement. *PRINT THE LETTER OF THE CORRECT ANSWER IN THE SPACE AT THE RIGHT.*

1. A physician orders the following pre-operative medications 1.___
   for a child: Demerol hydrochloride 8 mg.; Atropine
   sulfate 0.06 mg. On hand are the following vials:
   Meperidine (Demerol) hydrochloride 50 mg. in 1 cc.;
   Atropine sulfate 0.40 mg. in 1 cc.
   In order to administer the prescribed doses, the nurse
   should give _____ of meperidine and _____ of atropine.
   A. 0.16 cc.; 0.15 cc.   B. 0.26 cc.; 0.20 cc.
   C. 1 minim; 3 minims   D. 2 minims; 4 minims

2. To provide care to a patient who has lost a body part or 2.___
   valued function, which of these measures is ESSENTIAL to
   include in the care plan?
   A. Inviting the assistance of a person who has a similar
      handicap
   B. Encouraging an immediate independence in self-care
   C. Providing information to the patient about available
      prosthetic devices
   D. Allowing adequate time for the patient to work
      through his grief

Questions 3-9.

DIRECTIONS: Questions 3 through 9 are to be answered on the basis of the following information.

Ms. Gloria Goldstein, 40 years old, visits a physician because of pain in her left leg. The physician determines that Ms. Goldstein has thrombophlebitis in her left leg and hospital admission is arranged. Her orders include bed rest and bishydroxycoumarin (Dicumarol).

3. Bed rest is prescribed for Ms. Goldstein in order to   3.___
   A. promote fluctuations in the venous pressure of both
      extremities
   B. improve the capacity of the venous circulation in
      both extremities
   C. minimize the potential for release of a thrombus in
      the affected extremity
   D. prevent thrombus formation in the unaffected
      extremity

4. The EXPECTED action of Dicumarol is to   4.___
    A. dissolve a thrombus
    B. prevent extension of a thrombus
    C. promote healing of the infarction
    D. reduce vascular necrosis

5. To detect a common untoward effect of Dicumarol, the   5.___
nurse should assess Ms. Goldstein for the possible
development of
    A. generalized dermatitis   B. hematuria
    C. urinary retention   D. vitamin K deficiency

6. While Ms. Goldstein is receiving Dicumarol, she should   6.___
be monitored by which of these laboratory tests?
    A. Prothrombin time   B. Clotting time
    C. Red cell fragility   D. Platelet count

7. An order for which of these medications should be ques-   7.___
tioned because it is usually contraindicated for a
patient receiving Dicumarol?
    A. Cortisone
    B. Aspirin
    C. Chlorpromazine hydrochloride (Thorazine)
    D. Isoproterenol (Isuprel) hydrochloride

8. The nurse is talking with Ms. Goldstein on the third day   8.___
of her hospitalization. Suddenly, Ms. Goldstein, who is
in bed, complains of a sharp pain in the left side of her
chest. The physician establishes a diagnosis of pulmonary
embolus. Ms. Goldstein's orders include absolute bed
rest and heparin.
Which of these medications should be READILY available
while Ms. Goldstein is receiving heparin therapy?
    A. Procainamide (Pronestyl) hydrochloride
    B. Protamine sulfate
    C. Papaverine hydrochloride
    D. Calcium gluconate

9. At lunchtime one day, Ms. Goldstein, who is on a regular   9.___
diet, states that she does not feel hungry.
The nurse should
    A. encourage her to eat the full meal
    B. emphasize her need for protein
    C. limit her snacks
    D. allow her to eat as she likes

10. The BEST beginning point in offering support to a patient   10.___
in time of crisis is to
    A. tell the client what to do to solve the problem
    B. imply that the client is a competent person
    C. find a person or agency to take care of the problem
    D. remind the client that everyone has to cope with
       crises

Questions 11-16.

DIRECTIONS: Questions 11 through 16 are to be answered on the
               basis of the following information.

     Ms. Sylvia Capp, 53 years old, has a physical examination, and
it is determined that she is hypertensive. She attends the medical
clinic and is receiving health instruction and supervision. Ms.
Capp is to receive a thiazide drug and a diet low in fat, sodium,
and triglycerides.

11.   The finding that would constitute a significant index of   11.___
       hypertension is a
       A. pulse deficit of 10 beats per minute
       B. regular pulse of 90 beats per minute
       C. systolic pressure fluctuating between 150 and 160 mm.
          Hg.
       D. sustained diastolic pressure greater than 90 mm. Hg.

12.   The nurse asks Ms. Capp to select foods that best meet   12.___
       her diet prescription.
       Ms. Capp's knowledge of goods lowest in both fat and
       sodium would be ACCURATE if she selected
       A. tossed salad with blue cheese dressing, cold cuts,
          and vanilla cookies
       B. split pea soup, cheese sandwich, and a banana
       C. cold baked chicken, lettuce with sliced tomatoes,
          and applesauce
       D. beans and frankfurters, carrot and celery sticks,
          and a plain cupcake

13.   When teaching Ms. Capp about her diet, the nurse should   13.___
       include which of these instructions?
       A. Avoid eating canned fruits
       B. Season your meat with lemon juice or vinegar
       C. Restrict your intake of green vegetables
       D. Drink diet soda instead of decaffeinated coffee

14.   To assist Ms. Capp to comply with a low-fat diet, the   14.___
       information about fats that would be MOST useful to her
       is the
       A. amount of fat in processed meats
       B. method of preparing foods to limit the fat content
       C. comparison of hydrogenated fats to emulsified fats
       D. caloric differences of foods containing fats and
          carbohydrates

15.   Because Ms. Capp is receiving a thiazide drug, her diet   15.___
       should include foods that are high in
       A. calcium   B. potassium
       C. iron   D. magnesium

16. Ms. Capp tells the nurse that she smokes two packs of 16.___
cigarettes a day.
To initiate a plan that will assist Ms. Capp in overcoming her smoking habit, which of these actions by the
nurse would probably be MOST effective?
    A. Have her identify those times when she feels that
       she must have a cigarette
    B. Ask her to describe what she knows about the dele-
       terious effects of smoking on her condition
    C. Explain to her how smoking contributes to environ-
       mental pollution
    D. Impress on her the realization that smoking is a
       form of addiction that is no longer socially
       acceptable

Questions 17-25.

DIRECTIONS: Questions 17 through 25 are to be answered on the
basis of the following information.

Mr. Ethan Allen, 46 years old, is admitted to a center for the
treatment of persons who abuse alcohol. He had been drinking a quart
or more of liquor a day for 10 to 15 years. He was drinking up to
the time of his admission. His wife is with him.

17. Mr. Allen's immediate treatment is MOST likely to include 17.___
orders for
    A. oral fluids, ascorbic acid, and a narcotic
    B. a cool bath, a barbiturate, and blood lithium level
    C. full diet as tolerated, thiamine, and a tranquilizer
    D. a spinal tap, bromides, and restraints

18. If Mr. Allen develops delirium tremens, which of these 18.___
environmental factors is likely to be MOST disturbing?
    A. Strangers   B. Shadows
    C. Unfamiliar procedures   D. Medicinal odors

19. Ms. Allen says to the nurse, *I'd do anything to help my* 19.___
husband stop drinking.
The PRIMARY goal of the nurse's response should be to
    A. get Ms. Allen to clarify the problem as she sees it
    B. have Ms. Allen join Al-Anon
    C. tell Ms. Allen that she has done all she could to
       help her husband
    D. have Ms. Allen understand that alcoholism is a
       problem that only her husband can solve

20. In giving care to Mr. Allen, the nurse should be alert 20.___
for complications of withdrawal, which include
    A. aphasia   B. hypotension
    C. diarrhea   D. convulsions

21. After several weeks of group therapy, Mr. Allen says to
    the nurse, *I've never been able to face life without
    alcohol.*
    Which of the responses would initially be MOST appro-
    priate?
      A. I know how you feel, Mr. Allen. We all have diffi-
         culty in meeting some problems.
      B. But now you know where to go for help.
      C. Perhaps you can manage if you join Alcoholics
         Anonymous, Mr. Allen.
      D. That has been the way you have dealt with your
         problems.

    21.___

22. Mr. Allen's success in abstaining from drinking is
    thought to depend on his
      A. admission that his behavior is detrimental to him-
         self and his family
      B. conviction that he must change and has some capacity
         for change
      C. ability to express remorse
      D. having taken a pledge witnessed by fellow alcoholics

    22.___

23. Mr. Allen is started on disulfiram (Antabuse), which he
    will continue to take after discharge from the hospital.
    It should be emphasized to Mr. Allen that while he is on
    Antabuse, he must NEVER take
      A. elixir of terpin hydrate
      B. aspirin
      C. bicarbonate of soda
      D. antihistamines

    23.___

24. Patients such as Mr. Allen may develop Korsakoff's
    psychosis.
    Which of these symptoms is associated with this condition?
      A. Fantastic delusions and fear
      B. Sullenness and suspiciousness
      C. Amnesia and confabulation
      D. Nihilistic ideas and tearfulness

    24.___

25. The nurse explains Alcoholics Anonymous to Mr. Allen.
    An understanding implemented by Alcoholics Anonymous is
    that people
      A. feel less alone when they feel understood
      B. are more likely to be able to handle problems when
         they are alerted to them ahead of time
      C. are dependent upon their environment for cues that
         keep them oriented
      D. resort to defense mechanisms as a means of coping
         with anxiety

    25.___

KEY (CORRECT ANSWERS)

1. A		11. D	
2. D		12. C	
3. C		13. B	
4. B		14. B	
5. B		15. B	
6. A		16. A	
7. B		17. C	
8. B		18. B	
9. D		19. A	
10. B		20. D	

21. D
22. B
23. A
24. C
25. A

———

EXAMINATION SECTION
TEST 1

DIRECTIONS: Each question or incomplete statement is followed by several suggested answers or completions. Select the one that BEST answers the question or completes the statement. *PRINT THE LETTER OF THE CORRECT ANSWER IN THE SPACE AT THE RIGHT.*

1. A 59 year-old white male develops cancer of the larynx.   1.___
   Nursing care of this patient, who is undergoing a total
   laryngectomy, includes all of the following EXCEPT
      A. reinforcing the physician's teaching regarding loss
         of normal speech, breathing patterns, and sense of
         smell
      B. introducing the patient to changes in modes of
         communication, for example, esophageal speech and
         artificial larynx
      C. establishing methods of communication to be used in
         the immediately postoperative period, like magic
         slate and gestures
      D. none of the above

2. Postoperative nursing management of the patient in the   2.___
   previous question would NOT include
      A. promotion of wound drainage by elevating foot end of
         bed
      B. in order to prevent infection, monitoring sputum and
         drainage for changes in color, odor, and characteris-
         tics
      C. promotion of optimum ventilatory status
      D. assessment for respiratory complications, such as
         dyspnea, cyanosis, and tachpnea

3. Gastric secretions include all of the following EXCEPT   3.___
      A. pepsinogen
      B. hydrochloric acid
      C. cholesystokinin
      D. intrinsic factor and mucoid secretion

4. The one of the following that would NOT be part of the   4.___
   nursing care of a patient undergoing oxygen therapy
   through nasal cannula is
      A. instructing patient to breathe through his nose
      B. removing cannula and cleaning nares every 4-5 days
      C. providing mouth care every 2-3 hours
      D. assessing arterial PO_2 frequently

5. In the diagnostic workup of a 60 year-old male suspected   5.___
   of colonic carcinoma, barium enema is planned.
   A nurse would be expected to do all of the following
   EXCEPT
      A. explain to the patient that cramping may be experienced
         during the procedure

B. give the patient a semisolid diet prior to the
   procedure
C. administer laxatives or suppositories
D. give enemas until clear on the morning of the test

6. Regarding dumping syndrome occurring after gastric ulcer   6.___
   surgery, it is TRUE that
   A. there is abrupt emptying of stomach content into the
      intestine
   B. it is associated with the presence of hyperosmolar
      chyme in jejunum, which draws fluid by osmosis from
      extracellular fluid into the bowel
   C. its signs and symptoms include weakness, faintness,
      palpitations, and feeling of fullness
   D. all of the above

7. Nursing interventions in a case of intestinal obstruction   7.___
   would include all of the following EXCEPT to
   A. start with the prophylactic antibiotic to prevent
      intestinal infection
   B. monitor fluid and electrolyte balance
   C. accurately measure drainage from nasogastric tube
   D. prevent complication by measuring abdominal girth
      daily for increasing abdominal distension and monitor
      urine output

8. The FALSE statement regarding diverticulosis is: 8.___
   A. It may be present with alternating constipation and
      diarrhea with blood and mucus
   B. Women in their early thirties are more prone to
      developing diverticulosis
   C. The most common site is in the sigmoid colon
   D. A high residue diet should be included in the treat-
      ment plan

9. The one of the following factors NOT responsible for   9.___
   diverticulosis in a middle-aged man is
   A. stress
   B. congenital weakness of muscular fibers of the intes-
      tine
   C. increased use of laxatives and stool softeners
   D. dietary deficiency of roughage and fiber

10. Nursing intervention in the irrigation of a colostomy   10.___
    tube after bowel surgery would include all of the
    following EXCEPT
    A. filling irrigation bag with desired amount of water
       and hanging bag so the bottom is at shoulder height
    B. removing air from tubing and lubricating the tip of
       the catheter
    C. observing and recording amount and character of fecal
       return
    D. none of the above

11. A 46 year-old male is going to be discharged after a
    hemorrhoidectomy.
    The nurse would NOT be expected to instruct him regarding
    the
        A. high fiber diet and ingestion of at least 2000 cc a
           day
        B. continuation of antibiotics and analgesics for 15-20
           days after the operation
        C. use of stool softeners as needed until healing occurs
        D. sitz baths after each bowel movement for at least
           two weeks after surgery

11.___

12. A 62 year-old male with chronic renal failure is under-
    going hemodialysis.
    Nursing care of this patient before and during hemodialysis
    should include all of the following EXCEPT
        A. assessing vital signs before and every 30 minutes
           during the procedure
        B. ensuring bed rest with frequent position changes for
           comfort
        C. continuing antihypertensives, sedatives, and vaso-
           dilator to prevent a hypotensive episode
        D. monitoring closely for signs of bleeding since blood
           has been heparinized

12.___

13. In peritoneal dialysis, a specially prepared dialysate
    solution is introduced into the abdominal cavity.
    The nurse treating a patient on peritoneal dialysis
    should assess for
        A. peritonitis resulting from contamination
        B. protein loss, as they pass through the peritoneal
           membrane and are lost in dialysate
        C. respiratory difficulty from upward displacement of
           the diaphragm
        D. all of the above

13.___

14. A patient is going to be discharged with continuous
    ambulatory peritoneal dialysis.
    The nurse teaching him should emphasize all of the
    following points EXCEPT
        A. adherence to a high-fat diet
        B. looking for complications like contamination, obstruc-
           tion, and dialysate leak
        C. daily weights
        D. importance of periodic blood chemistries

14.___

15. A 58 year-old man who is a heavy cigarette smoker is
    diagnosed with bladder cancer.
    If surgery is planned, a nurse involved in the pre-
    operative preparation of this patient should
        A. assess the understanding and emotional response of
           the patient
        B. perform pre-operative bowel preparation for a proce-
           dure involving the ileum or colon

15.___

C. discuss with the patient the social aspects of stoma on his sexuality and body image
D. all of the above

16. During postoperative care of the above patient, nursing   16.___
intervention regarding prevention of skin irritation and
breakdown would NOT include that the nurse
    A. patch test all adhesives, sprays, and skin barriers
       before use
    B. implement measures to maintain urine alkalinity
    C. clean peristomal skin with soap and water
    D. place wick on stomal opening when appliance is off

17. Among the predisposing factors for stones anywhere in the   17.___
urinary tract are
    A. diets containing large amounts of calcium and oxalate
    B. increased uric acid levels
    C. sedentary lifestyle, immobility, family history of
       hyperparathyroidism, and gout or calculi
    D. all of the above

18. A 29 year-old male sustains a severe injury to his right   18.___
kidney. Transplantation of the right kidney is done.
Postoperative nursing intervention would include all of
the following EXCEPT to
    A. monitor fluid and electrolyte balance carefully
    B. discourage frequent and early ambulation
    C. assess for signs of rejection, such as decreased urine
       output, fever, pain, edema, increased blood pressure,
       and rise in serum creatinine
    D. monitor vital signs carefully, especially temperature

19. Postoperative nursing care of a patient undergoing a   19.___
nephrectomy for kidney donation would NOT require that
the nurse
    A. assess for urine output every hour, which should be
       at least 30-50 cc an hour
    B. discontinue all drugs as soon as the patient gets
       mobilized
    C. weigh the patient daily
    D. ask the patient to splint the incision while turning,
       coughing, and deep breathing

20. Which of the following statements about prostate cancer   20.___
is INCORRECT?
    A. Squamous cell carcinoma is the most common type of
       prostatic tumor.
    B. It is the second most common cause of cancer death
       in American males over age 55.
    C. A spread to seminal vesicle, bladder wall, and
       external sphincter are common.
    D. Most of the time it is asymptomatic.

21. Postoperative nursing intervention for a patient under-   21.___
    going prostatic surgery for a malignancy would include
    all of the following EXCEPT to
    A. ensure patency of three-way Foley's catheter
    B. monitor continuous bladder irrigation with sterile
       saline solution
    C. control bladder spasms by encouraging frequent walks
       and decreasing rate of continuous bladder irrigation
       if urine color is not red and clots are not present
    D. all of the above

22. Nursing care of a patient on traction after a fracture   22.___
    would NOT include
    A. maintaining proper alignment of the patient in such
       a way that the affected limb rests against the foot
       of the bed
    B. encouraging active exercises for the unaffected limbs
    C. observing for and preventing deep vein thrombosis
    D. performing neurovascular checks to the affected
       extremity

Questions 23-24.

DIRECTIONS: Questions 23 and 24 are to be answered on the basis
              of the following information.

    A 59 year-old woman has severe intolerable pain and disability
of the hip joint due to osteoarthritis. Total hip replacement is
performed.

23. Postoperative nursing care of this patient would include   23.___
    all of the following EXCEPT
    A. maintaining adduction of the affected limb at all
       times with adductor splints between the legs
    B. preventing external rotation by placing trochanter
       rolls along the legs
    C. preventing flexion at the hip
    D. turning only to the unoperative side if ordered

24. When the above patient is discharged, the nurse will NOT   24.___
    instruct her to
    A. avoid sitting in low chairs
    B. always cross the legs while sitting
    C. avoid bending down to put on shoes or socks
    D. use raised toilet set

25. Laminectomy has been done on a patient who has a herni-   25.___
    ated nucleus pulposus at the cervical spine.
    Postoperative nursing care of this patient would include
    all of the following EXCEPT
    A. slightly lowering the head end of the patient after
       cervical spine surgery
    B. applying a neck collar to avoid flexion if ordered
    C. checking dressing for hemorrhage, CSF leakage, and
       infection
    D. assessing for bladder and bowel function

26. Among the following, which one is NOT an indication of complete or partial hypophysectomy?
    A. Pituitary tumors
    B. Testisticular malignancy
    C. Metastatic cancer of the breast or prostate
    D. Diabetic retinopathy

26.___

27. After hypophysectomy through transphenoidal approach, postoperative nursing care would include all of the following EXCEPT
    A. performing frequent oral hygiene with soft swabs to cleanse the teeth and mouth, rinses, no toothbrushing
    B. administering mild analgesics for headaches as prescribed
    C. to avoid CSF leakage, encouraging patient to cough
    D. elevating head of bed to 30° to decrease headache and pressure on sella turcica

27.___

28. Proper nursing care of a patient who has an adrenalectomy done for Cushing's syndrome would be to
    A. observe for hemorrhage and shock by continuously monitoring vital signs and input and output
    B. maximize the aseptic techniques because the immuno-suppressive status of the patient can make him more susceptible to infection
    C. administer cortisone or hydrocortisone as ordered to maintain cortisol levels
    D. all of the above

28.___

29. Regarding intussusception, it is TRUE that
    A. it is most common in boys around the age of 6 months
    B. telescoping of one segment of the bowel into another can cause edema, obstruction, and necrosis of the bowel
    C. bloody mucus in stool is called currant-jelly stool
    D. all of the above

29.___

30. Vesicoureteral reflux will NOT predispose a child to
    A. urinary tract infection
    B. pyelonephritis from chronic UTIs
    C. goodpasture's syndrome
    D. hydronephrosis

30.___

KEY (CORRECT ANSWERS)

1. D	11. B	21. D
2. A	12. C	22. A
3. C	13. D	23. A
4. B	14. A	24. B
5. B	15. D	25. A
6. D	16. B	26. B
7. A	17. D	27. C
8. B	18. B	28. D
9. C	19. B	29. D
10. D	20. A	30. C

TEST 2

DIRECTIONS: Each question or incomplete statement is followed by several suggested answers or completions. Select the one that BEST answers the question or completes the statement. *PRINT THE LETTER OF THE CORRECT ANSWER IN THE SPACE AT THE RIGHT.*

1. A diabetic patient is discharged from the floor.   1.___
   The nurse will give all of the following advice regarding
   good foot care to prevent gangrene EXCEPT:
   A. Wash feet with mild soap and water to prevent drying
      and cracking
   B. Start with antibiotics prophylactically
   C. Cut toenails straight across
   D. Apply lanolin to feet to prevent drying and cracking

2. Nursing intervention in a patient with burns would NOT   2.___
   include
   A. administering powerful analgesics for relief of pain
   B. monitoring alterations in fluid and electrolyte
      balance
   C. stopping all antibiotics at once
   D. promoting maximal nutritional status by providing a
      high calorie, high protein diet with vitamin and
      mineral supplementation

3. Gastrointestinal complications can be prevented by the   3.___
   nurse's taking all of the following measures EXCEPT
   A. assisting with insertion of nasogastric tube to
      prevent stress ulcer and prophylactic administration
      of antacids
   B. discussions about peritoneal dialysis as a good
      treatment modality
   C. monitoring bowel sounds
   D. testing stools for occult blood

4. A tonsillectomy has been performed on a 15 year-old boy   4.___
   with recurrent tonsillitis.
   Postoperative nursing intervention will probably NOT
   include
   A. offering clear, cool, noncitrus,non-red fluids when
      the patient is awake and alert
   B. vigorous suctioning during initial postoperative care
   C. positioning the patient on his side or abdomen to
      facilitate drainage or secretion
   D. observing closely for hemorrhage

5. A 2 year-old boy has aspirated a foreign object.   5.___
   The nurse would do all of the following EXCEPT
       A. try meticulously to remove the object with the help
          of a finger
       B. after removal, place the child in a high humidity
          environment and treat secondary infection if appli-
          cable
       C. perform the Heimlich maneuver if indicated
       D. counsel the parents regarding age-appropriate
          behavior and safety precautions

6. In the postoperative nursing care of a patient who has   6.___
   surgery done for pyloric stenosis, a nurse would NOT be
   expected to
       A. strictly monitor input and output and daily weighing
       B. after feeding, place the patient on his left side
       C. observe the incision for signs of infection
       D. provide the patient with instructions concerning
          feeding and positioning

7. Pre-operatively, nursing intervention to prevent infection 7.___
   in exstrophy of the bladder would
       A. cover the exposed bladder with vaseline gauze
       B. change diaper frequently and keep the diaper loose-
          fitting
       C. keep the area clean, as urine on the skin will cause
          irritation and ulceration
       D. all of the above

8. _____ is NOT an associated anomaly of the exstrophy of   8.___
   the bladder.
       A. Vesicoureteral reflex   B. Epispadiasis
       C. Undescended testicles   D. Chordee

9. All of the following are potential complications follow-   9.___
   ing nasal surgery EXCEPT
       A. bronchiectasis
       B. contaminated nasal pack leading to local infection
       C. aspiration pneumonia
       D. pressure necrosis from packing

10. Pleural effusion is the collection of fluid in the   10.___
    pleural space.
    The one of the following NOT among its possible etiologies
    is
        A. pleuropulmonary infection such as pneumonia
        B. congestive heart failure, cirrhosis and nephrosis
        C. bronchiectasis
        D. disseminated cancer from lung and breast

11. During the management of pulmonary embolism, nursing   11.___
    intervention for restoring pulmonary function and correct-
    ing hemodynamic consequences includes
        A. preparing the patient for assisted ventilation when
           hypoxemia is due to local areas of pneumoconstriction
           and abnormalities of ventilation/perfusion ratio

B. assessing for hypoxia, headache, restlessness, apprehension, pallor, cyanosis, and behavioral changes
C. monitoring vital signs, ECG, and arterial blood gas levels for adequacy of oxygenation
D. all of the above

12. To maintain an open airway and assure adequate respiratory function after thoracic surgery, a nurse should do all of the following EXCEPT   12.___
    A. know that after surgery due to trauma to the tracheo-bronchial tube there is excessive secretion, decreased lung ventilation, and diminished cough reflex
    B. auscultate the chest for adequacy of air movement to detect bronchospasm and consolidation
    C. advise the patient to take high doses of broncho-dilators for symptomatic relief
    D. look and listen for evidence of obstruction while the patient breathes

13. Of the following types of anemia, the one which is NOT an indication for bone marrow transplantation is _____ anemia.   13.___
    A. hemolytic   B. aplastic
    C. sickle cell   D. Fanconi's

14. In the follow-up of a patient who had a pericardiocentesis done, the nurse should look for   14.___
    A. inadvertent puncture of the heart chamber
    B. dysrhythmias
    C. laceration of the coronary artery, myocardium, lung, stomach, and liver
    D. all of the above

15. The one of the following that is NOT among the clinical indications for placing a cardiac pacemaker is   15.___
    A. pericardial effusion
    B. supraventricular and ventricular tachyarrythmias
    C. mobitz type II second degree and complete heart block
    D. plan for prophylactic use before or following cardiac surgery and following acute MI

16. A 28 year-old male suffers a maxillofacial fracture after a vehicular accident. Nursing intervention for the monitoring and prevention of complications in this patient includes all of the following EXCEPT   16.___
    A. monitoring blood pressure, pulse, respirations, and temperature to note early onset of infection and/or aspiration
    B. observing facial nerve injuries for swelling, erythema, pain or warmth to detect infection
    C. maintaining an effective airway by putting the head of the bed down and elevating the foot end of the bed
    D. changing facial dressing as needed to prevent contamination

17. Possible etiological factors for the rupture of an   17.___
    intracranial aneurysm with subarachnoid hemorrhage
    include
    A. atherosclerosis
    B. intracranial arteriovenous malformation
    C. hypertensive vascular disease and head trauma
    D. all of the above

18. A 29 year-old man's traumatic spinal cord injury may   18.___
    manifest itself clinically in all of the following ways
    EXCEPT
    A. acute pain and tenderness in the neck and back along
       with numbness, tingling, burning, and muscle weakness
    B. due to loss of peripheral resistance, a marked
       increase in blood pressure
    C. loss of sweating and vasomotor tone below the level
       of the cord lesion
    D. sensory loss and motor paralysis below the level of
       lesion

19. In the pre-operative nursing intervention of a patient   19.___
    with retinal detachment, the nurse will most likely NOT
    A. provide emotional support during this time of stress
       and restriction
    B. discuss other treatment options with the patient
    C. instruct the patient to remain quiet to prevent
       further detachment of the retina
    D. wash the patient's face gently with an antibiotic
       solution to prevent infection

20. Regarding the postoperative nursing care of a patient   20.___
    with glaucoma,
    A. the patient should be mobilized as early as possible
    B. the head of the bed is elevated to promote the
       drainage of aqueous humor after trabeculectomy
    C. remind the patient that periodic eye check-ups are
       essential since pressure changes may occur
    D. all of the above

21. Nursing intervention for a patient with traumatic joint   21.___
    dislocation should NOT
    A. assist the patient with activities of daily living
       as needed
    B. make every effort to mobilize joints
    C. secure the patient's permission to undergo reduction
       of anesthesia if needed
    D. initiate health teaching concerning the need to
       comply with activity limitations, rehabilitation
       therapies, and long-term monitoring for sequelae

22. After fractures, all of the following complications asso-   22.___
    ciated with immobility may occur EXCEPT
    A. loss of range of motion due to contractures
    B. increased chance of malignancy

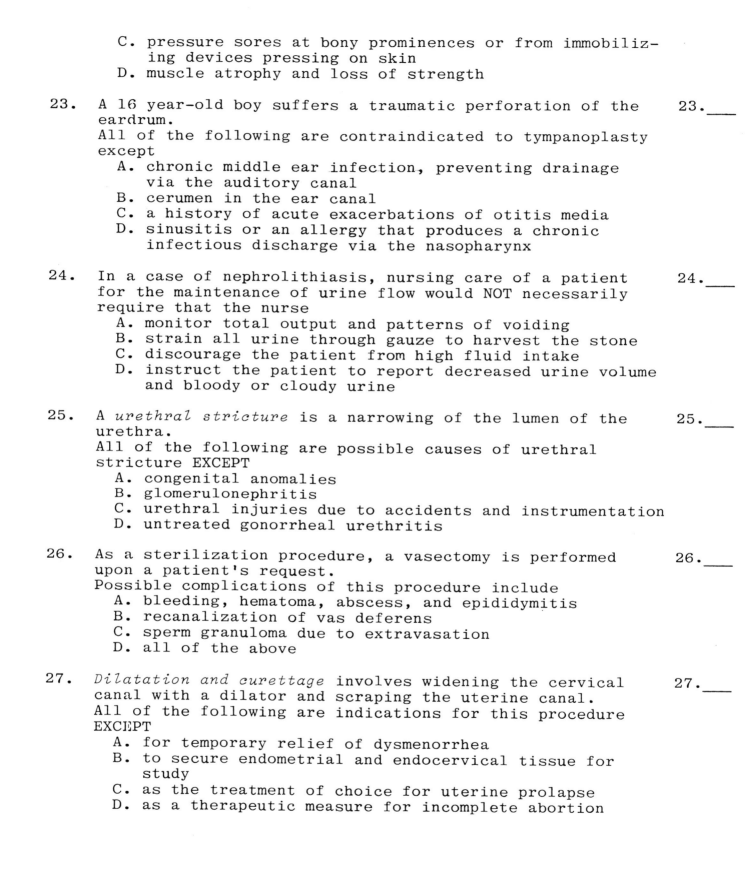

C. pressure sores at bony prominences or from immobiliz-
    ing devices pressing on skin
D. muscle atrophy and loss of strength

23. A 16 year-old boy suffers a traumatic perforation of the   23.___
     eardrum.
     All of the following are contraindicated to tympanoplasty
     except
         A. chronic middle ear infection, preventing drainage
             via the auditory canal
         B. cerumen in the ear canal
         C. a history of acute exacerbations of otitis media
         D. sinusitis or an allergy that produces a chronic
             infectious discharge via the nasopharynx

24. In a case of nephrolithiasis, nursing care of a patient   24.___
     for the maintenance of urine flow would NOT necessarily
     require that the nurse
         A. monitor total output and patterns of voiding
         B. strain all urine through gauze to harvest the stone
         C. discourage the patient from high fluid intake
         D. instruct the patient to report decreased urine volume
             and bloody or cloudy urine

25. A *urethral stricture* is a narrowing of the lumen of the   25.___
     urethra.
     All of the following are possible causes of urethral
     stricture EXCEPT
         A. congenital anomalies
         B. glomerulonephritis
         C. urethral injuries due to accidents and instrumentation
         D. untreated gonorrheal urethritis

26. As a sterilization procedure, a vasectomy is performed   26.___
     upon a patient's request.
     Possible complications of this procedure include
         A. bleeding, hematoma, abscess, and epididymitis
         B. recanalization of vas deferens
         C. sperm granuloma due to extravasation
         D. all of the above

27. *Dilatation and curettage* involves widening the cervical   27.___
     canal with a dilator and scraping the uterine canal.
     All of the following are indications for this procedure
     EXCEPT
         A. for temporary relief of dysmenorrhea
         B. to secure endometrial and endocervical tissue for
             study
         C. as the treatment of choice for uterine prolapse
         D. as a therapeutic measure for incomplete abortion

28. A nurse taking care of a patient after dilatation and curettage would NOT
    A. advise the patient to maintain bedrest for the remainder of the day to decrease cramping and bleeding
    B. advise the patient to refrain from sexual activity for at least one year
    C. monitor the patient's vital signs carefully
    D. advise the patient to use perineal pads at home and report fever, bleeding and/or severe cramping

28.___

29. *Hysterectomy* is the surgical removal of the uterus. All of the following are indications for hysterectomy EXCEPT
    A. second degree uterine prolapse
    B. malignant and/or non-malignant growth that should be removed
    C. endometriosis, when conservative management fails
    D. severe, life-threatening pelvic infection

29.___

30. Advantages of vaginal over abdominal hysterectomy include
    A. fewer surgical complications and shorter hospital stay
    B. no incision
    C. quicker recovery and less abdominal pain
    D. all of the above

30.___

KEY (CORRECT ANSWERS)

1. B	11. D	21. B
2. C	12. C	22. B
3. B	13. A	23. B
4. B	14. D	24. C
5. A	15. A	25. B
6. B	16. C	26. D
7. D	17. D	27. C
8. A	18. B	28. B
9. A	19. B	29. A
10. C	20. D	30. D

EXAMINATION SECTION
TEST 1

DIRECTIONS: Each question or incomplete statement is followed by several suggested answers or completions. Select the one that BEST answers the question or completes the statement. *PRINT THE LETTER OF THE CORRECT ANSWER IN THE SPACE AT THE RIGHT.*

1. A patient on tube feeding is at risk for entry of gastro-   1.___
   intestinal secretions, oropharyngeal secretions, or
   solids or fluids into the tracheobronchial passages.
   Nursing intervention in this case includes all of the
   following EXCEPT
   A. ruling out hypoactive peristalsis and abdominal
      distension with gastric contents
   B. maintaining patency and functioning of nasogastric
      suction apparatus
   C. raising the foot end of the patient's bed to prevent
      gastric reflux through gravity
   D. suctioning and clearing oropharyngeal secretions

Questions 2-4.

DIRECTIONS: Questions 2 through 4 are to be answered on the basis
            of the following information.

   A 26-year-old man is admitted in ICU after sustaining a head
injury in an automobile accident.

2. Nursing intervention for this patient includes assessment   2.___
   of
   A. temperature, pulse, respiration, and blood pressure
      almost every hour
   B. respiratory rate, depth and pattern
   C. chest and abdomen, and look for other sites of
      fracture
   D. all of the above

3. If after head injury in the above patient convulsion   3.___
   occurs, the nurse should take all of the following
   safety measures to prevent any further injury EXCEPT
   A. if possible, place a soft object between the patient's
      teeth before the tonic phase
   B. try to stop the patient's movements
   C. loosen all tight clothing
   D. remain in the patient's room

4. This patient has impaired gas exchange related to altered   4.___
   respiratory drive and cerebral dysfunction.
   Nursing care of this patient, to maintain pulmonary
   stability, would NOT include

    A. if respiratory distress is noted, observing closely, not leaving patient unattended, and notifying physician

    B. notifying physician of any decrease in PaO_2 or pH or any increase in $PaCO_2$

    C. preparing patient for endotracheal intubation if $Pa\ O_2$ decreases to 90 mmHg

    D. monitoring vital capacity, blood gases, and respiratory effort to assess respiratory status

5. A patient is at high risk for altered cerebral function related to head injury.
A nurse would be expected to observe, report, and record, every hour, all of the following EXCEPT

    A. sensory changes

    B. increased blood pressure with widened pulse pressure and cerebral perfusion pressure

    C. pupillary changes, such as change in size, equality, position, direct response, and consensual responses

    D. vomiting or incontinence

5.___

6. After a close head injury, a patient may have altered fluid and electrolyte balance.
To maintain a fluid and electrolyte balance, the nurse should

    A. administer IV fluid, record fluid intake, and weigh patient daily

    B. place a foley catheter and record daily urinary output

    C. monitor serum and urine electrolyte every 8 hours and check hematocrit and blood urea nitrogen levels daily

    D. all of the above

6.___

7. A patient is at high risk for ineffective thermoregulation related to altered hypothalamic process.
To maintain a temperature near normal, the nurse would do all of the following EXCEPT

    A. take the patient's temperature every 2 hours with a tympanic membrane, esophageal, or rectal sensor

    B. keep the room temperature at 30°C

    C. when temperature is elevated, bathe the patient with tepid water sponges rather than alcohol sponges

    D. make sure that fluid intake is at least 3000 ml/day as ordered

7.___

8. After a cerebrovascular accident, a patient is at high risk for gastrointestinal bleeding related to stress or steroid administration.
The resolution of gastric ulceration or bleeding would NOT require the nurse to

    A. monitor for signs of gastrointestinal bleeding, including abdominal tenderness, distension, hypotension, and sudden tachycardia

8.___

      B. check for occult blood from nasogastric aspirate
         and stool every shift on all unresponsive patients
      C. check gastric pH every day and keep it lower than
         3 with antacids
      D. monitor hemoglobin and hematocrit for changes
         indicative of bleeding

9. A patient with CVA is at high risk for systemic infection   9.___
related to invasive procedures or meningitis.
Nursing intervention to assess for signs of infection
would include
      A. monitoring temperature every 4 hours and obtaining
         blood, sputum, urine, and CSF cultures
      B. evaluating intravenous sites every 4-8 hours for
         signs of redness, tenderness, and phlebitis
      C. ensuring strict sterile techniques when assisting
         with such procedures as catheterization, tracheo-
         stomy tube suctioning, and dressing changes on
         central lines and on arterial lines
      D. all of the above

10. A major goal of therapy for intracranial hypertension is   10.___
to determine and, if possible, remove the cause of
elevated pressure.
In the management of intracranial hypertension, it is
NOT necessary to
      A. maintain arterial partial pressure of oxygen (PaO_2)
         greater than 70 torr.
      B. keep patient's head elevated 30-45 degrees and in
         neutral plane
      C. maintain systemic arterial pressure between 120-180
         mmHg systolic
      D. administer lidocaine intravenous bolus as pretreat-
         ment for suctioning and administer barbiturate and
         mannitol as needed

11. *Rebleeding* is a potential complication secondary to sub-   11.___
arachnoid hemorrhage after ruptured intracranial aneurysm.
Nursing intervention to prevent rebleeding includes
      A. ensuring bed rest in a quiet, darkened room with
         restricted visitors to lessen external stimuli
      B. avoiding any activity that could lead to increased
         ICP, such as neck hyperflexion, hyperextension or
         lateral hyperrotation that impedes jugular venous
         return and increases the ICP
      C. providing a high-fiber diet and stool softeners to
         prevent constipation, which leads to straining and
         increased risk of bleeding
      D. all of the above

12. In a patient with an intracranial tumor, signs of impend-   12.___
    ing brain herniation are present.
    A nurse, to decrease further complications, would do all
    of the following EXCEPT
        A. prepare to administer osmotic agents and/or diuretics
        B. notify a physician at once
        C. be sure that the head of the patient is not elevated
        D. if ventriculostomy catheter is placed, drain CSF as
           ordered

13. Lesions of the more anterior portion of the hypothalamus   13.___
    lead to hyperthermia.
    Nursing intervention in a case of malignant hyperthermia
    includes administering
        A. danrolene to rapidly decrease metabolism
        B. cold IV solutions and cool water sponge baths
        C. sodium bicarbonate to reverse metabolic and respira-
           tory acidosis and hyperventilating patient initially
        D. all of the above

14. Nursing intervention for the provision of adequate nutri-   14.___
    tion to the tissues and the correction of electrolyte
    imbalances in malignant hyperthermic patients include all
    of the following EXCEPT
        A. administering 50% dextrose and regular insulin as
           advised
        B. monitoring serum electrolytes and blood urea nitrogen
           and creatinine levels
        C. vigorous administration of sodium chloride and
           potassium supplements
        D. monitoring CPK levels for indications of muscle
           hyperactivity

15. *Clearance* is defined as the ability of the kidneys to   15.___
    clear substances from the plasma.
    Of the following, only _____ does NOT affect renal
    clearance.
        A. glomerular membrane permeability
        B. blood pressure and cardiac output
        C. hypothyroidism
        D. renal blood flow

16. *Hypokalemia* is a potassium deficit of the extracellular   16.___
    fluid, with a serum potassium level less than 3.5 MEQ/L.
    All of the following are findings of hypokalemia EXCEPT
        A. muscular weakness and cardiac irregularities
        B. decreased sensitivity to digitalis
        C. decreased reflexes, paresthesias, and confusion
        D. abdominal distortion and flatulence

17. Individuals with hypophosphatemia develop bleeding dis-   17.___
    orders from defective platelets and fragile red blood
    cell membranes.
    _____ does NOT lead to hypophosphatemia.

A. Prolonged use of IV dextrose infusions
B. Diabetic ketoacidosis
C. Malabsorption disorder
D. Lactic acidosis

18. A primary base bicarbonate deficit is referred to as   18.___
    metabolic acidosis.
    All of the following are causes of metabolic acidosis
    EXCEPT
    A. primary aldosteronism
    B. diabetic keto and lactive acidosis
    C. starvation and diarrhea
    D. uremia

19. *Acute tubular necrosis* refers to damage occurring within   19.___
    the epithelium of the tubular portions of the nephron.
    The ischemic causes of acute tubular necrosis do NOT
    include
    A. rhabdomyolisis
    B. excessive diuretic use
    C. burns and sepsis
    D. hemorrhage and peritonitis

20. *Acute renal failure* can be defined as any rapid decline   20.___
    in GFR with subsequent development of retention of
    metabolic waste products.
    All of the following are intrarenal causes of acute renal
    failure EXCEPT
    A. hypertensive and diabetic sclerosis
    B. toxic damage
    C. severe burns
    D. glomerulo and pyelonephritis

21. *Chronic renal failure* is defined as insidious and irre-   21.___
    versible damage to the kidney.
    Cardiovascular manifestations of chronic renal failure
    do NOT include
    A. hypertension
    B. dysrhythmias
    C. congestive cardiac failure and pericarditis
    D. hypovolemia

22. End-stage renal disease, or uremic syndrome, results   22.___
    from severely elevated BUN, creatinine, potassium and
    phosphate levels.
    Signs and symptoms of this disorder include
    A. restless legs and burning sensation of soles of feet
    B. flapping tremors of hands
    C. poor skin turgor, dependent edema, and easy bruising
    D. all of the above

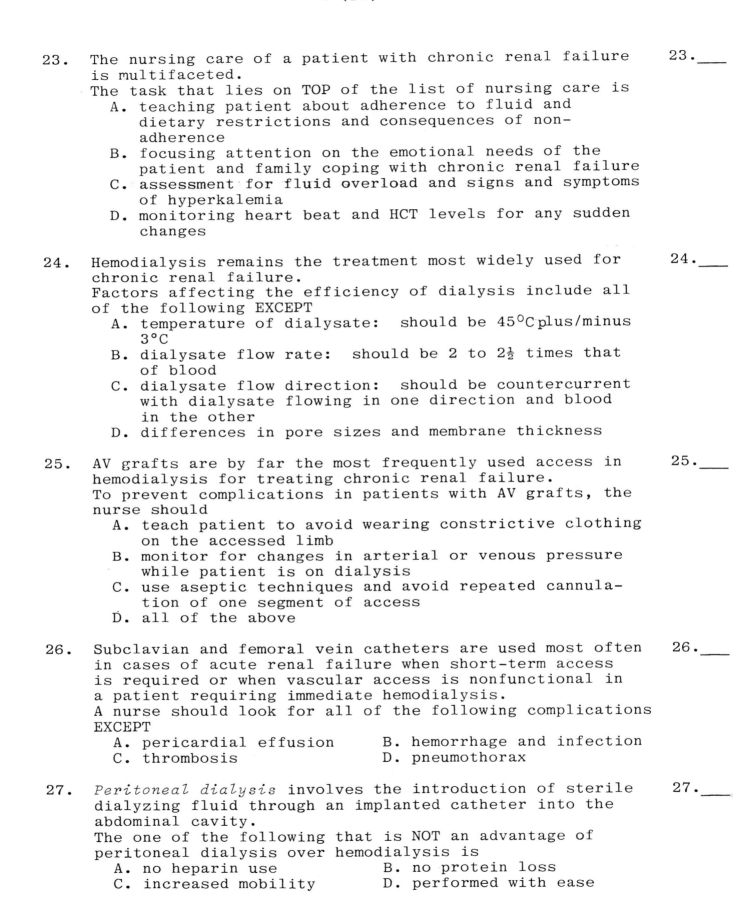

23. The nursing care of a patient with chronic renal failure   23.___
    is multifaceted.
    The task that lies on TOP of the list of nursing care is
    A. teaching patient about adherence to fluid and
       dietary restrictions and consequences of non-
       adherence
    B. focusing attention on the emotional needs of the
       patient and family coping with chronic renal failure
    C. assessment for fluid overload and signs and symptoms
       of hyperkalemia
    D. monitoring heart beat and HCT levels for any sudden
       changes

24. Hemodialysis remains the treatment most widely used for   24.___
    chronic renal failure.
    Factors affecting the efficiency of dialysis include all
    of the following EXCEPT
    A. temperature of dialysate: should be $45^{o}C$ plus/minus
       $3°C$
    B. dialysate flow rate: should be 2 to $2\frac{1}{2}$ times that
       of blood
    C. dialysate flow direction: should be countercurrent
       with dialysate flowing in one direction and blood
       in the other
    D. differences in pore sizes and membrane thickness

25. AV grafts are by far the most frequently used access in   25.___
    hemodialysis for treating chronic renal failure.
    To prevent complications in patients with AV grafts, the
    nurse should
    A. teach patient to avoid wearing constrictive clothing
       on the accessed limb
    B. monitor for changes in arterial or venous pressure
       while patient is on dialysis
    C. use aseptic techniques and avoid repeated cannula-
       tion of one segment of access
    D. all of the above

26. Subclavian and femoral vein catheters are used most often   26.___
    in cases of acute renal failure when short-term access
    is required or when vascular access is nonfunctional in
    a patient requiring immediate hemodialysis.
    A nurse should look for all of the following complications
    EXCEPT
    A. pericardial effusion   B. hemorrhage and infection
    C. thrombosis   D. pneumothorax

27. *Peritoneal dialysis* involves the introduction of sterile   27.___
    dialyzing fluid through an implanted catheter into the
    abdominal cavity.
    The one of the following that is NOT an advantage of
    peritoneal dialysis over hemodialysis is
    A. no heparin use   B. no protein loss
    C. increased mobility   D. performed with ease

28. While dealing with a patient on peritoneal dialysis, a
    nurse should be alert for
    A. fluid overload and blood-tinged effluent
    B. hernias and fluid overload
    C. peritonitis and catheter tunnel infection
    D. all of the above

    28.___

29. Nursing interventions to deal with the complication of
    fluid overload in a patient on peritoneal dialysis
    include all of the following EXCEPT
    A. decreasing the use of hypertonic solutions
    B. weighing patient frequently
    C. monitoring lung sounds and peripheral edema
    D. decreasing oral fluid intake

    29.___

30. Rejection of the transplanted kidney can occur during
    acute surgical implantation or months to years later.
    The one of the following that does NOT correctly describe
    acute renal transplant rejection is:
    A. Cell mediated immunity is involved, with T lympho-
       cytes slowly developing a sensitivity to antigens
       on foreign tissue
    B. It occurs either during surgery or promptly after
       transplant
    C. Occasionally, aggressive treatment with immuno-
       suppressives and radiation can stop the rejection
    D. Diagnosis can be made through monitoring serum
       creatinine levels, renal scan, ultrasonography,
       and even kidney biopsy

    30.___

KEY (CORRECT ANSWERS)

1. C	11. D	21. D
2. D	12. C	22. D
3. B	13. D	23. C
4. C	14. C	24. A
5. A	15. C	25. D
6. D	16. B	26. A
7. B	17. D	27. B
8. C	18. A	28. D
9. D	19. A	29. A
10. C	20. C	30. B

TEST 2

Each question or incomplete statement is followed by several suggested answers or completions. Select the one that BEST answers the question or completes the statement. *PRINT THE LETTER OF THE CORRECT ANSWER IN THE SPACE AT THE RIGHT.*

1. Nursing intervention in a patient with fluid volume deficit related to hyponatremia after sustaining a traumatic injury to the abdomen would include all of the following EXCEPT
   A. if patient is ambulatory, protect from falls until CNS symptoms and postural hypotension clears
   B. start with diuretics, especially thiazide and loop diuretics
   C. if performing nasogastric suctioning, irrigate tube with normal saline solution
   D. provide oral fluids, such as juice or bouillon, that are high in sodium

   1.___

2. Fluid retention during acute renal failure results from the function of compensatory mechanisms governing sodium and water retention.
   From a nursing point of view, outcome criteria in this case do NOT include
   A. edema or ascites absent or reduced to baseline
   B. lungs clear to auscultation and exertional dyspnea absent
   C. weight gain
   D. flat neck veins and blood pressure normal

   2.___

3. Proper nursing care of a patient with fluid volume deficit related to active blood loss includes all of the following EXCEPT
   A. securing an airway and administering high flow oxygen
   B. placing patient in supine position with head elevated to increase preload
   C. administering crystalloid solution, using fluid challenge techniques
   D. moving or repositioning patient minimally to decrease or limit tissue oxygen demands

   3.___

4. Which of the following is NOT a cause of traumatic rupture of the esophagus?
   A. Severe vomiting
   B. During endoscopy, traumatic insertion of a nasogastric tube
   C. Automobile accidents and gunshot wounds
   D. Ingestion of corrosive chemicals

   4.___

5. Risk factors for death from upper GI bleeding include   5.___
   A. age over 60
   B. requiring a transfusion of five or more units of
      blood and H/O recent major operation, trauma, and
      sepsis
   C. disease in three organ systems
   D. all of the above

6. Acute pancreatitis is caused chiefly by gallstones and   6.___
   alcoholism.
   Nursing intervention in the management of acute pancrea-
   titis includes all of the following EXCEPT
   A. continuous monitoring of central venous pressure or
      pulmonary artery pressure to yield information
      about fluid volume
   B. alertness for development of complications
   C. effective analgesia and chest auscultation
   D. continuous ECG monitoring for any cardiac complica-
      tion

7. Intestinal ischemia occurs in patients older than 50 years   7.___
   of age who also have histories of atherosclerosis, cardiac
   failure, or hemodynamic disorders.
   Conditions associated with intestinal ischemia include
   A. thrombosis or embolus in splanchnic bed
   B. polyarteritis nodosa or Buerger's disease
   C. vasculitis secondary to collagen disease
   D. all of the above

8. Acute intestinal obstruction occurs when bowel contents   8.___
   fail to move forward.
   Nursing care of a patient with intestinal obstruction
   includes all of the following EXCEPT
   A. discouragement of nasogastric tube insertion
   B. monitoring patient closely for electrolyte imbalance,
      e.g., hyponatremia and hypokalemia
   C. administration of antipyretics to treat fever
   D. maintaining accurate intake and output

9. A *perforated viscus* is a hole in the bowel that results   9.___
   in spillage of contents into the peritoneal cavity.
   Which of the following is NOT a cause of colorectal
   perforation?
   A. Trauma, such as gunshot or knife wound
   B. Pericolic abscess, appendix, and diverticulum
      rupture
   C. colorectal carcinoma
   D. ingested foreign bodies, such as pits or bones

10. Nursing care of a patient with colorectal perforation   10.___
    includes
    A. assessing vital signs hourly
    B. assessing patient closely for signs of peritonitis,
       such as abdominal pain, rigidity, fever, tachycardia,
       and tachypnea

      C. ordering blood cultures and antibiotics for febrile
         episodes
      D. all of the above

11. A *fistula* is an abnormal communication between two or   11.___
    more structures or spaces.
    Of the following, the conditions that predispose to
    fistula formation include
      A. Crohn's disease and ulcerative colitis
      B. irradiation
      C. diverticulitis and small bowel obstruction
      D. all of the above

12. All of the following factors delay or prevent spontaneous   12.___
    closure of fistulas EXCEPT
      A. complete disruption of bowel continuity
      B. increased vascularity
      C. epithelial-lined tract contiguous with the skin
      D. foreign bodies in the fistulous tract

13. *Pseudomembranous enterocolitis* is an antibiotic-associated 13.___
    diarrhea in which the bowel mucosa and submucosa become
    inflamed and necrosis ensues.
    Nursing care of the patient with pseudomembranous entero-
    colitis would NOT include
      A. perianal skin protection
      B. care of nasogastric tube
      C. monitoring vital signs frequently to evaluate fluid
         and electrolyte imbalances secondary to losses
      D. because of the risk of toxic megacolon and perfora-
         tion, regular abdominal assessments

14. Nursing goals in fistula management include   14.___
      A. patient mobility and comfort
      B. skin protection and nutritional support
      C. drainage containment and odor control
      D. all of the above

15. Diabetic ketoacidosis is a serious complication of   15.___
    diabetes mellitus.
    Increased endogenous glucose is a potential cause of
    diabetic ketoacidosis and can be caused by all of the
    following EXCEPT
      A. decreased growth hormone
      B. increased glucagon
      C. increased sympathetic response, as in stressful
         events such as injury, surgery, infection, and
         emotional trauma
      D. increased dietary intake

16. A patient's hydration status is severely compromised in   16.___
    ketoacidosis.
    Nursing intervention to check the hydration status of a
    patient in diabetic ketoacidosis would NOT include
    monitoring

A. blood pressure changes, neck veins' filling, and
   body weight measurement
B. EEG continuously
C. central venous pressure and pulmonary arterial wedge
   pressure
D. hourly intake and output, and skin moisture and
   turgor

17. During the management of diabetic ketoacidosis, hypo-   17.___
    kalemia can occur within the first 4 hours of the
    rehydration-insulin treatment.
    The nurse on duty should be alert for all of the signs
    and symptoms of hypokalemia which include all of the
    following EXCEPT
    A. continuous ECG monitoring showing prolonged QT
       interval, a flattened or depressed T wave, and
       depressed ST segment
    B. respiratory arrest
    C. bradycardia and increased gastrointestinal motility
    D. muscle weakness, hypotension, and a weak pulse

18. Diabetes insipidus occurs when there is an insufficiency   18.___
    or hypofunctioning of antidiuretic hormone.
    The one of the following that is NOT a cause of central
    diabetes insipidus is
    A. congenital defects of the hypothalamic hypophysial
       system (HHS)
    B. primary and metastatic malignancies involving HHS
    C. trauma, infection, or surgery on HHS
    D. compulsive water drinking

19. Injuries to the aorta can occur through either a blunt   19.___
    or a penetrating mechanism, and predominantly result
    from motor vehicle accidents.
    Aortic disruption can be manifested by all of the
    following signs and symptoms EXCEPT
    A. hoarseness or stridor and dysphagia
    B. upper extremity hypotension and lower extremity
       hypertension
    C. hypovolemic shock and paraplegia
    D. anterior or posterior thoracic pain

20. Radiographic evidence of aortic disruption on an upright   20.___
    anterior posterior view will NOT include
    A. loss of aortic knob
    B. pleural capping
    C. shortening of superior mediastinum
    D. tracheal and esophageal deviation to the right

21. Aortic injury should be HIGHLY suspected in _____   21.___
    fractures.
    A. thoracic spine
    B. multiple left rib (especially left ribs 1, 2, or 3)
    C. scapular and sternal
    D. all of the above

22. Anaphylaxis is a potentially life-threatening allergic   22.___
    reaction.
    Nursing care of a patient with an acute hypersensitivity
    reaction would include all of the following EXCEPT
       A. assessment and support of respiratory and cardio-
          vascular function
       B. starting with the appropriate antibiotic treatment
       C. identification and removal of the offending antigen
          and allergin
       D. education and referral of patient to prevent life-
          threatening events

23. In tension pneumothorax, injury permits atmospheric air   23.___
    to enter into the pleural space during inspiration, but
    it cannot leave during expiration.
    Clinical manifestations of tension pneumothorax do NOT
    include
       A. marked respiratory distress
       B. dullness to percussion
       C. tracheal and apical heart beat shifts to an
          unaffected site
       D. restlessness, agitation, and crepitus

24. Pericardial tamponade results from an injury to the heart   24.___
    causing blood or fluid collection in the pericardial sac.
    Tamponade manifests itself by all of the following signs
    and symptoms EXCEPT
       A. widened pulse pressure and hypertension
       B. pulses paradoxus
       C. progressive venous distension in the neck and arms
          leading to elevated neck vein
       D. muffled heart sounds

25. Aspirin poisoning is NOT manifested by   25.___
       A. hyperpnea and hyperthermia
       B. respiratory acidosis and hyperkalemia
       C. GI hemorrhage and vomiting
       D. hypertension and dehydration

26. Shock is a clinical syndrome characterized by a reduction   26.___
    in effective circulating blood volume and inadequate
    perfusion to the cells.
    Causative factors in bacteremic shock, especially gram
    negative sepsis, include
       A. bowel perforation
       B. pyelonephritis
       C. acute cholecystitis and bacterial endocarditis
       D. all of the above

27. ADH is the hormone directly responsible for maintaining   27.___
    fluid balance within the body.
    Nursing interventions in a patient of fluid volume deficit
    related to decreased secretion of ADH would include all of
    the following EXCEPT

A. monitoring for signs of critical volume deficits, i.e., hypotension, fall in pulmonary artery pressures, and tachycardia
B. avoiding replacement of losses with intravenous dextrose solutions because of the risk of water intoxication
C. anticipating administration of demeclocycline
D. after hypophysectomy, teaching patient to monitor intake and output and document daily weight

28. Pulmonary diseases believed to stimulate the baroreceptors and serve as potential causes of a syndrome of inappropriate antidiuretic hormone secretion include   28.___
    A. pulmonary tuberculosis
    B. chronic obstructive pulmonary disease
    C. viral and bacterial pneumonia and cystic fibrosis
    D. all of the above

29. Nursing interventions in a patient with fluid volume excess related to increased secretion of ADH do NOT include   29.___
    A. monitoring patient closely for evidence of cardiac decompensation caused by excessive preload
    B. with physician's collaboration, administering intravenous hypertonic sodium chloride to temporarily correct hyponatremia
    C. administering vasopressin intravenously
    D. maintaining fluid restriction and monitoring hydration status

30. In the management of a burn patient, after debridement the wound should be left open.   30.___
    All of the following are advantages of the open method EXCEPT
    A. easy assessment of wound
    B. need for strict isolation techniques
    C. dressings would limit the range of motion
    D. decreased risk of diminishing circulation

31. Disseminated intravascular coagulation is a hemorrhagic disorder produced by the effects of both thrombotic and fibrinolytic processes.   31.___
    Which of the following obstetrical disorders is involved in the causation of DIC?
    A. Dead fetus syndrome   B. Toxemia of pregnancy
    C. Amniotic fluid embolism   D. All of the above

32. All of the following are organs usually damaged by disseminated intravascular coagulation EXCEPT the   32.___
    A. heart   B. kidney
    C. pituitary gland D. lungs

33. In laboratory findings, the one of the following that does   33.___
    NOT favor a diagnosis of disseminated intravascular coa-
    gulation is
    A. hyperfibrinogenemia
    B. prolonged prothrombin time
    C. elevated levels of fibrin-split products
    D. thrombocytopenia

34. In the nursing care of a patient with DIC, the precau-   34.___
    tionary steps that should be taken by the nurse to
    prevent hemorrhage include avoiding the use of
    A. intramuscular injections
    B. rectal temperatures, vaginal or rectal suppositories,
       enemas and digital examination of rectum and vagina
    C. aspirin and many nonestreodal anti-inflammatory drugs
    D. all of the above

35. Nursing interventions in a patient with hopelessness   35.___
    related to failing or deteriorating physical condition
    include all of the following EXCEPT
    A. helping patient establish short- and long-term goals
       and look for alternatives
    B. offering information before events occur
    C. supporting patient's sense of security and inner
       strengths and facilitating close personal contacts
    D. none of the above

    _____

KEY (CORRECT ANSWERS)

1. B	11. D	21. D	31. D
2. C	12. B	22. B	32. C
3. B	13. B	23. B	33. A
4. A	14. D	24. A	34. D
5. D	15. A	25. B	35. D
6. D	16. B	26. D	
7. D	17. C	27. C	
8. A	18. D	28. D	
9. C	19. B	29. C	
10. D	20. C	30. B	

EXAMINATION SECTION
TEST 1

DIRECTIONS: Each question or incomplete statement is followed by several suggested answers or completions. Select the one that BEST answers the question or completes the statement. *PRINT THE LETTER OF THE CORRECT ANSWER IN THE SPACE AT THE RIGHT.*

1. While evaluating a case of infertility in a 27 year-old   1.___
   female, endometrial tissue is found attached to the ovary
   on laparoscopy. A diagnosis of endometriosis is made by
   the examining gynecologist. The concerned patient asks
   you what the usual manifestations of endometriosis are.
   Your reply should NOT include a mention of
   A. dysmenorrhea
   B. dyspareunia
   C. irregular menses, cyclic rectal bleeding, and
      hematuria
   D. high-grade fever

2. The drug MOST commonly used in the medical management of   2.___
   endometriosis is
   A. tomaxifen   B. danazol
   C. methotrexate   D. rifampin

3. A nurse involved in the management of a case of endometri- 3.___
   osis should do all of the following EXCEPT :
   A. provide emotional support by including the patient
      and her family in the treatment plan
   B. encourage the patient to try position changes for
      sexual intercourse if there is dyspareunia
   C. teach her how to apply local antibiotic cream to the
      affected area
   D. encourage the use of heating pads and analgesics

4. During the management of endometriosis, medical hypophy-   4.___
   sectomy can be produced by the continued administration of
   A. gonadotropin-releasing hormone agonists
   B. corticosteroids
   C. progestogens
   D. danazol

Questions 5-6.

DIRECTIONS: Questions 5 and 6 are to be answered on the basis of
           the following information.

   A 25 year-old woman comes to the emergency room with complaints
of thick, white vaginal discharge with severe vulvar itching. She
further tells the physician that she has taken amoxacillin for a
urinary tract infection for 1 week. On examination, a beefy red
appearance of the vagina is found.

5. This presentation classically suggests   5.___
   A. trichomonal vaginalis   B. nesseria gonorrhea
   C. candida albicans   D. G. vaginalis

6. The BEST treatment suggestion for this patient is   6.___
   A. clotrimazole and miconazole
   B. metronidazole
   C. sulphonamides
   D. acyclovir

Questions 7-8.

DIRECTIONS: Questions 7 and 8 are to be answered on the basis
             of the following information.

    A 22 year-old woman comes to the gynecologic clinic with
complaints of grey, frothy, malodorous profuse discharge. The
discharge is also accompanied by pruritis. Her sexual partner
also has mild discharge and pruritis. On examination, she has
strawberry spots on her vagina and cervix.

7. What is the MOST likely diagnosis?   7.___
   A. Candida albicans
   B. Trichomonas vaginalis
   C. Herpes simplex Type II disease
   D. Traumatic vaginitis

8. The BEST treatment for this condition is   8.___
   A. acyclovir   B. surgical D & C
   C. metronidazole   D. miconazole

Questions 9-10.

DIRECTIONS: Questions 9 and 10 are to be answered on the basis
             of the following information.

    A 29 year-old woman is presented in the gynecologic clinic
with watery discharge. Laboratory evaluation shows clue cells
and fishy odor when wet mount specimen is mixed with potassium
hydroxide.

9. The organism responsible for this presentation is MOST   9.___
   likely
   A. candida albicans
   B. gardnerella vaginalis
   C. herpes simplex genitalis
   D. T. vaginalis

10. In the management of this patient, all of the following   10.___
    may be advised EXCEPT
    A. oral metronidazole
    B. vaginal creams containing sulphonamides

C. intravenous clindamycin for severe cases
D. treatment of sexual partners to prevent reinfection

Questions 11-13.

DIRECTIONS: Questions 11 through 13 are to be answered on the basis of the following information.

A 17 year-old girl is presented in the gynecologic clinic with burning, itching, dysuria and tenderness of vulva. She is sexually active. On examination, vesicles are present and accompanied by signs of inflammation. Local lymphadenopathy is also present.

11. The causative agent is PROBABLY   11.____
    A. herpes simplex virus II   B. G. vaginalis
    C. chlamydia trachomitis   D. candida albicans

12. In treating this patient, the drug of choice is   12.____
    A. metenidazole   B. penicillin
    C. acyclovir   D. miconazole

13. A nurse involved in the management of this patient should   13.____
    advise her to do all of the following EXCEPT
    A. apply wet dressing locally
    B. take sitz baths with boric acid solution for sympto-
       matic relief
    C. use analgesics as advised by the physician
    D. apply gentacin cream locally at least twice a day

14. Hyperplastic dystrophies are present in a menopausal   14.____
    woman with constant pruritis leading to excoriations.
    The BEST treatment a physician can prescribe is
    A. fluorinated steroid cream
    B. topical testosterone preparation
    C. gentacin cream
    D. sulphonamide-containing cream

15. With reference to the dysfunction of uterine bleeding,   15.____
    which of the following definitions is INCORRECT?
    A. Menorrhagia - Prolonged and excessive bleeding at
       regular intervals
    B. Metrorrhagia - Bleeding that occurs at irregular
       but frequent intervals
    C. Menometrorrhagia - Prolonged bleeding occurring at
       irregular intervals
    D. Oligomenorrhea - Infrequent bleeding occurring less
       than 21 days apart

16. All of the following should be done to avoid pregnancy   16.____
    as a result of rape EXCEPT
    A. administration of clomophine citrate
    B. diethylstilbesterol 25 mg twice a day for 5 days
    C. HCG β-subunit determination
    D. insertion of an intrauterine device

17. All of the following tests are indicated in the initial   17.___
    screening of a pregnant woman EXCEPT
       A. blood group and RH typing
       B. serologic testing for syphilis
       C. alpha fetoprotein level
       D. rubella antibody titer

18. _____ will NOT affect the outcome of pregnancy.   18.___
       A. Syphilis   B. Tuberculosis
       C. Gonorrhea   D. Rubella

19. A 20 year-old, normally menstruating woman suddenly   19.___
    develops a high grade fever of 102°F with vomiting and
    profuse watery diarrhea. Initially, she has hypotension,
    and later she goes into shock. Her urine and blood
    samples are taken. She has a history of tampon use.
    A diagnosis of toxic shock syndrome is made on culture
    reports.
    The organism MOST commonly responsible for toxic shock
    syndrome is
       A. staphylococcus aureus   B. B. hemolytic streptococci
       C. nesseria gonorrhea   D. E. coli

20. A menstruating woman should   20.___
       A. alternate the use of pads with tampons
       B. avoid using super-absorbent tampons
       C. change tampons frequently and not wear one longer
          than 8 hours
       D. all of the above

Questions 21-22.

DIRECTIONS: Questions 21 and 22 are to be answered on the basis
              of the following information.

    A 32 year-old woman, Para II, Gravida II, comes to the clinic
with 10 weeks of amenorrhea and mild abdominal distension. The
patient has only complained of vomiting for the last 2-3 days.

21. The POSSIBLE diagnosis is   21.___
       A. ovarian tumor
       B. gestational trophoblastic disease
       C. pelvic inflammatory disease
       D. all of the above

22. During the initial evaluation of this patient, she is   22.___
    found to be HCG positive in urine.
    What is the next BEST diagnostic test?
       A. Ultrasound of abdomen
       B. Serum HCG
       C. Vaginal smear for staining and culture
       D. Amniocentesis

Questions 23-24.

DIRECTIONS: Questions 23 and 24 are to be answered on the basis
              of the following information.

     A 24 year-old prostitute comes to the clinic with a chancre
on her vulvovaginal region. Her ulcer base is necrotic, surrounded
by red margin. Further examination shows inguinal adenopathy. Gram
staining shows chaining appearance.

23.   The MOST common etiology is   23.___
      A. H. ducreyi   B. N. gonorrhea
      C. H. vaginalis   D. T. pallidium

24.   The BEST treatment in this case is   24.___
      A. metronidazole   B. ampicillin
      C. tetracyclines   D. acyclovir

25.   Scabies   25.___
      A. can be transmitted by nonsexual means such as sharing
         cloths and bedding
      B. is caused by a mite sarcoptes scabiei
      C. presents with severe intermittent itching
      D. all of the above

KEY (CORRECT ANSWERS)

1. D   11. A
2. B   12. C
3. C   13. D
4. A   14. A
5. C   15. D

6. A   16. A
7. B   17. C
8. C   18. B
9. B   19. A
10. C   20. D

21. D
22. A
23. A
24. C
25. D

TEST 2

1. The loss of _____ leads to stress urinary incontinence after the distortion of a normal anatomic urethrovesical relationship.
   A. normal urethral length
   B. posterior urethrovesical angle
   C. hormonal effects of hormones in the postmenopausal period
   D. normal urethral position when supine

   1.___

2. All of the following are legitimate non-pharmacological measures for the prevention of osteoporosis in a menopausal woman EXCEPT
   A. no smoking or alcohol drinking
   B. regular weight-bearing exercises
   C. avoidance of sex
   D. good nutrition containing calcium and vitamin D

   2.___

3. A nurse attending in a case of a postmenopausal woman would most likely NOT
   A. assess her genitalia for elasticity and atrophy
   B. inform the woman that her sexual function is going to be decreased
   C. if the woman desires, provide her with information regarding estrogen replacement
   D. advise a good balanced diet to prevent osteoporosis

   3.___

4. All of the following increase the incidence of cervical cancer EXCEPT
   A. marriage or conception at an old age
   B. multiple sexual partners
   C. cigarette smoking
   D. immunosuppression

   4.___

5. A 64 year-old woman, four days after a radical hysterectomy for endometrial carcinoma, develops sudden shortness of breath, right-sided chest pain, hypotension, and a low grade temperature.
   The MOST likely diagnosis is
   A. myocardial infarction   B. sepsis
   C. pulmonary embolism   D. pneumothorax

   5.___

6. _____ is a complication of oral contraceptives.   6.___
    A. Thromboembolism   B. Hypertension
    C. Liver tumor   D. All of the above

7. All of the following are signs and symptoms of invasive   7.___
carcinoma of the cervix EXCEPT
    A. malodorous bloody discharge
    B. deep pelvic pain
    C. intermenstrual bleeding
    D. postcoital or irregular bleeding

8. Before performing a voluntary sterilization, a physician   8.___
does NOT have to inform the patient that
    A. the procedure is temporary
    B. the operation will result in sterility
    C. there are alternative forms of contraception
    D. there is no guarantee of sterility

9. Consent for voluntary sterilization cannot be obtained   9.___
if the patient is
    A. under 21 years of age
    B. either in labor or having an abortion
    C. under the influence of alcohol or drugs
    D. all of the above

10. While counseling a family for artificial insemination by   10.___
donor, a physician has a duty to explain all of the
following possibilities EXCEPT
    A. no guarantee of pregnancy
    B. chance of endometrial carcinoma increases
    C. possibility of birth defects
    D. despite screening, chances of acquiring a sexually
       transmitted disease

11. A 20 year-old multipara comes to the obstetric clinic for   11.___
her first antenatal visit. She is 10 weeks pregnant.
About 4 weeks before, her chest x-ray was done after a
blunt trauma to the thoracic cage.
The physician should advise her
    A. to think about abortion
    B. that her risk of having a fetus with congenital
       defects is not increased above the baseline risk
       for all pregnancies
    C. that her risk is not increased after a chest x-ray
    D. that her risk is increased about 25%

12. All of the following statements about human papilloma   12.___
virus are correct EXCEPT:
    A. It is associated with hepatic carcinoma
    B. Genital warts are caused by this virus
    C. It is associated with squamous cell carcinoma
    D. Sexual transmission is not the only mode of trans-
       mission

13. In the pretreatment staging evaluation, _____ is considered mandatory.   13.___
    A. intravenous pyelogram
    B. barium enema
    C. cytoscopy and proctosigmoidoscopy under anesthesia
    D. all of the above

14. In the follow-up of a patient with cervical cancer, it is NOT necessary to do   14.___
    A. a CT scan of the head   B. pap smears
    C. periodic chest x-rays   D. an intravenous pyelogram

15. Histologically, the type of carcinoma MOST common in the endometrium is a(n)   15.___
    A. squamous cell carcinoma
    B. adenocarcinoma
    C. adenoacanthoma
    D. transitional cell carcinoma

16. Which one of the following is NOT a characteristic symptom of a patient with ovarian cancer?   16.___
    A. Pelvic mass
    B. Lower abdominal pain
    C. Intermenstrual bleeding
    D. Abdominal distension caused by ascites

17. All of the following statements about dysgerminoma – a germ cell tumor of the ovary – are correct EXCEPT: They   17.___
    A. have a glomerulus-like structure
    B. are the most common germ cell tumor
    C. are exquisitely radiosensitive
    D. have a great tendency for lymphatic invasion

18. Nursing intervention in a case of a patient who has a hysterectomy done due to endometrial carcinoma does NOT include   18.___
    A. instituting sitz baths or wet dressing to alleviate perineal discomfort
    B. monitoring signs and symptoms of bladder infection by regularly checking intake and output and bladder distension
    C. administering prophylactic heparin as prescribed
    D. advising complete sexual abstinence

19. A patient of uterine prolapse is on the floor and you, the nurse in charge of that patient, advise her to do all of the following EXCEPT   19.___
    A. pelvic floor exercises
    B. avoid pregnancy for 3 years
    C. control pain with analgesics, heating pads, and sitz baths
    D. increase fluids to decrease bladder infection

20. A 65 year-old woman comes to the clinic with complaints   20.___
    of pruritis and foul smelling discharge. She has a
    history of infection with human papilloma virus. On
    examination, she has a reddened, slightly ulcerated
    lump on the labio majora with local lymphadenopathy.
    The MOST likely diagnosis is
    A. squamous cell carcinoma of the vulva
    B. prolapse of the uterus
    C. clear cell carcinoma of the vagina
    D. metastasis from endometrial carcinoma

21. The complications of vulvectomy include   21.___
    A. wound breakdown
    B. lymphadema and leg cellulitis
    C. vaginal stenosis
    D. all of the above

22. Which of the following statements is NOT true regarding   22.___
    breast self-examination (BSE)?
    A. Nurses play an important role in motivating women
       towards BSE by teaching them that this is an
       inexpensive, risk-free way to detect cancer.
    B. 90% of cancers are found by women themselves.
    C. 80% of breast lumps are malignant.
    D. It is important to examine the entire breast by
       deep palpation.

23. All of the following American Cancer Society guidelines   23.___
    for mammographic screening of asymptomatic women are
    legitimate EXCEPT for the suggestion of a(n)
    A. baseline mammogram for all women at age 35-40 years
    B. mammography at 1-2 year intervals from ages 40-49
    C. annual mammography for women 50 years or older
    D. mammography every third month for women over 65 years

24. The one of the following that is NOT a definitive risk   24.___
    factor for CA breast is
    A. prior history of breast cancer
    B. late menarche and early menopause
    C. prolonged unopposed estrogen usage
    D. someone in the family (e.g., mother and sister) have
       cancer

25. The ABSOLUTE contraindication to the use of oral contra-   25.___
    ceptives is
    A. diabetes mellitus
    B. depression
    C. a cerebrovascular accident
    D. sickle cell disease

KEY (CORRECT ANSWERS)

1. B		11. B	
2. C		12. A	
3. B		13. D	
4. A		14. A	
5. C		15. B	
6. D		16. C	
7. C		17. A	
8. A		18. D	
9. D		19. B	
10. B		20. A	

21. D
22. C
23. D
24. B
25. C

EXAMINATION SECTION
TEST 1

DIRECTIONS: Each question or incomplete statement is followed by several suggested answers or completions. Select the one that BEST answers the question or completes the statement. *PRINT THE LETTER OF THE CORRECT ANSWER IN THE SPACE AT THE RIGHT.*

Questions 1-10.

DIRECTIONS: Questions 1 through 10 are to be answered on the basis of the following information.

Rosa Dawson, a primigravida, comes to the antepartal clinic accompanied by her husband. This is Rosa's first prenatal visit.

1. Presumptive signs and symptoms (subjective) for pregnancy   1.___
    do not include
    A. amenorrhea   B. urinary frequency
    C. weight change   D. irritability

2. All of the following are known as probable signs and symp-   2.___
    toms (objective) for pregnancy EXCEPT
    A. uterine enlargement
    B. ballottement
    C. quickening
    D. Braxton Hicks' contractions

3. Positive signs and symptoms of pregnancy include   3.___
    A. presence of chorionic gonadotrophin hormone
    B. fetal heartbeat detection as early as eight weeks
       with an electronic device
    C. demonstration of fetal outline by ultrasound after
       third week
    D. all of the above

4. Rosa now needs to consume an extra amount of iron in her   4.___
    meals.
    The BEST source for Rosa to meet her increased daily iron
    requirement is
    A. adding at least two extra pounds of beef to her daily
       diet
    B. consuming at least six glasses of milk daily
    C. taking ferrous sulphate preparations with a vitamin
       C source
    D. including extra fruits in her daily diet

5. Rosa informs the health care staff that she has noticed   5.___
   her husband's gaining weight and suffering from fatigue
   and nausea throughout her pregnancy.
   This phenomenon is known as
      A. motivation   B. identification
      C. mitleiden   D. bondage

6. Rosa comes to the antepartal unit for a nonstress test   6.___
   after experiencing pregnancy-induced hypertension at
   34 weeks' gestation.
   Of the following, the MOST accurate statement about this
   test is that it
      A. determines fetal-maternal placental function
      B. is considered positive if there are no decelerations
      C. is considered positive if there are no fetal heart-
         beats
      D. is non-invasive and observes the response of fetal
         heart rate to the stress of activity

7. Rosa's doctor orders an L/S ratio for her.   7.___
   The nurse knows that this test is an assessment of
      A. fetal renal maturity and function
      B. fetal lung maturity through measurement of lung
         surfactants, using amniotic fluid
      C. bilirubin level, using amniotic fluid
      D. the level of maternal-fetal estriol production

8. An oxytocin challenge test is done to determine fetal   8.___
   well-being.
   The results of this test are considered
      A. *positive* if persistent late decelerations occur in
         more than 50 percent of contractions
      B. *positive* if persistent late decelerations occur in
         more than 75 percent of contractions
      C. *negative* if there are three contractions in ten
         minutes, lasting two minutes without late decelera-
         tion
      D. *negative* if there are six contractions in ten minutes,
         lasting forty seconds without late deceleration

9. Rosa comes to the clinic for evaluation after experiencing 9.___
   contractions throughout the night.
   If Rosa is experiencing Braxton Hicks contractions, the
   nursing assessment will reveal that the contractions
      A. are confined to the upper back
      B. are intensified by excessive rest
      C. are intensified by walking about
      D. do not increase in frequency or intensity

10. Rosa delivers a healthy eight pound boy and wants to   10.___
    breastfeed.
    In teaching Rosa about breastfeeding, all of the following
    information provided by the nurse would be helpful EXCEPT:
       A. Breastfeeding provides the exact type and distribution
          of nutrients needed by a human newborn in the amounts
          required

B. Breastfeeding is initiated by prolactin, which
   stimulates milk production
C. Ovulation is suppressed and pregnancy is impossible
   while breastfeeding
D. Oxytocin causes *let-down* or delivery of milk to
   the nursing baby

11. A pregnant woman notices enlargement of her breast,   11.___
    darkening of nipple, and widening of areola. Veins also
    become visible in the breast.
    All of the following are conditions besides normal
    pregnancy that can produce this breast picture EXCEPT
       A. hyperprolactinemia
       B. calcitonin-producing tumors
       C. pseudocyesis
       D. pre-menstrual syndrome

12. Pregnancy-induced causes of skin changes, such as linea   12.___
    nigra, chloasma, and vascular marking, do NOT include
       A. increased melanocyte-stimulating hormone
       B. increased estrogen
       C. decreased melanocyte-stimulating hormone
       D. stretching and atrophy of connective tissue

13. Constipation is a common complaint during the first and   13.___
    last trimesters of pregnancy.
    To relieve constipation, the nurse should advise the
    patient to make all of the following dietary changes
    EXCEPT
       A. increase daily intake of fruit and vegetables
       B. choose unrefined grains, which contain more fiber
       C. decrease daily fluid intake
       D. include prunes or prune juice, which have a natural
          laxative effect

14. The FALSE statement regarding changes in the cardio-   14.___
    vascular system as a result of pregnancy is:
       A. The heart is displaced to the left and upward
       B. Diastolic murmurs are common in pregnancy
       C. There is an exaggerated splitting of the first heart
          sound
       D. There is a loud, easily heard third heart sound

15. Height of fundus roughly measures the fetal growth or   15.___
    duration of pregnancy.
    Of the following measurements of uterine growth and
    estimated fetal growth, it is INCORRECT that fundus at
    _____ is equal to _____ weeks of gestation.
       A. symphasis pubis; 6
       B. umbilicus; 20
       C. 28 cm. from top of symphasis pubis; 28
       D. lower border of rib cage; 36

16. A nurse should advise the pregnant woman to report at once to the clinic with any unusual signs.
NOT included among these unusual signs requiring a visit to the clinic is
    A. abnormal or severe abdominal pain
    B. chilling fever or burning on urination
    C. ankle edema
    D. vaginal bleeding, new or old blood

16.___

17. A fundal height greater than expected period of gestation suggests all of the following EXCEPT
    A. oligohydramnios   B. miscalculated due date
    C. multiple pregnancy   D. hydatiform mole

17.___

18. Amniocentesis is a procedure in which amniotic fluid is removed from the uterine cavity by insertion of a needle through the abdominal and uterine walls and into the amniotic sac.
During amniocentesis, it is NOT the nurse's responsibility to
    A. reduce the anxiety related to the procedure
    B. reduce the pain and discomfort related to the procedure
    C. start with the prophylactic antibiotic after the procedure
    D. reduce the potential for traumatic injury to the fetus, placenta, or maternal structure

18.___

19. To minimize the chances of traumatic injury, either to the mother or fetus during amniocentesis, it is TRUE that
    A. if the fetus is more than 20 weeks of gestation, the woman should empty her bladder before the procedure
    B. the nurse should obtain maternal vital signs and a 20-minute fetal heart tracing to serve as a baseline to evaluate possible complications
    C. the nurse should monitor the woman during and following the procedure for signs of premature labor or bleeding
    D. all of the above

19.___

20. The *non-stress test* (NST) is used to evaluate fetal heart rate accelerations that normally occur in response to fetal activity in a fetus in good condition.
Indications for NST include all of the following EXCEPT
    A. 30th week of gestation
    B. RH sensitization
    C. suspected intrauterine growth retardation
    D. sickle cell disease, maternal diabetes, and hyperthyroidism

20.___

21. During non-stress testing, the nurse should   21.___
    A. place the woman in semi-Fowler's position to monitor fetal and uterine activity externally
    B. evaluate the response of fetal heart rate immediately following fetal activity
    C. monitor the mother's blood pressure and uterine activity for deviations during the procedure
    D. all of the above

22. A *contraction stress test* is used to evaluate the ability   22.___
    of a fetus to withstand the stress of uterine contractions
    as would occur during labor.
    All of the following are indications for a contraction
    stress test EXCEPT
    A. evidence of potential fetal distress
    B. woman with a reactive non-stress test
    C. history of previous stillbirth
    D. abnormal estriol values

23. Contraindications to a contraction stress test do NOT   23.___
    include
    A. prolonged pregnancy
    B. woman with previous cesarean birth
    C. third trimester bleeding
    D. premature rupture of membranes

24. A nurse attending during contraction stress testing   24.___
    should do all of the following EXCEPT
    A. obtain a 30-minute strip of fetal heart rate and uterine activity for baseline data
    B. place the woman in a sitting position
    C. have the woman void
    D. administer diluted oxytocin via an infusion pump and keep increasing oxytocin every 20-30 minutes, until three contractions occur within 10 minutes

25. To avoid constipation, a pregnant woman should   25.___
    A. perform adequate daily exercise
    B. establish regular patterns of elimination
    C. take in additional fluids and dietary roughage
    D. all of the above

26. By the 10th lunar month, the fetus is supposed to have   26.___
    reached all of the following developmental milestones
    EXCEPT
    A. lanugo almost absent
    B. testes begins descent to scrotal sac
    C. vernix caseosa mainly on back
    D. ample subcutaneous fat

27. Regarding sexual activity during pregnancy, it is NOT   27.___
    true that
    A. there is no contraindication to intercourse during
       pregnancy
    B. women may experience heightened sexual activity
       during the second trimester
    C. the female inferior position is more comfortable
       in the latter half of pregnancy
    D. women may find deep penile penetration uncomfortable

28. Nursing intervention to help the pregnant woman in her   28.___
    employment planning would provide the advice that
    A. there is no reason to stop working unless complica-
       tions arise
    B. exposure to toxic substances, such as chlorinated
       hydrocarbons, lead, benzene, toluene, mercury, and
       radioactive substances, should be avoided
    C. it is desirable to avoid severe physical strain and
       get adequate periods of rest
    D. all of the above

29. In the health teaching of a pregnant woman, the nurse   29.___
    should advise cessation of smoking because of the
    increased risk of complications.
    NOT among these risked complications is
    A. spontaneous abortion
    B. neonatal death increasing directly with increasing
       level of maternal smoking during pregnancy
    C. birth of a high birth weight infant
    D. fetal death

30. Nursing intervention to set a good daily nutrition plan   30.___
    must contain iron because iron performs all of the
    following functions EXCEPT
    A. providing iron for fetal development
    B. enhancing the light and dark adaptation of vision
    C. maintaining mother's stores of iron
    D. maintaining hemoglobin level of mother

KEY (CORRECT ANSWERS)

1. D	11. B	21. D
2. C	12. C	22. B
3. B	13. C	23. A
4. C	14. B	24. B
5. C	15. A	25. D
6. D	16. C	26. B
7. B	17. A	27. C
8. A	18. C	28. D
9. D	19. D	29. C
10. C	20. A	30. B

TEST 2

DIRECTIONS: Each question or incomplete statement is followed by several suggested answers or completions. Select the one that BEST answers the question or completes the statement. *PRINT THE LETTER OF THE CORRECT ANSWER IN THE SPACE AT THE RIGHT.*

1. Nursing advice to relieve respiratory discomfort associated with pressure of the enlarged uterus on the diaphragm include providing relief by   1.___
   A. assuming semi-Fowler's position arranged with pillow
   B. good posture and standing tall
   C. eating small, frequent meals, preventing increased pressure from full stomach
   D. all of the above

2. Calcium should be an important dietary constituent of the nutrition plan of a pregnant woman because it provides all of the following important functions EXCEPT   2.___
   A. skeletal structures of the fetus
   B. maintenance of healthy skin
   C. production of breast milk
   D. blood coagulation, neuro-muscular irritability, and muscle contractility

3. *Fetoscopy* is the insertion of a fiberoptic instrument into the uterine cavity to examine the fetus visually or to obtain blood, placental or tissue samples for identification, and diagnosis of   3.___
   A. congenital anomalies or teratogenic-induced malformations
   B. hemoglobinopathies such as sickle cell anemia and beta-thalassemia
   C. sex-linked autosomal abnormalities or neural tube disorders
   D. all of the above

4. Percutaneous umbilical cord blood sampling is used to identify fetal blood dyscrasias and also for fetal karyotyping.
   Complications of this procedure involve all of the following EXCEPT   4.___
   A. prematurity   B. infections
   C. postmaturity   D. fetal loss

5. The one of the following that is NOT a possible complication of chorionic villous biopsy is   5.___
   A. rupture of membranes
   B. incidence of fetal loss of about 55%
   C. maternal tissue contamination
   D. spontaneous abortion

6. By the 9th lunar month, the fetus is supposed to reach   6.___
    all of the following developmental milestones EXCEPT
       A. 320 mm. crown-rump length and 2500 gms weight
       B. fingernails reach fingertips
       C. testes in inguinal canal
       D. skin is pink and smooth

7. If a couple at risk for passing along a genetic defect   7.___
    chooses to begin a pregnancy, chorionic villi sampling
    may be performed as early as the fifth week of pregnancy.
    Chorionic villi sampling is indicated if
       A. the woman is a carrier of an x-linked disorder
       B. both parents are carriers of a metabolic disease
       C. either partner is a known balanced translocation
          carrier
       D. all of the above

8. After chorionic villi sampling, a woman is found to have   8.___
    a fetus with Down's syndrome.
    All of the following are signs of Down's syndrome EXCEPT
       A. webbing of neck   B. protruding tongue
       C. epicanthal folds   D. hypotonia

9. A nurse should have all of the legal guidelines for   9.___
    genetic screening in her mind before performing the
    procedure.
    The one of the following statements NOT in keeping with
    these guidelines is:
       A. People desiring genetic counseling should sign an
          informed consent form before the procedure
       B. Results may be given to persons other than those
          directly involved
       C. Participation in a genetic screening program must
          be elective, not mandatory
       D. Results must not be withheld from individuals

10. After genetic counseling, a fetus is found to have   10.___
    Klinefelter's syndrome.
    Klinefelter's syndrome manifests itself by all of the
    following clinical signs EXCEPT
       A. small testes   B. gynecomastia
       C. cat-like cry   D. infertility

11. It is INCORRECT that after the 4th lunar month of gesta- 11.___
    tion the fetus'
       A. rudimentary kidneys secrete urine
       B. sex is not differentiated
       C. heartbeat is present
       D. nasal septum and palate close

12. Which of the following is a basic principle that guides nursing practices in the care of women?
   A. Health promotion and disease prevention are more satisfying for the consumer and more cost effective for society
   B. Nursing services are targeted towards helping women develop a sense of mastery of their bodies and their roles in culture
   C. The health of one individual within a social system, such as a family, influences all the other members
   D. All of the above

   12.___

13. Any maternal condition that impairs the blood flow to the placenta causes impairment of oxygen suppy to the fetus, resulting in fetal distress and increased level of corticosteroids, which triggers the elaboration of surfactant in alveolar cells, causing accelerated maturity. All of the following maternal conditions lead to accelerated maturity EXCEPT
   A. chronic glomerulonephritis
   B. hyperthyroidism
   C. sickle cell disease
   D. narcotic addiction

   13.___

14. Specific physiologic alteration resulting from pregnancy may cause neurologic or neuromuscular symptomatology, such as
   A. compression of pelvic nerves or vascular stasis
   B. edema involving the peripheral nerves which may result in carpal tunnel syndrome during the last trimester
   C. acroesthesia, i.e., numbness and tingling of the hands
   D. all of the above

   14.___

15. The mother-child relationship progresses through pregnancy as a developmental process.
   Which of the following developmental tasks are identified in the evolution of this relationship?
   To
   A. accept the biologic fact of pregnancy
   B. accept the growing fetus as distinct from the self and as a person to nurture
   C. prepare realistically for the birth and parenting of the child
   D. all of the above

   15.___

16. Nursing interventions to prevent potential intrauterine infection and reduce anxiety of injury to fetus after sexual intercourse during pregnancy include all of the following EXCEPT
   A. inform woman that intercourse is safe as long as the membranes are intact
   B. caution against use of hot tub

   16.___

C. advise that intercourse is strongly contraindicated during the end of the second trimester and onwards
D. review signs of ruptured membranes

17. To determine the expected date of delivery, the nurse should use
    A. information from the patient's history and then apply Naegle's Rule
    B. ultrasound
    C. fundal height measurements
    D. all of the above

17.___

18. To reduce nausea in a pregnant woman, a nurse should advise her to
    A. eat small, frequent meals instead of three large ones
    B. avoid eating fried or greasy foods, especially before bed
    C. keep crackers or other dry carbohydrates at the bedside
    D. all of the above

18.___

19. *Varicose veins* are large, distended, tortuous superficial veins that may occur during pregnancy.
    To help prevent varicose veins, _____ should be avoided.
    A. obesity
    B. wearing loose clothing
    C. lengthy standing or sitting
    D. constipation and bearing down with bowel movements

19.___

20. For the prevention and treatment of joint pain, backache, and pelvic pressure in a pregnant woman, nursing suggestions would include
    A. maintaining good posture and body mechanics
    B. wearing low-heeled shoes
    C. pelvic floor exercises, rest, and reassurance
    D. all of the above

20.___

21. Heartburn is a frequent complication occurring in the first trimester of pregnancy.
    Nursing advice to prevent and treat heartburn would include all of the following EXCEPT
    A. avoid fatty foods and large meals
    B. take sips of milk for temporary relief
    C. use baking soda to reduce symptoms
    D. maintain good posture

21.___

22. GI tract motility is slowed down because of the effect of progesterone, leading to constipation.
    In the prevention and treatment of constipation, a nurse would NOT suggest that a patient
    A. ingest mineral oil
    B. drink six glasses of water per day
    C. use relaxation techniques and deep breathing
    D. avoid taking stool softeners, laxatives, or other drugs without first consulting a physician

22.___

23. Nursing care of a pregnant woman with headaches would   23.___
    include
    A. emotional support   B. prenatal teaching
    C. conscious relaxation   D. all of the above

24. In the general nursing care plan for a pregnant woman,   24.___
    a nurse should educate the woman about
    A. good nutrition, eating habits, and favorable weight
       gain
    B. the importance of maintaining an exercise program
    C. safety hazards relevant to work and travel
    D. all of the above

25. A nurse caring for a woman experiencing anxiety and   25.___
    negative feelings towards her body should
    A. discuss with her the normal physiologic processes
       responsible for changes in body shape and pigmenta-
       tion
    B. assess the relationship of the couple
    C. discuss with her maternity clothing that will
       enhance the woman's professional image and self-
       concept
    D. all of the above

26. To help a woman with the problem of leukorrea, the nurse   26.___
    should talk with her, discussing
    A. what leukorrea is and what causes it
    B. signs to watch for impending leukorrhea
    C. types of undergarments that aid in controlling
       problems with leukorrhea
    D. all of the above

27. All of the following are signs and symptoms of preterm   27.___
    labor EXCEPT
    A. uterine contractions that occur every 10 minutes or
       more often
    B. decrease in vaginal discharge
    C. abdominal cramping with or without diarrhea
    D. pelvic pressure that feels like the baby is pushing
       down constantly or intermittently

28. Hospital, not home, birth is indicated for women   28.___
    A. who cannot be transferred easily to a hospital should
       the need arise unexpectedly
    B. who are opposed to home birth
    C. with inadequate home facilities
    D. all of the above

29. General goals regarding maternal and fetal nutrition   29.___
    include
    A. involving the woman as a participant in her own care
    B. ensuring optimum nutrition for the gravida and her
       fetus
    C. ensuring optimum nutrition for women of childbearing
       age
    D. all of the above

30. To prepare a woman for amniocentesis, it is NOT necessary   30.___
    to
    A. place the woman in a sitting position with her hands
       under her head or across her chest
    B. take baseline vital signs and fetal heart rate
    C. prepare the abdomen with a shave and a scrub with
       povidone-iodine
    D. pre-medicate if ordered by physician

    ———————

KEY (CORRECT ANSWERS)

1. D	11. B	21. C
2. B	12. D	22. A
3. D	13. A	23. D
4. C	14. D	24. D
5. B	15. D	25. D
6. C	16. C	26. D
7. D	17. D	27. B
8. A	18. D	28. D
9. B	19. B	29. D
10. C	20. D	30. A

———————

EXAMINATION SECTION

TEST 1

DIRECTIONS: Each question or incomplete statement is followed by several suggested answers or completions. Select the one that BEST answers the question or completes the statement. *PRINT THE LETTER OF THE CORRECT ANSWER IN THE SPACE AT THE RIGHT.*

1. Which of these occurrences in a postpartal woman would   1.___
    be MOST indicative of an abnormality?
    A. A chill shortly after delivery
    B. A pulse rate of 60 the morning after delivery
    C. Urinary output of 3,000 ml. on the second day after
       delivery
    D. An oral temperature of 101°F. (38.3°C.) on the third
       day after delivery

2. While discussing nutrition with the nurse, a woman who is   2.___
    a primigravida says that she eats an egg for breakfast
    every day.
    The woman should be informed that the absorption of iron
    from the egg would be BEST facilitated by the woman's
    also eating _____ at the same meal.
    A. toast   B. butter
    C. orange juice   D. bacon

Questions 3-8.

DIRECTIONS: Questions 3 through 8 are to be answered on the
           basis of the following information.

    Ms. Judy Lee, 28 years old and gravida I, is attending the
antepartal clinic regularly. Ms. Lee is carrying twins. In the
38th week of gestation, she is admitted to the hospital in labor.
Her membranes have ruptured.

3. Since Ms. Lee's admission, the nurse has been able to   3.___
    hear and count the heartbeats of both twins. Suppose
    that at a later time during Ms. Lee's labor, the nurse
    can hear only one heartbeat, even after several attempts.
    Which of these interpretations of this finding would be
    ACCURATE?
    A. Inaudibility of one of the heartbeats can result from
       a change in the position of the twins, but it could
       also be due to fetal distress; prompt evaluation of
       the situation by the physician is mandatory.
    B. Muffled fetal heartbeats are common when uterine
       contractions are strong and frequent, as they are in
       a multiple pregnancy; more frequent evaluation of
       the fetal heartbeats is advisable.

    C. Inability to hear one heartbeat in a twin pregnancy
       can normally be expected at intervals throughout
       labor; no action is indicated.
    D. Inability to hear fetal heartbeats in a twin pregnan-
       cy does not indicate fetal difficulty unless accom-
       panied by additional symptoms; amniotic fluid should
       be examined for meconium staining.

4. Ms. Lee's labor progresses, and she delivers spontaneous-   4.___
   ly two girls - one weighs 4 lbs. (1,814 gm.) and the other
   weighs 4 lb. 8 oz. (2,041 gm.). The twins are transferred
   to the premature nursery, and Ms. Lee is transferred to
   the postpartum unit.
   Which of these concepts should be MOST basic to planning
   care for the Lee twins?
    A. Circulatory function is enhanced by frequent change
       of position.
    B. A well-lubricated skin is resistant to excoriation
       and damage.
    C. A premature infant's rectal temperature reflects the
       infant's ability to conserve heat.
    D. Optimal environmental temperature results in minimal
       oxygen consumption in the premature infant.

5. The method used for a premature infant's first formula   5.___
   feeding and the time at which it is begun will be based
   CHIEFLY upon the infant's
    A. birth weight
    B. degree of hydration
    C. level of physiologic maturity
    D. total body surface

6. The smaller of the Lee twins is to be gavaged.   6.___
   In determining the location of the catheter after its
   insertion into the infant, it would be MOST desirable
   to insert
    A. the tip of a large syringe into the catheter and with-
       draw an amount of air equal to the amount of feeding
    B. a few drops of sterile water into the catheter, hold
       the end of the catheter below the level of the
       infant's stomach, and observe it for drainage of
       gastric contents
    C. about 0.5 to 1 ml. of air into the catheter and
       listen to the infant's abdomen with a stethoscope
    D. about 5 ml. of sterile water into the catheter and
       observe the infant's respirations

7. On her second postpartum day, Ms. Lee says to the nurse,   7.___
   I've been to the bathroom four times in the past hour to
   urinate. The funny thing about it is that I only pass a
   small amount of urine each time.
   Which of these initial actions by the nurse would demonstrate the BEST judgment?
    A. Palpate Ms. Lee's abdomen for bladder distention.
    B. Explain to Ms. Lee that frequent voiding is expected
       during the first few days after delivery.

C. Advise Ms. Lee to use a bedpan for her next voiding.
D. Discuss with Ms. Lee the relationship between trauma during delivery and signs of bladder irritation during the postpartum period.

8. On the third postpartum day, Ms. Lee is discharged. The twins are to remain until they have reached an appropriate weight. When the twins are to be discharged, Mr. and Ms. Lee come to the hospital to take them home. Which of these statements, if made by Ms. Lee, would indicate the BEST understanding of her babies' needs?
   A. Our babies' needs are different from those of full-term infants, and we will do all we can to protect them.
   B. We are going to try very hard to counteract the effects of our babies' having been born prematurely.
   C. For a while the smaller baby will need special attention, and then we will be able to treat both of our babies similarly.
   D. We expect to enjoy our babies and will give them the kind of care babies need.

8.___

Questions 9-18.

DIRECTIONS: Questions 9 through 18 are to be answered on the basis of the following information.

Ms. Angela Dobbs, 32 years old and gravida I, is now in her third trimester of pregnancy. She has had diabetes mellitus since the age of 16 and has been attending the antepartal clinic regularly for the past 5 months.

9. Compared with Ms. Dobbs' insulin requirements when she was not pregnant, it can be expected that the insulin dosage during her third trimester will
   A. remain the same
   B. be increased
   C. be decreased
   D. be increased or decreased, depending upon fetal activity

9.___

10. At 30 weeks' gestation, Ms. Dobbs has an ultrasonic examination.
    The results of this examination disclose information about the fetus'
    A. circulatory function
    B. gestational age
    C. presence of surfactant
    D. presence of congenital defects

10.___

11. Because the incidence of fetal death is higher in women who have diabetes mellitus, indications of placental insufficiency should be suspected if Ms. Dobbs has a(n)
    A. sustained drop in her blood glucose level
    B. urinary output of more than 1500 ml. a day
    C. increase in the secretion of gonadotropin
    D. albumin content in her urine of +1

11.___

12. At 35 weeks' gestation, Ms. Dobbs is admitted to the   12.___
    hospital for evaluation of her pregnancy and diabetic
    status. Ms. Dobbs is to have a urinary estriol level
    determination.
    Which of these instructions should be among those given
    to her about collecting the urine for this procedure?
    Collect
        A. the first morning specimen before eating breakfast
        B. a specimen about an hour after the evening meal
        C. a twenty-four hour specimen
        D. a clean-voided specimen

13. Ms. Dobbs is to have an amniocentesis done to determine   13.___
    the lecithin/sphingomyelin (L/S) ratio.
    The purpose of this study is to
        A. assess placental functioning
        B. assess the amount of fetal body fat
        C. determine fetal kidney functioning
        D. determine fetal pulmonary maturity

14. Ms. Dobbs has a cesarean section and is delivered of a   14.___
    boy who weighs 8 lb. 4 oz. (3,742 gm.). He is trans-
    ferred to the intensive care nursery. Ms. Dobbs is
    transferred to the postpartum unit from the recovery
    room.
    Postpartum orders for Ms. Dobbs include an estrogen
    preparation to
        A. promote sodium excretion
        B. suppress the production of chorionic gonadotropin
        C. inhibit secretion of the lactogenic hormone
        D. diminish lochial flow

15. Two hours after delivery, the nurse observes that Baby   15.___
    Boy Dobbs is lethargic and has developed mild generalized
    cyanosis and twitching.
    In view of the fact that his mother has diabetes
    mellitus, the infant is PROBABLY exhibiting symptoms of a
        A. low blood sugar level   B. high CO_2 level
        C. subnormal temperature   D. withdrawal from insulin

16. Because Ms. Dobbs has diabetes mellitus, her infant   16.___
    should be assessed for the presence of
        A. a blood group incompatibility
        B. meconium ileus
        C. phenylketonuria
        D. a congenital abnormality

17. Ms. Dobbs is bottle-feeding her baby. Ms. Dobbs, who   17.___
    has previously observed a demonstration of diapering,
    is changing her baby's diaper for the first time, under
    the supervision of the registered nurse. Ms. Dobbs is
    holding the baby's feet correctly, but when she starts to
    raise his legs to remove the diaper, the feet slip from
    her grasp, and the baby's legs drop back onto the
    mattress of the bassinet. The baby whimpers briefly, and
    Ms. Dobbs looks dismayed.

Which of these responses by the nurse would be BEST?
A. I'll show you again how to change the baby's diaper, Ms. Dobbs.
B. I'll diaper the baby for you this time, Ms. Dobbs.
C. You've almost got it, Ms. Dobbs. Try again?
D. Why are you so nervous, Ms. Dobbs?

18. Some time after discharge, Ms. Dobbs calls the hospital to report the loss of her baby's birth certificate. Where would it be BEST for her to apply for a duplicate? The   18.___
A. record room of the hospital where the baby was born
B. agency that records vital statistics for the community in which the baby was born
C. Census Bureau
D. National Office of Vital Statistics

Questions 19-25.

DIRECTIONS: Questions 19 through 25 are to be answered on the basis of the following information.

Ms. Linda Young, a 17-year-old high school student, attends the antepartal clinic on a regular basis. This is Linda's first pregnancy.

19. Linda is now 7 months pregnant.   19.___
In assessing whether Linda is retaining abnormal amounts of fluid, it would be ESPECIALLY significant that she has gained
A. 3 lb. (1,361 gm.) during the past week
B. 4½ lb. (2,041 gm.) since her last clinic visit a month ago
C. 11 lb. (4,990 gm.) in the second trimester of pregnancy
D. 14 lb. (6,350 gm.) since the onset of pregnancy

20. Which of these measures will contribute MOST to the prevention of postpartal uterine infections?   20.___
A. Routine use of serologic tests for syphilis early in the antepartal period
B. Limitation of sexual intercourse during the last six weeks of pregnancy
C. Maintenance of cleanliness of the perineal area during labor
D. Taking showers or sponge baths exclusively during the last six weeks of pregnancy

21. At term, Linda is admitted to the hospital in active labor. Linda's cervix is 2 cm. dilated and 80% effaced. Which of these interpretations of these findings is CORRECT?   21.___
The
A. cervix is 2 cm. short of complete dilatation, and it is 80% thinner than it was before labor started

    B. cervix is still 2 cm. long, and 80% of the thinning
       of the cervix is completed
    C. walls of the cervix are 2 cm. thick, and 80% of the
       widening of the cervical opening has been achieved
    D. opening of the cervix is 2 cm. wide, and the cervical
       canal is 80% shorter than normal

22. Linda has an episiotomy and delivers a 7 lb. (3,175 gm.)   22.___
    boy. Baby Boy Young is transferred to the nursery and
    Linda is transferred to the postpartum unit. Linda plans
    to bottle-feed her baby. The nurse is assessing Baby Boy
    Young.
    Which of these observations, if made, would be considered
    characteristics of a newborn?
    A. Branlike desquamation of the hands and fee; alternat-
       ing limpness and stiffness of the body; and pink,
       moist skin
    B. Cool, mottled hands and feet; quivering lower jaw;
       and flexion of body parts
    C. Clenched fists; arching of the back when recumbent;
       and frequent crying
    D. Butterfly-shaped area of pigmentation at the base of
       the spine; extension of the arms and legs when the
       head is turned to the side; and diaphragmatic
       breathing

23. When Linda has been admitted to the postpartum unit,   23.___
    she says to the nurse, *I'm so glad my baby is a boy.*
    Maybe Jack will marry me now because he'll be so proud
    to have a son.
    It is probably MOST justifiable to say that Linda
    A. wants to get married in order to gain her independence
       from her family
    B. is capable of subordinating her personal needs to the
       needs of others
    C. is showing a beginning awareness of the problems
       associated with having a baby out of wedlock
    D. lacks insight into the factors that contribute to a
       successful marriage

24. When Baby Boy Young is brought to his mother for the   24.___
    first time to be fed, Linda asks the nurse, *What's wrong*
    with my baby's eyes? He looks cross-eyed.
    Which of these initial responses by the nurse would
    probably be MOST helpful?
    A. Babies seem to be cross-eyed for a while after birth
       because the muscles in their eyes aren't able to
       work together.
    B. You feel that your baby's eyes are abnormal?
    C. I can see that you're upset about this. It would be
       advisable for you to talk with the doctor about it.
    D. Your baby will appear cross-eyed for some time
       because his eyes won't be completely developed until
       he is about six months old.

25. When Linda is talking with the nurse about feeding her baby, she says, *I've heard that if I breastfed him, he'd develop a close feeling toward me more quickly. I had planned to bottle-feed him.* The nurse's initial reply should convey which of these understandings about the development of a mother-child relationship?

25. ___

   A. A satisfactory mother-child relationship will develop more readily through breastfeeding than bottle-feeding.

   B. Holding the baby during bottle-feeding will help to promote a good mother-child relationship.

   C. The times at which the baby is fed by the mother will affect the quality of the mother-child relationship more than the feeding method.

   D. Since bottle-feeding is less complicated than breastfeeding, the mother will be able to focus more attention on mothering functions such as cuddling and talking while the baby is eating.

KEY (CORRECT ANSWERS)

1. D		11. A	
2. C		12. C	
3. A		13. D	
4. D		14. C	
5. C		15. A	
6. C		16. D	
7. A		17. C	
8. D		18. B	
9. B		19. A	
10. B		20. C	

21. D
22. B
23. D
24. A
25. B

TEST 2

DIRECTIONS: Each question or incomplete statement is followed by several suggested answers or completions. Select the one that BEST answers the question or completes the statement. *PRINT THE LETTER OF THE CORRECT ANSWER IN THE SPACE AT THE RIGHT.*

1. The instructions that are ESPECIALLY important to give   1.___
to a pregnant woman who has heart disease are:
   A. Increase protein intake
   B. Take no drugs unless they have been prescribed
   C. Limit high-calorie foods
   D. Avoid fatigue

Questions 2-9.

DIRECTIONS: Questions 2 through 9 are to be answered on the basis of the following information.

Ms. Mary White, 35 years old, is pregnant for the third time. She is receiving antepartal care from a private physician. Ms. White is in the seventh month of pregnancy and has symptoms of preeclampsia.

2. The physician instructs Ms. White not to eat foods which   2.___
have a high sodium content. The nurse tells Ms. White
about foods containing sodium and then asks her to identi-
fy foods lowest in sodium.
Which of these foods, if selected by Ms. White, would be
CORRECT?
   A. Creamed chipped beef on dry toast
   B. Cheese sandwich on whole wheat toast
   C. Frankfurter on a roll
   D. Tomato stuffed with diced chicken

3. In Ms. White's 39th week of gestation, her physician   3.___
recommends that she be hospitalized. When the physician
leaves after examining Ms. White, Ms. White says to the
nurse, *It's easy for you people to say, "Go to the
hospital," but it's not so easy for me to do it. I
can't go just like that!*
After acknowledging her feeling, which of these approaches
by the nurse would probably be BEST?
   A. Stress to Ms. White that her husband would want her
      to do what is best for her health.
   B. Explore with Ms. White ways that immediate hospitali-
      zation could be arranged.
   C. Repeat the physician's reasons for advising immediate
      hospitalization for Ms. White.
   D. Explain to Ms. White that she is ultimately respon-
      sible for her own welfare and that of her baby.

4. Ms. White is admitted to the hospital.   4.___
   Because of the possibility of convulsive seizures, which
   of these articles should be readily available for Ms.
   White's care?
   A. Oxygen and suction machine
   B. Suction machine and mouth care tray
   C. Mouth care tray and venous cutdown set
   D. Venous cutdown set and oxygen

5. The next morning, Ms. White tells the nurse that she   5.___
   thinks she is beginning to have contractions.
   For the timing of uterine contractions, it is recommended
   that she place
   A. her hands on the upper part of the abdomen, on oppo-
      site sides, and curve them somewhat around the
      uterine fundus
   B. the heel of the hand on the abdomen, just above the
      umbilicus, and press firmly
   C. her hand flat on the abdomen over the uterine fundus,
      with the fingers apart, and press lightly
   D. her hand in the middle of the upper part of the
      abdomen and then move the hand several times to
      different parts of the upper abdomen during each
      contraction

6. Ms. White goes into labor.   6.___
   If Ms. White were to complain of a severe headache while
   she is in labor, the nurse should INITIALLY
   A. put Ms. White flat in bed with one pillow under her
      head
   B. take Ms. White's blood pressure
   C. check Ms. White's chart to determine whether she has
      recently received an analgesic
   D. count the fetal heart rate

7. Ms. White delivers a girl. Baby White's Apgar score at   7.___
   1 minute is 8.
   The CHIEF purpose of the first Apgar scoring of a newborn
   is to
   A. obtain a baseline for comparison with the infant's
      future development
   B. evaluate the efficiency of the infant's vital func-
      tions
   C. assess the effectiveness of the initial care given to
      the infant
   D. determine the presence of gross malformations in
      the infant

8. Ms. White is transferred to the postpartum unit, and   8.___
   Baby Girl White is transferred to the newborn nursery.
   Ms. White had a normal vaginal delivery, but is having
   difficulty voiding in the early postpartum.
   The cause of her difficulty is MOST likely due to
   A. decreased abdominal pressure and trauma to the trigone
      of the bladder

B. decreased blood volume and increased production of
estrogen and progesterone
C. increased bladder tone and emotional stress
D. constriction of the kidney pelves and ureters

9. Ms. White is bottle-feeding her baby.   9.___
Which of these manifestations developing in her nipples
or breasts on the third day after delivery would be NORMAL?
A. Decrease in secretion from the breasts
B. Engorgement of the breasts
C. Inversion of the nipples
D. Tenderness and redness of the nipples

Questions 10-11.

DIRECTIONS: Questions 10 and 11 are to be answered on the basis
of the following information.

Ms. Ellen Stone, an 18-year-old primigravida, is brought to the
hospital in early active labor. She has received no antepartal care
during her pregnancy.

10.   Which of these observations of Ms. Stone would be the   10.___
MOST reliable indication that she is in true labor?
A. Strong, intermittent uterine contractions
B. Progressive cervical effacement and dilatation
C. Rupture of the membranes
D. Engagement of the presenting part

11.   During the first stage of Ms. Stone's labor, which of   11.___
these measures by the nurse would be MOST supportive of
her?
A. Administering sufficient analgesia to minimize pain
from uterine contractions and encouraging her to
remain on her back
B. Keeping her informed about the progress of her labor
and helping her to relax between contractions
C. Having her hold on to the nurse's hand during the
height of contractions and reminding her to breathe
rapidly with her mouth open
D. Telling her to bear down with her contractions and
instructing her to sleep between contractions

Questions 12-21.

DIRECTIONS: Questions 12 through 21 are to be answered on the
basis of the following information.

Ms. Karen Newman, a 26-year-old multipara, is pregnant. Her
obstetric history includes 2 full-term pregnancies terminating in
normal deliveries and, prior to her present pregnancy, a spontaneous abortion at 14 weeks' gestation. She is receiving antepartal
care from a private physician.

12. On the basis of Ms. Newman's obstetric history, she is
    designated as a gravida _____, para _____.
      A. III; II   B. III; IV   C. IV; II   D. IV; III

12.___

13. Ms. Newman weighs 152 lb. (68.95 kg.) at the end of the
    fourth month of gestation. Her weight before she became
    pregnant was 135 lb. (61.23 kg.), which was normal for
    her age and body build.
    It is justifiable to say that Ms. Newman's 17-lb.
    (7.72 kg.) weight gain for her stage of pregnancy is
      A. below average   B. average
      C. somewhat above average   D. excessive

13.___

14. Ms. Newman tells the nurse that her 2½-year-old son,
    Danny, tends to be jealous and that she is worried about
    how he may react to the new baby.
    The nurse's reply should indicate that jealousy in a
    2½-year-old
      A. can be lessened by providing a mother-substitute for
         the child when the mother first returns home from
         the hospital
      B. can be suppressed if the child's contact with the
         new baby is restricted
      C. cannot be handled by reasoning with the child
      D. cannot be dealt with therapeutically

14.___

15. Ms. Newman is 2 weeks past term. She is admitted to the
    hospital for induction of labor with an oxytocic drug.
    Upon admission, Ms. Newman is permitted to have liquids
    by mouth.
    Which of these foods would probably be CONTRAINDICATED
    for her?
      A. Tea with lemon   B. Ginger ale
      C. Milk   D. Gelatin dessert

15.___

16. Which of these findings, if present in Ms. Newman, would
    it be ESSENTIAL for the registered nurse to report to
    the physician before the oxytocic infusion is started?
      A. Low backache
      B. A rise in blood pressure from 122/80 to 130/84
      C. An increase in pulse rate from 88 to 98
      D. Regular contractions of 60 seconds' duration

16.___

17. Ms. Newman has an intravenous infusion running, to which
    oxytocin injection (Pitocin) has been added.
    Which of these conditions would warrant IMMEDIATE dis-
    continuation of Ms. Newman's intravenous infusion of
    Pitocin?
      A. Increase in show
      B. Rupture of the membranes
      C. A sustained uterine contraction
      D. A fetal heart rate of 120 during a contraction

17.___

18. Ms. Newman has an order for 100 mg. of meperidine   18.____
    (Demerol) hydrochloride.
    Which of these groups of signs in Ms. Newman would MOST
    clearly indicate that a dose of Demerol could be given
    to her with safety?
    Cervical dilatation, _____ cm.; presenting part at _____
    station; uterine contractions q. _____ minutes, lasting
    _____ seconds; fetal heart rate, _____ beats per minute.
       A. 3; 0; 10; 45; 100   B. 4; 0; 3; 50; 172
       C. 5; -1; 5; 40; 144   D. 7; -1; 2; 60; 120

19. In view of the fact that Ms. Newman had general anes-   19.____
    thesia, it would be safe to start giving her oral fluids
    A. after she voids for the first time
    B. after she has coughed voluntarily
    C. when her pulse rate is 70 beats per minute
    D. when she has rested for about an hour after admission
       to the postpartum unit

20. Penicillin ointment rather than silver nitrate is used   20.____
    in the prophylactic eye care of Baby Boy Newman to
    A. promote a more lasting bacteriostatic effect
    B. gain a more rapid systemic effect
    C. administer therapeutic amounts with greater ease
    D. cause less irritation of the conjunctivae

21. Six weeks after the birth of her baby, Ms. Newman returns 21.____
    to the clinic for a routine follow-up visit. At the
    clinic, Ms. Newman says to the nurse, *Having so many
    children makes it very hard for us to manage, but my
    husband won't do anything to prevent me from getting
    pregnant. He gets angry when I even mention the idea.*
    Which of these approaches by the nurse is LIKELY to be
    MOST useful?
    A. Give Ms. Newman a pamphlet for her husband that
       describes various contraceptive methods.
    B. Ask Ms. Newman to have her husband accompany her to
       the clinic to talk with the nurse about contracep-
       tion.
    C. Refer Ms. Newman to an agency that provides family
       planning services.
    D. Find out from Ms. Newman if her husband would be
       willing to accept a method of contraception that
       would not involve him directly.

Questions 22-30.

DIRECTIONS: Questions 22 through 30 are to be answered on the
                  basis of the following information.

    Ms. Barbara Wing, 21 years old, attends the antepartal clinic
for the first time when she has missed two menstrual periods. The
physician determines that she is pregnant and finds her to be in
good health. This is her first pregnancy.

22. ·During Ms. Wing's initial conference with the registered
    nurse, she mentions that although she usually feels well,
    there are times when she feels tired.
    Which of these responses by the nurse would be BEST?
    A. Fatigue is normal when the body is adjusting to the
       pregnant state. Let's talk about your daily schedule
       so we can plan extra rest for you.
    B. It will be necessary for you to cut down on your
       usual activities and try to get more rest. About
       how many hours of sleep do you get at night?
    C. Your fatigue is probably due to hormonal changes
       that occur in early pregnancy. As your body adapts
       to the demands of your developing baby, this feeling
       will pass.
    D. Your fatigue at this time indicates that you probably
       will have to give special consideration to rest, and
       possibly even to diet, throughout your pregnancy.

22.___

23. Ms. Wing is to include extra amounts of vitamin C in her
    diet.
    She should be instructed that the juice that has the
    LEAST vitamin C per average serving is
    A. canned apple   B. canned tomato
    C. fresh grapefruit   D. frozen orange

23.___

24. Ms. Wing's pregnancy progresses normally.
    In the latter part of the third trimester, Ms. Wing
    should be advised to take which of these precautions
    relative to bathing?
    A. Take sponge baths exclusively
    B. Avoid using bath salts
    C. Bathe only in tepid water
    D. Place nonskid material at the bottom of the bathtub

24.___

25. Ms. Wing is at term and in early active labor when she
    is brought to the hospital by her husband. Mr. and Ms.
    Wing attended a series of preparation for childbirth
    classes.
    Such a program is MOST likely to be successful if the
    A. parents and the medical and nursing staff have
       accepted the philosophy, principles, and techniques
       of the classes
    B. physician is present during labor and gives support
       to the mother
    C. nurse who is to stay with the mother during labor
       and delivery is prepared to assist the father in
     · coaching his wife
    D. mother and father are truly prepared for their roles
       during labor and delivery

25.___

26. The nurse makes all of the following observations of Ms.
    Wing during the second stage of her labor.
    Which one would be of GREATEST significance in terms of
    her welfare and that of her baby?
    A(n)
    A. sudden increase in blood-tinged show
    B. change in the baseline blood pressure from 110/80
       to 90/60

26.___

C. fetal heart rate of 152 to 160 beats per minute
between contractions
D. increase in maternal pulse rate from 90 to 95 beats
per minute during contractions

27. Ms. Wing has an episiotomy and delivers a girl weighing   27.___
7 lb. 5 oz. (3,317 gm.).
Which of these observations of Ms. Wing would indicate
that normal placental separation is occurring?
She has
A. hardening and thickening of the exposed portion of
the umbilical cord, softening of the uterine fundus,
and a steady stream of blood from the vagina
B. strong uterine contractions, recession of the
uterine fundus below the symphysis pubis, and
temporary absence of vaginal bleeding
C. gaping of the vulva in conjunction with strong
uterine contractions, rapid enlargement of the
uterus, and oozing of blood from the vagina
D. increased protrusion of the umbilical cord from the
vagina, the uterus' becoming globular-shaped, and
a sudden spurting of blood from the vagina

28. Ms. Wing is transferred to the postpartum unit, and Baby   28.___
Girl Wing is transferred to the newborn nursery.
In examining Ms. Wing's episiotomy incision, which of
these positions would be appropriate for the patient and
would BEST help to minimize strain on the sutures?
A. Prone   B. Knee-chest
C. Sim's   D. Trendelenburg

29. Which of these measures, if carried out before Baby Girl   29.___
Wing's discharge, will PROBABLY contribute to Ms. Wing's
confidence in her ability to care for her baby?
A. Having Ms. Wing observe demonstrations of infant
care in which equipment commonly found in the home
is used
B. Having Ms. Wing take care of the baby in the hospital
under the guidance of the registered nurse
C. Arranging for Mr. Wing to learn how to assist Ms.
Wing with caring for the baby
D. Arranging to have the community health nurse visit
with Ms. Wing and discuss areas that are of concern
to Ms. Wing

30. Mr. and Ms. Wing discuss birth control with the nurse.   30.___
In selecting a method of birth control, the Wings should
give priority to
A. Ms. Wing's age
B. the length of their marriage
C. the technique they find most acceptable
D. the success rate of a particular method

KEY (CORRECT ANSWERS)

1. D	11. B	21. D
2. D	12. C	22. A
3. B	13. D	23. A
4. A	14. C	24. D
5. C	15. C	25. A
6. B	16. D	26. B
7. B	17. C	27. D
8. A	18. C	28. C
9. B	19. B	29. B
10. B	20. D	30. C

EXAMINATION SECTION
TEST 1

DIRECTIONS: Each question or incomplete statement is followed by several suggested answers or completions. Select the one that BEST answers the question or completes the statement. *PRINT THE LETTER OF THE CORRECT ANSWER IN THE SPACE AT THE RIGHT.*

1. A 21 year-old female develops tender breasts on the third   1.___
   day after delivery.
   The organism which is the MOST likely cause of this
   condition is
      A. staphylococcus aureus   B. streptococcus viridins
      C. klebsiella pneumoniae   D. haemophilis influenzae

2. Which one of the following cancers responds WELL to   2.___
   chemotherapeutic agents?
      A. Ovarian carcinoma   B. Cervical carcinoma
      C. Chosiocarcinoma   D. Carcinoma of the breast

3. The loss of more than 500 cc blood at the time of delivery   3.___
   or immediately thereafter is considered postpartum
      A. hematoma   B. thrombosis
      C. hemorrhage   D. none of the above

4. All of the following factors are major causes of postpartum   4.___
   hemorrhage EXCEPT
      A. uterine atony
      B. laceration of the birth canal
      C. placenta accreta
      D. complete expulsion of the placenta

5. Assessment findings of postpartum hemorrhage generally do   5.___
   NOT include
      A. uterus indicates lacerations when firm with excess
         bleeding
      B. dark red blood with clots
      C. with retained placental fragments, delay of up to
         six weeks
      D. with severe blood loss, signs and symptoms of shock

6. The clinical manifestations of postpartal hemorrhage   6.___
   include a blood loss of greater than 500 cc
      A. within 24 hours prior to delivery in early postpartal
         hemorrhage
      B. after the first 24 hours in late postpartal hemorrhage
      C. both A and B
      D. none of the above

7. Which of the following would be the CORRECT nursing   7.___
   diagnosis for postpartal hemorrhage?
   Fluid volume deficit related to blood loss secondary to
   A. uterine atony
   B. retained placental fragments
   C. lacerations
   D. all of the above

8. All of the following are appropriate nursing interventions   8.___
   for postpartal hemorrhage EXCEPT:
   A. Dim the light of the patient's room and leave her
      all alone in order for her to be able to take a good
      rest
   B. Monitor maternal vital signs for indications of shock
   C. If bleeding occurs, monitor fundus every 15 minutes
      for 1 hour when stable, then at appropriate intervals
   D. Keep the patient warm

Questions 9-12.

DIRECTIONS: Questions 9 through 12 are to be answered on the
             basis of the following information.

     A young, newly-delivered woman arrives at the emergency room.
She complains of feeling pain in her legs and pelvic region. After
preliminary examination by the physician, she is diagnosed with
thrombophlebitis.

9. The lady asks the nurse about the meaning of thrombophle-   9.___
   bitis.
   The nurse explains to the lady that thrombophlebitis
   A. is the formation of a thrombus when a vein wall is
      inflamed
   B. may be seen in the veins of the legs or pelvis
   C. may result from an increase in the circulating
      clotting factors in pregnant and newly-delivered
      women
   D. all of the above

10. While assessing the lady, the nurse expects to notice   10.___
    A. pain, redness, and edema over the affected area
    B. elevated temperature and chills
    C. possible decreased peripheral pulses
    D. all of the above

11. The MOST appropriate nursing diagnosis for thrombophle-   11.___
    bitis would be
    A. potential altered respiratory function related to
       excess work
    B. acute pain related to inflammation and impaired
       circulation
    C. potential altered health maintenance related to lack
       of exercise
    D. all of the above

12. The patient seems to be uncomfortable because of pain in
    the affected area.
    The BEST nursing intervention to make the patient feel
    comfortable quickly would be to
       A. provide a bed cradle to keep sheets off her legs
       B. allow the patient to express her fears and reactions
          to her condition
       C. teach the patient not to massage her legs
       D. administer analgesics as ordered

12._____

Questions 13-16.

DIRECTIONS: Questions 13 through 16 are to be answered on the
             basis of the following information.

    35 year-old, newly delivered Ann Martin comes to the hospital
emergency room with complaints of feelings of discomfort in the
region of her uterus and episodes of backaches and bleeding. After
being examined by the physician, she is diagnosed with *subinvolution*.

13. To be able to assess Ann well, the nurse should know that
    subinvolution
       A. is the failure of the uterus to revert to the pre-
          pregnant state through gradual reduction in size and
          placement
       B. may be caused by infection and retained placental
          fragments in the uterus
       C. may be caused by tumors in the uterus
       D. all of the above

13._____

14. While assessing Ann, the nurse finds out that
       A. the uterus is enlarged
       B. the fundus appears to be lower in the abdomen than
          anticipated
       C. lochia progressed from rubra to alba
       D. all of the above

14._____

15. In subinvolution, the ACTUAL cause of possible leukorrhea
    and backache is
       A. retained placental fragments
       B. tumors in the uterus
       C. infection
       D. all of the above

15._____

16. The nursing intervention that would be MOST helpful to
    improve Ann's condition would be to
       A. tell Ann not to worry about slight bleeding
       B. instruct Ann to report abnormal bleeding to her
          physician
       C. administer oxytocic medication ordered by the head
          nurse
       D. none of the above

16._____

Questions 17-20.

DIRECTIONS: Questions 17 through 20 are to be answered on the basis of the following information.

30-year-old Laura Smith comes to the hospital two weeks after her delivery with complaints of breast pain and fever. After being examined by a physician in the emergency room, she is diagnosed with mastitis.

17.   Mrs. Smith has been admitted to the postpartal care unit.   17.___
      The nurse taking care of Mrs. Smith knows that mastitis
      is caused by
         A. excessive milk production
         B. pumping the breast with an electric pump
         C. the invasion of the breast tissue by pathogenic
            organisms
         D. none of the above

18.   While assessing Mrs. Smith, the nurse notices   18.___
         A. redness and hardened area in the breast
         B. elevated temperature and pulse
         C. chills and tachycardia
         D. all of the above

19.   Mrs. Smith has a fever of 104.2°F and is ordered by her   19.___
      physician to stop nursing her baby for the present time.
      Which of the following nursing interventions would be of
      HIGHEST priority in this situation?
         A. Have Mrs. Smith wear a well-fitting bra for support.
         B. Apply ice packs to reduce pain due to excessive
            collection of milk in the breasts resulting from
            ceased nursing.
         C. Teach Mrs. Smith the importance of handwashing before
            nursing.
         D. Help Mrs. Smith with milk expression on a regular
            basis to prevent engorgement.

20.   The BEST treatment for mastitis is the administration of   20.___
         A. antibiotics, antipyretics, and analgesics as ordered
            by the physician
         B. antipyretics
         C. analgesics
         D. essential vitamins and minerals

21.   There is reversal of all of the following anatomic and   21.___
      auscultatory changes of the cardiovascular system in
      the postpartum period EXCEPT
         A. cardiac enlargement
         B. valvular defects
         C. cardiac displacement due to increased uterine size
         D. abnormal sounds

22. Besides anatomic changes, what other changes may be
    expected in the cardiovascular system of a postpartal
    woman?   22.___
    A. Blood volume drops sharply after delivery and returns
       to non-pregnancy level in 4 weeks
    B. Cardiac output declines gradually to non-pregnant
       level after initial 48 hours
    C. Minimal or no changes in blood pressure or pulse
       after delivery
    D. All of the above

23. Nursing intervention in a postpartal woman taking stool   23.___
    softener includes assessing for
    A. bowel activity   B. diarrhea
    C. any abdominal cramping D. all of the above

24. The one of the following changes NOT expected in the gall   24.___
    bladder of a postpartal woman is
    A. gall bladder emptying increases
    B. risk of gall stones increases
    C. bile flow decreases
    D. liver function studies are no longer abnormal

25. In order to ensure adequate immunologic status, a nurse   25.___
    should,
    A. if patient has signs and symptoms of postpartal
       infection, administer antibiotic
    B. to prevent isoimmunization, most RH negative women
       receive RH immune globulin
    C. if patient lacks immunity for rubella, immunize her
       before discharge
    D. all of the above

KEY (CORRECT ANSWERS)

1. A   11. B
2. C   12. D
3. C   13. D
4. D   14. A
5. C   15. C

6. B   16. B
7. D   17. C
8. A   18. D
9. D   19. D
10. D   20. A

21. B
22. D
23. D
24. B
25. D

TEST 2

DIRECTIONS: Each question or incomplete statement is followed by several suggested answers or completions. Select the one that BEST answers the question or completes the statement. *PRINT THE LETTER OF THE CORRECT ANSWER IN THE SPACE AT THE RIGHT.*

1. The postpartal risk factor for puerperal infection includes all of the following EXCEPT
   A. inadequate infection control
   B. lack of prenatal care
   C. postpartal hemorrhage
   D. retained placental fragments

   1.__

2. The MOST common cause of postpartal hemorrhage is
   A. laceration of the vagina
   B. retained placental fragments
   C. uterine atony
   D. laceration of the cervix

   2.__

3. Postpartal hemorrhage occurs when a patient loses more than _____ ml of blood during or after the third stage of labor.
   A. 50   B. 200   C. 350   D. 500

   3.__

4. The sequelae of severe postpartal hemorrhage do NOT include
   A. anterior pituitary gland necrosis
   B. lung infarction
   C. hepatitis
   D. renal failure

   4.__

5. To ensure early detection of hemorrhage, the nurse should review the client's chart carefully for
   A. cesarean delivery   B. prolonged labor
   C. uterine atony   D. all of the above

   5.__

6. Documentation for the patient with postpartal hemorrhage should include the documentation for any postpartal complications, as well as all of the following, EXCEPT
   A. uterine tone and bladder status
   B. cup measurement
   C. fluid status including urine output every 24 hours for at least 72 hours
   D. effectiveness of oxytocic therapy

   6.__

7. The MOST common cause of puerperal fever is
   A. urinary tract infection
   B. genital tract infection
   C. pneumonia
   D. atelectasis

   7.__

8. NOT included among the common signs and symptoms of   8.___
   postpartum endometritis is
      A. foul lochia   B. fever
      C. seizures   D. peripheral leukocytosis

9. The MAJOR predisposing factor for pelvic infection in a   9.___
   postpartal woman is
      A. cesarean section
      B. multiparity
      C. failure to progress in labor
      D. obesity

10. Pelvic immobility and subsequent joint injury may occur   10.___
    if the patient
       A. is obese
       B. has a small pelvis
       C. had her legs positioned improperly during delivery
       D. was anemic

11. The eclamptic patient has a nursing diagnosis of high   11.___
    risk for injury related to seizure secondary to
    eclampsia.
    To help ensure the patient's safety in case of seizure,
    the nurse should
       A. make sure bed rails are padded
       B. keep an airway at the bedside
       C. keep oxygen and suction apparatus readily available
       D. all of the above

12. Among the following, which is NOT a predisposing condition   12.___
    for venous thrombosis in a postpartal woman?
       A. Preeclampsia
       B. IV heparin use
       C. Immobility
       D. Increased fibrinolysis inhibition

13. A nurse who is taking care of a patient with deep venous   13.___
    thrombosis should be aware of a potential complication of
    DVT, which is
       A. pulmonary embolism   B. hyperthermia
       C. cerebral edema   D. pericardial effusion

14. For the patient with venous thrombosis, an APPROPRIATE   14.___
    nursing evaluation statement may include that the
    patient('s)
       A. condition remained stable with no signs of pulmonary
          embolism
       B. is increasing distances without pain
       C. leg circumference decreased
       D. all of the above

15. The MOST common cause of postpartal mastitis is   15.___
       A. staphylococcus aureus   B. haemophilus influenzae
       C. E. coli   D. klebsiella pneumoniae

Questions 16-17.

DIRECTIONS: Questions 16 and 17 are to be answered on the basis
of the following information.

The time involved in caring for a neonate may seem overwhelming
to the new mother. Her concept of herself as a mother may hinge on
her ability to feed the neonate and cope with the neonate's crying.
When feeding does not go well or the neonate is fretful, she feels
she has failed.

16.   As a nurse, you should   16.___
    A. send her to the psychiatric ward
    B. explore the childcare options
    C. admit her to the hospital
    D. none of the above

17.   The different interventions for this mother include   17.___
    A. mobilizing the patient's support system
    B. referring the patient to a support group
    C. instructing the patient to break down large tasks
       into small, manageable parts
    D. all of the above

18.   When assessing a patient for substance abuse, a PHYSICAL   18.___
sign that the nurse may observe is
    A. memory loss   B. needle marks on the skin
    C. violent behavior   D. frequent mood swings

19.   Mrs. George, a primigravida patient who is breastfeeding,   19.___
is going to be discharged soon.
What patient teaching information should the nurse include
in her discharge plan to prevent mastitis?
    A. Breastfeed the infant at least every 2 to 3 hours
    B. Begin breastfeeding with the affected breast and
       continue with this breast until it is completely soft
    C. To allow the breast to empty completely, do not wear
       a brassiere or other restrictive clothing when breast-
       feeding
    D. All of the above

20.   In a discharge teaching plan for a patient with thrombo-   20.___
embolic disease, the nurse should NOT tell her to
    A. wear an elastic support stocking
    B. perform prescribed leg exercises
    C. frequently massage and/or rub the affected extremity
    D. not to sit or stand for a long period

21.   The amount and duration of lochia - postpartal vaginal   21.___
discharge - correlate with endometrial healing and
regeneration.
All of the following statements about lochia discharge
are true EXCEPT:

A. Women who have cesarean deliveries exhibit a heavier lochia flow of longer duration than those who deliver vaginally.
B. The first stage of lochia contains a mixture of mucus, tissue debris, and blood.
C. The second stage contains more serous and paler fluids.
D. The final stage contains creamy white, brown, or colorless discharge consisting mainly of serum and white blood cells.

22. Lochia is considered abnormal if it contains any of the following EXCEPT   22.___
    A. large clots or tissue fragments
    B. blood or mucus
    C. a foul or offensive odor
    D. relapse to a previous stage

23. The postpartal period typically brings complete resolution of pregnancy-related respiratory changes and associated complaints.   23.___
    These changes and complaints do NOT include
    A. shortness of breath
    B. chest and rib discomfort
    C. decreased tolerance for physical exertion
    D. none of the above

24. As progesterone level declines, oxygen demand decreases and the uterus no longer impinges on the diaphragm.   24.___
    It is also TRUE that
    A. tidal volume, minute volume, and vital capacity decrease to non-pregnancy values
    B. function residual capacity rises to non-pregnancy level
    C. both of the above
    D. none of the above

25. All of the following are signs of postpartal hemorrhage EXCEPT   25.___
    A. decreased pulse and respiratory rate, with increased blood pressure
    B. boggy uterus
    C. both of the above
    D. none of the above

KEY (CORRECT ANSWERS)

1. B	6. C	11. D	16. B	21. A
2. C	7. B	12. B	17. D	22. B
3. D	8. C	13. A	18. B	23. D
4. B	9. A	14. D	19. D	24. C
5. D	10. C	15. A	20. C	25. C

EXAMINATION SECTION

TEST 1

DIRECTIONS: Each question or incomplete statement is followed by
several suggested answers or completions. Select the
one that BEST answers the question or completes the
statement. *PRINT THE LETTER OF THE CORRECT ANSWER IN
THE SPACE AT THE RIGHT.*

1. Mothers of infants and toddlers should be instructed that   1.___
    diets for their children that include milk at the expense
    of other foods are MOST likely to result in the develop-
    ment of a deficiency in
        A. iron   B. carbohydrate
        C. vitamin D   D. vitamin K

2. A 1-week-old boy, weighing 6 pounds, has just been   2.___
    returned to the pediatric unit after having surgery for
    an intestinal obstruction. He has nasogastric suction
    and is receiving intravenous fluids via a venous cutdown.
    In addition to meeting the infant's special needs, which
    of these measures would be ESSENTIAL?
        A. Restraining all four of the baby's extremities
        B. Handling the baby as little as possible
        C. Explaining the equipment used in the baby's treatment
           to his mother so that she can assist the nurse with
           his care
        D. Spending time stroking the baby

3. A mother makes all of these comments about her infant   3.___
    daughter to the physician.
    Which one describes a characteristic MORE likely to be
    observed in an infant with hypothyroidism than in a
    normal 3-month-old infant?
        A. She smiles a lot.
        B. She's so good and she never cries.
        C. She notices her toys and she knows my voice.
        D. She seems to spend a great deal of time watching her
           hands.

Questions 4-7.

DIRECTIONS: Questions 4 through 7 are to be answered on the basis
               of the following information.

    Bruce Alfonse, 9 years old, has an acute asthmatic attack and
is admitted to the hospital because he did not respond to treatment
in the emergency room. He has had bronchial asthma since early
childhood.

4. Bruce is to receive 100 mg. of aminophylline intravenous-   4.___
    ly.
    If the ampules of aminophylline available on Bruce's unit
    contain aminophylline gr. 7$\frac{1}{2}$ in 10 cc. of solution, how
    much solution from the ampule will contain 100 mg. of
    aminophylline?
        A. 2 cc.   B. 4 cc.   C. 6 cc.   D. 8 cc.

5. Which of these events in Bruce's life would be MOST likely   5.___
    to cause an increase in the frequency and intensity of his
    asthmatic attacks?
      A. Ms. Alfonse's buying new furniture for Bruce's bed-
         room
      B. The Alfonse's moving to another city
      C. Mr. Alfonse's being away from home on business for
         several days
      D. Bruce's favorite grandparent's coming to visit for
         a week

6. An IMPORTANT objective of the medical and nursing manage-   6.___
    ment of Bruce should be to help him to
      A. accept the fact that he cannot be like other children
         and that he will have to limit his goals
      B. accept his condition and live a productive life
      C. understand the underlying cause of his condition
      D. accept being dependent upon his mother until he is
         in his middle teens

7. The nurse is planning Bruce's care.   7.___
    Consideration should be given to the fact that most normal
    8-year-olds
      A. prefer to associate with a peer of the same sex
      B. seek opportunities for socializing with older boys
      C. enjoy small heterosexual groups
      D. function best as a member of a large group of some-
         what younger boys and girls

Questions 8-13.

DIRECTIONS: Questions 8 through 13 are to be answered on the
             basis of the following information.

Jeff Green, age 2½, sustained a simple fracture of the shaft
of the left femur when he fell down stairs at home. Upon his
admission to the hospital, Jeff is placed in Bryant's traction.

8. Among the equipment used in the application of Bryant's   8.___
    traction is
      A. adhesive material on the skin of both limbs
      B. metal calipers in the malleoli of both ankles
      C. a Kirschner wire in the affected femur
      D. a Thomas splint on the fractured extremity

9. During his first two days in the hospital, Jeff lies   9.___
    quietly, sucks his thumb, and does not cry.
    It is MOST justifiable to say that he
      A. has made a good adjustment to the traction
      B. is accustomed to being disciplined at home
      C. has confidence in the nurses caring for him
      D. is experiencing anxiety

10. Prior to his admission, Jeff was partially bowel-trained,   10.___
    but now he defecates involuntarily.
    The nurse's approach to this problem should be based on
    which of these assessments?
       A. What is Jeff's reaction to his soiling
       B. How compulsive is Jeff about cleanliness
       C. Is Jeff too young for bowel training
       D. Is bowel training important for Jeff

11. Ms. Green is upset because when she comes to visit,   11.___
    Jeff turns his head away from her and holds his arms
    out to the nurse.
    It is probably MOST justifiable to say that Jeff
       A. is angry with his mother for leaving him in the
          hospital
       B. is testing the relationship between his mother and
          the nurse
       C. now has a stronger emotional tie with the nurse
          than with his mother
       D. is consciously trying to make his mother jealous

12. One day when the nurse offers Jeff a cookie, he says *No!*   12.___
    and at the same time holds out his hand for it.
    Which of these interpretations of Jeff's behavior is
    PROBABLY justifiable?
       A. His mother has forbidden sweets, and he is in con-
          flict about accepting any.
       B. He is confused about the meaning of yes and no.
       C. His negativism is a beginning attempt at independence.
       D. He is unaccustomed to being offered choices.

13. To prevent accidents such as Jeff's among toddlers, which   13.___
    one of the following measures would probably help MOST?
       A. Having carpeting on stairs
       B. Using adjustable gates on stairways
       C. Providing the toddler with a plentiful supply of
          play materials in one room
       D. Keeping the toddler in a playpen placed near the
          mother's work area

Questions 14-19.

DIRECTIONS: Questions 14 through 18 are to be answered on the
             basis of the following information.

     Adam Crane, 13 years old, is admitted to the hospital for
treatment of acute rheumatic fever. He is placed on bed rest.

14. Adam MOST probably has which of these groups of symptoms   14.___
    that are characteristic of acute rheumatic fever?
       A. Swelling of the fingers, petechiae, and general
          malaise
       B. Nodules overlying bony prominences, dependent edema,
          and elevated blood pressure
       C. Bleeding gums, dyspnea, and failure to gain weight
       D. Fever, rash, and migratory joint pain

15. Adam is receiving a corticosteroid drug.   15.__
    He should be observed for common side effects of this
    type of drug therapy, such as
       A. hypotension   B. weight loss
       C. pallor   D. acne

16. An oral potassium preparation is ordered for Adam.   16.__
    The CHIEF purpose of this drug for him is to
       A. promote excretion of bacterial toxins
       B. prevent hypokalemia
       C. enhance the action of the corticosteroid drug
       D. reduce the electrical potential of the cardiac
          conduction system

17. Adam's blood tests include all of the following results.   17.__
    Which of these results would be MOST indicative of
    improvement in his condition?
       A. Positive C-reactive protein
       B. Hemoglobin, 14.0 Gm. per 100 cc. of blood
       C. White blood cell count, 11,000 per cu. mm. of blood
       D. Decreasing erythrocyte sedimentation rate

18. Permanent functional impairment would MOST likely result   18.__
    if Adam developed
       A. erythema marginatum   B. polyarthritis
       C. carditis   D. subcutaneous nodules

19. Recurrent attacks of rheumatic fever in Adam can BEST be   19.__
    prevented by
       A. keeping him on prophylactic drug therapy for an
          indefinite period
       B. including foods in his diet that are rich in vitamins
          and minerals
       C. improving his family's socioeconomic condition
       D. providing daily afternoon rest periods for him for
          about a year after recovery from an acute attack

Questions 20-25.

DIRECTIONS: Questions 20 through 25 are to be answered on the
                 basis of the following information.

    Daniel Rich, 6 weeks old, is admitted to the pediatric unit
with pyloric stenosis. He is to have a pyloromyotomy.

20. Daniel's parents tell the nurse that they do not quite   20.__
    understand what the doctor has told them about the
    operation, and they ask for clarification.
    Which of these explanations to the parents would be MOST
    appropriate?
       A. Daniel's stomach is contracted and its capacity
          diminished, making it necessary for the doctor to
          dilate it with instruments.

B. Nerves have produced contraction of certain muscles in Daniel's stomach called sphincters, and these nerves must be cut in order to produce relaxation.
C. Constricting bands of tissue in the middle of Daniel's stomach, which are causing vomiting, will be resected.
D. The doctor will make a cut in a tight muscle at the bottom of Daniel's stomach, which has caused his symptoms.

21. Preoperatively, Daniel is to receive 0.15 mg. (gr. 1/400) of atropine sulfate.
If a vial containing 0.4 mg. (gr. 1/150) in 1 cc. of solution is used to prepare Daniel's dose, how much of the stock solution should be given to him?
_____ cc.
   A. 0.28   B. 0.33   C. 0.38   D. 0.43
   21.___

22. Daniel should be observed for early symptoms of side effects of atropine, which include
A. vomiting and subnormal temperature
B. lethargy and bradycardia
C. rapid respirations and flushed skin
D. muscle spasms and diaphoresis
   22.___

23. Daniel has a pyloromyotomy.
Assuming that Daniel's operation is successful, his parents should be informed that his convalescence can be expected to be
A. *gradual*, with the persistence of mild preoperative symptoms for a few weeks
B. *prolonged*, with gradual reduction and eventual disappearance of preoperative symptoms over a period of a few months
C. *brief*, but with periodic recurrence of preoperative symptoms during his first 6 months of life
D. *rapid*, and characterized by the absence of preoperative symptoms
   23.___

24. Daniel is now 8 weeks old.
He should be expected to
A. cry when a stranger approaches
B. pay attention to a voice
C. laugh aloud
D. make sounds such as *ba-ba* and *da-da*
   24.___

25. In response to Ms. Rich's questions, the nurse discusses with her the introduction of new foods into Daniel's diet.
Which of these suggestions by the nurse would be MOST appropriate?
A. Whenever a new food is added to Daniel's diet, decrease the amount of milk offered to him.
B. Give Daniel new foods one at a time.
C. Allow Daniel to touch each new solid food before he tastes it.
D. Mix new foods with a small amount of some food Daniel has previously had.
   25.___

KEY (CORRECT ANSWERS)

1. A			11. A	
2. D			12. C	
3. B			13. B	
4. A			14. D	
5. B			15. D	
6. B			16. B	
7. A			17. D	
8. A			18. C	
9. D			19. A	
10. A			20. D	

21. C
22. C
23. D
24. B
25. B

TEST 2

DIRECTIONS: Each question or incomplete statement is followed by several suggested answers or completions. Select the one that BEST answers the question or completes the statement. *PRINT THE LETTER OF THE CORRECT ANSWER IN THE SPACE AT THE RIGHT.*

1. Parents are given information relative to the nutrition   1.___
   of normal newborn infants.
   Which of the following statements is INACCURATE?
   A. Formulas made of modified cow's milk are well
      absorbed.
   B. A high protein intake assures a rapid growth rate.
   C. The total daily intake of nutrients is more important
      than the size or frequency of individual feedings.
   D. Infants born of well-nourished mothers are likely to
      have adequate stores of nutrients at birth.

2. A 3-year-old has nephrosis and marked ascites.   2.___
   In which position is she likely to be MOST comfortable?
   A. Semi-Fowler's   B. Sims'
   C. Dorsal recumbent   D. Prone

3. A 5-year-old with leukemia is to be discharged because   3.___
   his condition is in a state of remission.
   It will be MOST helpful to the child when he is at home
   if his parents understand that
   A. the child's condition is terminal, and it will be
      their responsibility to make him as happy as possible
      without making demands upon him
   B. they should guide their child, encouraging him and
      setting limits for him, so that he may develop to
      his full potential
   C. it will not be necessary for them to control their
      child's behavior because his condition makes him
      aware of his own limitations
   D. it will be important for them to develop a carefully
      planned schedule for the child that will conserve
      his strength

Questions 4-7.

DIRECTIONS: Questions 4 through 7 are to be answered on the
            basis of the following information.

    Josh Greene, 9½ months old, is admitted to the hospital. He
has a provisional diagnosis of intussusception.

4. Josh MOST probably has which of these symptoms that are 4.___
   characteristic manifestations of the onset of intussusception in an infant?
     A. Abdominal distention and coffee-ground vomitus
     B. Hyperpyrexia and rectal prolapse
     C. Passage of large amount of flatus associated with
        straining
     D. Paroxysmal abdominal pain accompanied by screaming

5. When the physician tells Mr. and Ms. Greene that immediate 5.___
   surgery will be necessary if Josh's diagnosis is confirmed,
   they are reluctant to give permission for the operation.
   If surgery is not performed soon after a diagnosis of
   intussusception is made, which of these conditions is
   LIKELY to result?
     A. Chronic ulcerative colitis
     B. Megacolon
     C. Meckel's diverticulum
     D. Gangrene of the bowel

6. A barium enema is ordered to help confirm Josh's diagnosis. 6.___
   An additional reason why a barium enema is ordered for
   Josh at this time is that it may result in
     A. elimination of offending toxins
     B. diminution of microbial flora of the intestine in
        preparation for surgery
     C. control of bleeding due to the barium's astringent
        effect on the bowel lining
     D. reduction of the telescoped bowel segment

7. Josh has intussusception, and the condition is corrected 7.___
   by surgery. His recovery is satisfactory.
   When Josh begins to feel better, the play material that
   would probably be MOST appropriate for him is a
     A. mobile
     B. beanbag
     C. roly-poly animal with a weighted base
     D. tinker toy with parts securely fastened

Questions 8-15.

DIRECTIONS: Questions 8 through 15 are to be answered on the
             basis of the following information.

Amy Simpson, 13½ years old, is in the hospital for treatment
of newly diagnosed diabetes mellitus. A teaching program for Amy
and her mother has been instituted by the nursing staff.

8. To plan a teaching program for Amy, the nurse should con- 8.___
   sider that the factor that will have the GREATEST influence
   on its success is
     A. the child's age
     B. the child's parents' acceptance of the diagnosis
     C. whether or not teaching is done consistently by the
        same nurse
     D. whether or not teaching is limited to one-hour periods

9. When teaching Amy and her parents about insulin, it is   9.___
important to include the fact that insulin
   A. requirements will decrease with age
   B. dosage is determined, primarily, on the basis of
      daily food intake
   C. dosage, after adolescence, can be adjusted by the
      person in terms of variations in physical activity
   D. will be needed for life

10. One morning when the nurse goes to help Amy with morning   10.___
care, Amy is argumentative and restless. She makes
unkind remarks to the other children.
It is essential for the nurse to give IMMEDIATE considera-
tion to which of these questions?
   A. Does Amy need a more structured plan of care?
   B. When did Amy have her insulin and did she eat her
      breakfast?
   C. Was there some incident that occurred the previous
      day that has upset Amy?
   D. Is Amy bored and does she need help in selecting
      recreational activities that will utilize her
      excess energy?

11. One day Amy asks the nurse, *Will I be able to go with*   11.___
the gang after school to get ice cream or a hot dog?
Which of these responses by the nurse would give Amy
accurate information?
   A. You can go with the group, but the hot dogs, ice
      cream, and other foods that they eat are prohibited
      for you. Your friends will learn to be considerate
      of your special needs.
   B. Both hot dogs and ice cream contain valuable nutri-
      ents. But if you have a hot dog, don't eat the
      roll.
   C. You can have a hot dog if you omit a corresponding
      amount of food from your next meal. Since sweets
      are not good for you, avoid foods like ice cream.
   D. Being with your friends is important. You can eat
      a hot dog or ice cream sometimes. We'll help you
      learn how to choose foods.

12. One day Amy tells her mother and the nurse that she does   12.___
not want to give herself insulin. Her mother says to her,
You don't have to give yourself the injection if you
don't want to. I'll do it for you.
Which of these understandings should be the basis of the
nurse's response?
   A. The mother must be helped to understand the importance
      of the girl's participation in her own care.
   B. The girl needs to assume responsibility for her
      treatment; therefore, Amy and her mother should be
      taught separately.
   C. Children with diabetes often rebel against puncturing
      themselves with needles, and teaching should be dis-
      continued until signs of readiness are demonstrated.
   D. The reaction of the mother is normal and should be
      overlooked.

13. A few days before Amy is discharged, her scout leader   13.___
    visits her. The scout leader stops at the nurses' station
    before leaving and says, *The troop is going on a four-day
    camping trip next month. Amy is very eager to go, and
    I'd like to have her come. But I'm rather concerned about
    having her out in the woods with us.*
    Before replying, which of these questions should the nurse
    consider?
        A. Are such trips contraindicated for children who have
           diabetes?
        B. Would it be too hazardous for Amy to attempt the trip
           so soon after her hospitalization?
        C. Will there be an adult accompanying the children who
           has had experience with children who have diabetes?
        D. Does Amy have enough information about her condition
           so that she is unlikely to have any difficulty?

14. Ms. Simpson says to the nurse, *Amy has never been a*   14.___
    *complainer. I'm afraid that she will not tell me if
    she doesn't feel well before she goes to school.*
    Which of these responses by the nurse would be MOST
    helpful to Amy's mother?
        A. It will be important to find out how Amy is feeling
           without stressing symptoms in talking with her.
        B. It is the school nurse's responsibility to help you
           with problems like this.
        C. Since Amy behaves this way, it will be necessary for
           you to question her frequently about how she feels.
        D. You don't need to worry about this because when Amy
           leaves the hospital her diabetes will be controlled.

15. In the management of a child with diabetes mellitus,   15.___
    occasional minimal glycosuria may be allowed.
    The purpose of this management is to
        A. retard degenerative tissue changes
        B. detect early symptoms of impending coma
        C. reduce the incidence of insulin shock
        D. facilitate diet supervision

Questions 16-22.

DIRECTIONS: Questions 16 through 22 are to be answered on the
             basis of the following information.

Jimmy Brown, 6 years old, is brought to the hospital immediately
after sustaining burns that occurred in his home when he pulled a pan
of boiling water off the stove. He has severe burns, mostly third
degree, of the anterior chest, upper arms, forearms, and hands.

Jimmy is placed in a single room. An intravenous infusion is
started, an indwelling urethral (Foley) catheter is inserted, and
pressure dressings are applied to his burned areas.

16. Jimmy develops burn shock.
    He can be expected to exhibit
    A. restlessness and bradycardia
    B. air hunger and hyperreflexia
    C. intense pain and convulsions
    D. pale, clammy skin and thirst

16.___

17. To plan for Jimmy's fluid replacement needs, it should
    be noted that the
    A. younger the child, the greater amount of fluid he
       needs in proportion to his body weight
    B. proportion of body weight contributed by water is
       smaller during early childhood than it is during
       adulthood
    C. fluid needs per kilogram of body weight are variable
       until the kidneys become functionally mature at
       adolescence
    D. total volume of extracellular fluid per kilogram of
       body weight increases gradually from birth to
       adolescence and then stabilizes at the adult level

17.___

18. On admission, Jimmy's rectal temperature was 99°F.
    (37.2°C.) Twelve hours later, it is 101.6°F. (38.7°C.).
    On the basis of the information provided about him, it
    is MOST justified to say that it
    A. is an expected development in injuries such as Jimmy's
    B. is indicative of damage to Jimmy's heat-control
       center
    C. is a manifestation of rapidly spreading infection
    D. has resulted chiefly from a marked increase in serum
       potassium

18.___

19. Twenty-four hours after his admission, Jimmy complains
    that his chest dressing feels too tight.
    The nurse should FIRST
    A. check Jimmy's respirations
    B. loosen the chest bandage
    C. call the doctor
    D. find out whether Jimmy has a p.r.n. order for an
       analgesic

19.___

20. When selecting a site for the administration of a paren-
    teral drug to Jimmy, it would be MOST important for the
    nurse to consider that
    A. impaired circulation hampers drug absorption
    B. decreased blood volume shortens the period of drug
       action
    C. drug action is potentiated by increased amounts of
       circulating epinephrine
    D. concentration of blood plasma in the tissues poten-
       tiates the desired effects of drugs

20.___

21. Which of these meals for Jimmy would be HIGHEST in   21.___
    proteins and calories?
       A. Vegetable soup, cottage cheese on crackers, apple-
          sauce, hot chocolate
       B. Cheeseburger, french fried potatoes, carrot sticks,
          cantaloupe balls, milk
       C. Fresh fruit plate with sherbet, buttered muffin,
          slice of watermelon, fruit-flavored milk drink
       D. Chicken noodle soup, cream cheese and jelly sandwich,
          buttered whole kernel corn, orange sherbet, cola
          drink

22. Jimmy is scheduled to go to the physical therapy depart-   22.___
    ment at 9:30 A.M. every day. One morning at 8:30, after
    Jimmy has had his breakfast, the nurse who goes in to
    bathe him finds him sound asleep.
    Which of these actions by the nurse would demonstrate
    the BEST judgment?
       A. Allow Jimmy to sleep until necessary equipment for
          his bath is gathered and then wake him for the
          procedure.
       B. Let Jimmy sleep and postpone his bath until sometime
          later in the day.
       C. Wake Jimmy gently and bathe him, explaining to him
          that he can rest when he returns from physical
          therapy
       D. Bathe Jimmy as quickly as possible and then let him
          sleep until it is time to go for physical therapy.

Questions 23-24.

DIRECTIONS: Questions 23 through 24 are to be answered on the
               basis of the following information.

    Ralph Dunn, 15 years old, is admitted to the hospital for
treatment of ulcerative colitis.

23. Ralph is receiving methantheline (Banthine) bromide.   23.___
    The CHIEF purpose of this drug for Ralph is to
       A. suppress inflammation of the bowel
       B. reduce peristaltic activity
       C. neutralize acid in the gastrointestinal tract
       D. increase bowel tone

24. Ralph is on a low-residue, high-protein, high-calorie   24.___
    diet.
    To meet the requirements of Ralph's diet prescription,
    the nurse should guide Ralph to select as an evening
    snack
       A. a roast beef sandwich
       B. strawberry shortcake with whipped cream
       C. canned peaches
       D. fresh orange juice

25. The nurse is discussing nutrition with the mother of two   25.___
    sons, a preadolescent and an adolescent.
    The mother should be instructed that in terms of nutri-
    tional needs, as compared with most normal preadolescent
    boys, MOST normal adolescent boys need _____ calories
    _____ protein.
    A. more; but less   B. more; and more
    C. fewer; but more   D. fewer; and less

―――――

KEY (CORRECT ANSWERS)

1.	B	11.	D
2.	A	12.	A
3.	B	13.	C
4.	D	14.	A
5.	D	15.	C
6.	D	16.	D
7.	C	17.	A
8.	B	18.	A
9.	D	19.	A
10.	B	20.	A

21. B
22. B
23. B
24. A
25. B

―――――

EXAMINATION SECTION
TEST 1

DIRECTIONS: Each question or incomplete statement is followed by several suggested answers or completions. Select the one that BEST answers the question or completes the statement. *PRINT THE LETTER OF THE CORRECT ANSWER IN THE SPACE AT THE RIGHT.*

1. Which approach by the nurse to a newly admitted toddler, who is not acutely ill, and to his mother would probably be MOST reassuring to both?   1.___
   A. Getting acquainted with the toddler before discussing his likes and dislikes with the mother
   B. Having the mother hold the toddler while questioning her about his habits
   C. Leaving the toddler with the play lady in the playroom while talking with the mother about his habits and preferences
   D. Holding the toddler while asking the mother questions about his habits

2. The nurse is assessing whether a normal 5-year-old is achieving the primary developmental task for children of his age.   2.___
   If the child is achieving this task, the child's behavior should indicate that he is developing a sense of
      A. trust   B. identity   C. intimacy   D. initiative

3. The mother of a 1-year-old and a 3-year-old is talking with the nurse about the eating habits of her children.   3.___
   In comparing the eating habits of most normal children of those ages, which DIFFERENCE is likely to be evident?
   A. The food intake of a 3-year-old will be about three times greater than that of a 1-year-old.
   B. A 1-year-old will have stronger food preferences than a 3-year-old.
   C. A 3-year-old will do more fingering of foods than a 1-year-old.
   D. The appetite of a 3-year-old is likely to be more capricious than that of a 1-year-old.

Questions 4-7.

DIRECTIONS: Questions 4 through 7 are to be answered on the basis of the following information.

Liz Thomas, 18 months old, is admitted to the hospital with symptoms of a subdural hematoma.

4. Liz's mother asks about her daughter's diagnosis.   4.___
She should be told that a subdural hematoma is
   A. under the outer layer of the meninges
   B. between the inner layer of the meninges and the
      brain
   C. in the soft tissues of the scalp
   D. under the periosteum and above the meninges

5. Liz has a craniotomy with removal of a hematoma. Her   5.___
condition is good. Mr. and Ms. Thomas are suspected
of physically abusing Liz.
The day after Liz's surgery, a nurse's aide says to the
nurse, *Every time I see Ms. Thomas, I see red. How
could any adult, least of all a mother, deliberately
hurt a little child?*
Which of these initial responses by the nurse would
probably be MOST helpful to the aide?
   A. Making judgments about parents' actions is not
      appropriate for nursing personnel.
   B. You must not let Ms. Thomas know how you feel.
   C. It is an upsetting situation, isn't it?
   D. There is no legal proof that Liz's parents have
      been abusing her.

6. Which of these measures is MORE important for toddlers   6.___
who have been battered than for other hospitalized
toddlers?
   A. Providing opportunities for physical activity
   B. Arranging to have them cared for consistently by
      the same personnel
   C. Scheduling specific visiting times for parents
   D. Providing opportunities for play with other toddlers

7. A staff nurse asks the nurse in charge, *Suppose I report*   7.___
*to the appropriate agency that a child in my community
has sustained a multiplicity of unexplained injuries
and may have been abused by the parents. What could
happen to me for reporting this information?*
If the state in which the nurse lives has a child abuse
law that covers nurses, it would be CORRECT to say that
he/she will be
   A. legally liable if a suit for slander is brought by
      the child's parents
   B. immune from legal action as a consequence of making
      the report
   C. exempt from appearing in court in defense of the
      child if a suit develops
   D. none of the above

Questions 8-11.

DIRECTIONS: Questions 8 through 11 are to be answered on the basis
               of the following information.

Gary Pott, 6 months old, is brought to the clinic by his mother.
Gary has phenylketonuria and is on a phenylalanine-controlled diet.

8. The nurse encourages Ms. Pott to keep Gary on the pre-   8.___
    scribed diet.
    The nurse should include in her teaching plan the under-
    standing that phenylketonuria is thought to be the
    result of
        A. insufficient fat intake during early infancy
        B. deficiency of an enzyme needed to utilize galactose
           during early infancy
        C. inability of the infant to metabolize one of the
           essential amino acids
        D. abnormal accumulation of lipids in the cells of
           infants

9. Ms. Pott should be instructed that the food that is   9.___
    HIGHEST in phenylalanine is
        A. fruits   B. fats   C. breads   D. jams

10. Ms. Pott tells the nurse that although her husband is   10.___
    working, his salary is small and they are having diffi-
    culty covering the cost of Gary's special feedings,
    along with other expenses.
    Which of these actions would BEST exemplify the CORRECT
    role of the nurse in this situation?
        A. Help Ms. Pott to reassess her budget.
        B. Refer Ms. Pott to the doctor.
        C. Make an appointment for Ms. Pott with the social
           worker.
        D. Report Ms. Pott's problem to the local department of
           welfare.

11. All of the following descriptions of Gary's behavior are   11.___
    typical of a normal 6-month-old infant EXCEPT that he
        A. raises himself to a sitting position, but he cannot
           lie down without help
        B. babbles, but the babbling is not in response to a
           specific situation
        C. can hold a small object simultaneously in each hand,
           but he drops one or both of them after a short period
        D. bends his fingers to grasp an object, but he does
           not use a pincer motion to pick up an object

Questions 12-16.

DIRECTIONS: Questions 12 through 16 are to be answered on the basis
of the following information.

One-month-old Susan Black is brought to the well child unit by her
mother for her first clinic visit.

12. To assess the adequacy of an infant's weight, the MOST   12.___
important index is the
A. age at which the infant doubles his birth weight
B. relationship between the infant's increase in height
and weight
C. infant's total weight gain since birth
D. pattern of the infant's weight gain

13. Ms. Black tells the nurse that she gives Susan twice   13.___
the prescribed amount of a multivitamin preparation
because the prescribed amount seems so small.
The nurse's response should MOST certainly include the
fact that
A. it is uneconomical to give vitamins in excess of
body requirements
B. an infant's growth rate can be accelerated by
vitamins in excess of the recommended daily requirements
C. metabolic processes are stimulated by large amounts
of vitamins
D. excessive amounts of fat-soluble vitamins can be
toxic

14. Examination reveals a possible congenital dislocation   14.___
of Susan's left hip.
Which of these observations of an infant would be an
early symptom of unilateral congenital dislocation of
the hip?
A. Flexion of the leg on the affected side and exten-
sion of the other leg when in the supine position
B. Absence of a gluteal fold on the affected side
C. Limited abduction of the hip on the affected side
D. Prominence of the hip on the unaffected side

15. Susan is referred to an orthopedic clinic, and a diagno-   15.___
sis of congenital dislocation of the left hip is established. A splint that holds Susan's legs in frog
position is used in her initial care.
When Susan is 10 months old, she is admitted to the
hospital; and, with closed manipulation, the head of
her left femur is placed in the acetabulum. A hip spica
cast is then applied. The cast extends from her waist-
line to below the knee on the left side and to a point
above the knee on the right side.

Which of these measures would probably be MOST helpful
in preventing Susan from becoming unresponsive and
withdrawn while she is hospitalized?
   A. Placing her in a room with several other infants
      the same age as she is
   B. Providing her with a variety of toys that she can
      handle
   C. Arranging for her mother to help with her care each
      day
   D. Keeping her regimen of care the same each day

16. If treatment for unilateral congenital dislocation of   16.___
    the hip had been delayed for Susan until after she
    walked, she would have been LIKELY to develop
   A. scoliosis and scissors gait
   B. pigeon toes and knock-knees
   C. a limp and lordosis
   D. waddling gait and knock-knees

Questions 17-25.

DIRECTIONS: Questions 17 through 25 are to be answered on the basis
              of the following information.

     Mr. Ted Wynn, 17 years old, awakens one night because he is having
difficulty breathing and noticeable wheezing on expiration. He is
admitted to the hospital. He has a history of asthmatic attacks.
His orders include isoproterenol (Isuprel) hydrochloride. Pulmonary
function studies and other diagnostic tests will be done after his
acute episode subsides.

17. The nurse should observe Mr. Wynn for   17.___
   A. pallor and dyspnea
   B. bradycardia and diplopia
   C. diarrhea and elevated blood pressure
   D. tachycardia and headache

18. All of the following information is provided by Mr. Wynn.   18.___
    The provoking factor of his asthmatic attack is probably
    that he
   A. wore a new suit made of a synthetic material two
      days ago
   B. smoked more cigarettes than usual during the past
      week
   C. has been up date at night playing cards with his
      friends
   D. slept on a new feather pillow

19. During the night, Mr. Wynn perspires profusely.   19.___
    The nurse should
   A. inform the physician
   B. watch him for signs of hypovolemic shock
   C. cover him with another blanket
   D. change his gown and sheets as needed

20. The MAJOR purpose of pulmonary function tests for
Mr. Wynn is to
    A. determine his exercise tolerance
    B. determine which areas of his lungs are affected
    C. evaluate the extent of his ventilatory deficiency
    D. evaluate the adequacy of his cardio-pulmonary
       circulation

20.___

The next morning, Mr. Wynn has an acute asthmatic attack.
Epinenphrine hydrochloride (Adrenalin) is administered
to him.

21. The nurse should observe Mr. Wynn for vasoconstricting
effects of Adrenalin, which include
    A. drowsiness and hypotension
    B. throbbing headache and tremor
    C. flushed face and increase in body temperature
    D. polyuria and urticaria

21.___

22. During the asthmatic attack, Mr. Wynn spontaneously
assumes an upright sitting position, which
    A. relieves the intrapleural pressure on the diaphragm
    B. stimulates the pleural reflex
    C. increases the muscle tone of the bronchioles
    D. permits a more efficient use of the muscles of
       respiration

22.___

23. All of the following measures should be carried out
during Mr. Wynn's asthmatic episode EXCEPT
    A. keeping his environment quiet
    B. offering him sips of water
    C. teaching him how to deep-breathe and cough
    D. noting the amount and characteristics of his sputum

23.___

24. Mr. Wynn had all of the following diseases during his
childhood.
Which one may have had a relationship to his present
illness?
    A. Rheumatic fever   B. Otitis media
    C. Chickenpox   D. Eczema

24.___

25. A desensitization program is prescribed for Mr. Wynn.
He should be informed that the outcome of the program
is usually MOST dependent upon the
    A. patient's age
    B. patient's response to antihistamines
    C. patient's ability to develop blocking antibodies
    D. type of serum used for the patient

25.___

KEY (CORRECT ANSWERS)

1.	B		11.	A
2.	D		12.	D
3.	D		13.	D
4.	A		14.	C
5.	C		15.	C
6.	B		16.	C
7.	B		17.	D
8.	C		18.	D
9.	C		19.	D
10.	C		20.	C

21. B
22. D
23. C
24. D
25. C

TEST 2

DIRECTIONS: Each question or incomplete statement is followed by several suggested answers or completions. Select the one that BEST answers the question or completes the statement. *PRINT THE LETTER OF THE CORRECT ANSWER IN THE SPACE AT THE RIGHT.*

1. The following four children completed their primary tetanus immunization 2 years ago.
Which child would be MOST likely to receive a booster dose of toxoid now?
   A. Bill, who sustained several long scratches on his bare legs while climbing on a backyard fence
   B. Sue, who is hospitalized and having emergency treatment for a perforated appendix
   C. John, who is having dental treatment for an abscessed impacted molar
   D. Amy, who walked barefoot around a vacation ranch and cut her foot on a broken bottle

1.____

2. The eating habits of most healthy young adolescents probably BEST reflect their need to
   A. conform to peer behavior
   B. look like a favorite adult
   C. spend short periods at a variety of activities
   D. have new experiences

2.____

3. A mother calls a neighbor who is a nurse and says that her toddler ate an unknown plant in the backyard and now appears ill.
In addition to telling the mother to call a doctor immediately, which of the following advice would it be APPROPRIATE for the nurse to give the woman?
   A. Obtain a urine specimen from the child.
   B. Have the child drink an ounce of mineral oil.
   C. Put the child to bed and elevate his extremities.
   D. Make the child vomit and save the vomitus.

3.____

4. The CHIEF difficulty in establishing a therapeutic relationship with most children who are autistic stems from the fact that they
   A. have a functional hearing defect
   B. are mentally retarded as well as mentally ill
   C. behave in a manner difficult to understand
   D. are unable to follow directions

4.____

5. Which of these measures is the MOST important one to consider in the home management of a young child who is mentally retarded?
   A. Having the same person teach him all new activities
   B. Limiting the amount of stimulation he receives from his environment

5.____

C. Maintaining a consistent routine for the performance of his activities of daily living
D. Teaching him amenities that will help him to be accepted by others

6. An infant has erythroblastosis fetalis (hemolytic disease of the newborn).
The parents should be informed that the development of jaundice in the infant is caused by
   A. an overproduction of erythrocytes
   B. an abnormal production of melanin
   C. excessive destruction of red blood cells
   D. hypobilirubinemia

6._____

7. A child with an eye infection is to have physiologic saline eye irrigations.
When carrying out an eye irrigation, it is CORRECT to
   A. use a solution in which there is a tablespoon of salt in each quart of water
   B. use only enough pressure to maintain a steady flow of solution along the lower conjunctival sac
   C. direct the flow of solution toward the inner surface of the upper lid
   D. keep the head flat

7._____

Questions 8-14.

DIRECTIONS: Questions 8 through 14 are to be answered on the basis of the following information.

Lisa Smith, 2 years old, is admitted to the hospital with acute otitis media of the right ear. Her body temperature is elevated.

8. Lisa's susceptibility to otitis media is due to the fact that the
   A. eustachian tube is short and wide in children
   B. causitive organism is part of the normal flora in throats of children
   C. external ear in children is less effective in resisting the entrance of foreign objects
   D. inner ear in children is markedly immature

8._____

9. Lisa is to have a tepid sponge bath.
To achieve the desired outcome of this procedure, the nurse should
   A. stroke Lisa's skin to cause friction
   B. give Lisa warm fluids to drink
   C. allow moisture on Lisa's skin to evaporate
   D. lower the temperature of Lisa's room

9._____

10. Lisa has severe pain in her right ear.
    The pain of acute otitis media is due CHIEFLY to
    A. reduced tension on structures in the vestibular
       portion of the inner ear
    B. constriction of the endolymphatic spaces in the
       labyrinth of the inner ear
    C. increased pressure of fluid in the middle ear
    D. irritation of the stapes in the middle ear

10.___

11. Lisa is to receive 100,000 U. of an oral suspension of
    penicillin four times a day. A bottle containing
    300,000 U. of penicillin in 5 cc. of solution is to be
    used to prepare Lisa's dosage.
    How much solution will contain the amount of penicillin
    prescribed for Lisa?
    _____ cc.
    A. 0.7   B. 1.7   C. 2.7   D. 3.7

11.___

12. Lisa's condition improves.
    Ms. Smith says to the nurse, *I need to go home to see how
    my mother is making out with my other children; but each
    time I try to leave, Lisa gets so upset that I just can't.*
    Which of these responses by the nurse would probably be
    BEST?
    A. Lisa is now well enough to be without you. Why don't
       you try slipping away when she falls asleep?
    B. Stress is not good for Lisa even though her condition
       is improved. Is it possible for you to find out
       about the children without leaving Lisa?
    C. Your feeling torn about whether to stay or go is
       understandable when Lisa needs you too. Whenever
       you're ready to go, let me know and I'll stay with
       her.
    D. Lisa needs to be more independent of you now. Your
       being away from her for a while will help her.

12.___

13. Lisa has a temper tantrum one morning while her mother
    is bathing her. Ms. Smith asks the nurse how the behavior
    should be handled.
    In replying, the nurse should include that this behavior
    in 2-year-olds
    A. indicates regression
    B. suggests a poorly developed sense of trust
    C. should be controlled by parental discipline
    D. is a normal outlet for tension

13.___

14. A member of the nursing team remarks to the team leader,
    *Lisa whines and fusses all the time her mother is with
    her. She quiets down as soon as she leaves but cries
    when she comes back. I wonder if it's good for her to
    visit so often.*
    Which of these responses would probably help the team
    member MOST to think through the problem?
    A. This is a characteristic trait of children this age.
       Haven't you noticed it in others?

14.___

B. This behavior may be indicative of a disturbed mother-child relationship. You should continue to watch them closely.
C. Even if the mother upsets the child, she should be encouraged to continue to visit as often as she can.
D. Is it possible that her mother's being with her enables her to express her unhappiness?

Questions 15-21.

DIRECTIONS: Questions 15 through 21 are to be answered on the basis of the following information.

When 16-month-old Ann Wolfe is admitted to the hospital, she has a temperature of 104°F. (40°C.), petechiae, and purpuric areas on her skin. A diagnosis of meningococcal meningitis is established.

15.   Ann has opisthotonos.
Which of these positions will be BEST for her while she has this symptom?
    A. Semi-Flowler's   B. Side-lying
    C. Dorsal recumbent   D. Prone   15._____

16.   While Ann is acutely ill, which of these measures will be ESSENTIAL in her care?
    A. Reducing environmental stimuli
    B. Maintaining optimum nutrition
    C. Preventing the development of herpetic lesions of the lips
    D. Exercising her extremities passively several times a day   16._____

17.   Ann is being watched for signs of adrenal insufficiency. Which of these symptoms are characteristic of this condition?
    _____ blood pressure and _____.
    A. Normal; increasing pulse rate
    B. Rising; weak, thready pulse
    C. Falling; weak, thready pulse
    D. Fluctuating; decreasing pulse rate   17._____

18.   Ann is receiving both an antibiotic and a sulfonamide. Because she is receiving a sulfonamide, which of these daily measures will be ESPECIALLY important for her?
    A. Weighing her and observing her for edema
    B. Giving her extra fluids and measuring her fluid intake and output
    C. Taking her blood pressure and her apical pulse at regular, specified intervals
    D. Observing her frequently for signs of photophobia and hyperreflexia   18._____

19. A spinal tap is done to assess Ann's response to therapy.   19.___
    Which change in Ann's spinal fluid would be indicative
    of improvement in her condition?
       A. *Increase* in cell count
       B. *Increase* in specific gravity
       C. *Decrease* in sugar
       D. *Decrease* in protein

20. Ann responds favorably to treatment and is convalescing.   20.___
    In order to meet Ann's nutritional needs, her food plan
    should be based on which of these needs of normal 16-
    month-old children?
       A. Their diets should include a variety of foods that
          they can eat by themselves.
       B. Liquids and semiliquids are best for them.
       C. Preference should be given to their favorite foods.
       D. Milk is of greater importance to them than solids.

21. After Ann recovers, which type of immunity to the   21.___
    meningococcus will she have?
       A. Passive acquired   B. Cellular
       C. Natural   D. Active acquired

Questions 22-24.

DIRECTIONS: Questions 22 through 24 are to be answered on the basis
              of the following information.

    Suzanne Edwards, 6 years old, is admitted to the hospital for
probable repair of a ventricular septal defect. This is Suzanne's
third hospital admission.

22. Suzanne has a cardiac catheterization.   22.___
    For the first few hours after the cardiac catheteriza-
    tion, which of these nursing measures will be ESSENTIAL
    for her?
       A. Keeping the head of her bed elevated 30 degrees
       B. Encouraging her to cough forcefully at regular inter-
          vals
       C. Checking her temperature every hour
       D. Taking her pulse frequently in the extremity used
          for the cutdown

23. In preparing Suzanne for the proposed surgery, which   23.___
    characteristic of 6-year-old children should be given
    GREATEST consideration by the nurse?
       A. Concrete experiences are most meaningful.
       B. The ability to think abstractly is well-developed.
       C. Cause and effect relationships are readily understood.
       D. The ability to distinguish between fantasy and
          reality is well-developed.

24. Suzanne has open-heart surgery for repair of a ventricu-   24.____
    lar septal defect. She is then transferred to the
    intensive care unit.
    During Suzanne's surgery, her femoral arteries were
    cannulated.
    As a result of this procedure, it is ESSENTIAL postopera-
    tively for the nurse to make frequent checks of Suzanne's
    A. urinary output
    B. pedal pulses
    C. rectal temperature
    D. ability to move her lower extremities

25. A woman phones a nurse at home and says that her son fell   25.____
    and broke his eyeglasses and that she thinks some glass
    may have penetrated one eye.
    The nurse advises immediate medical attention and that in
    the meanwhile it would be MOST important for the mother to
    A. apply a pressure dressing to the affected eye and
       keep the child in an erect sitting position
    B. examine the affected eye to determine whether any
       glass can be easily removed and apply petrolatum
       (Vaseline) on the outer surface of the eyelid
    C. loosely cover both eyes and have the child remain
       quiet
    D. gently irrigate the affected eye with a copious
       amount of boiled table salt solution that has cooled
       and leave the eye uncovered

KEY (CORRECT ANSWERS)

1. D		11. B	
2. A		12. C	
3. D		13. D	
4. C		14. D	
5. C		15. B	
6. C		16. A	
7. B		17. C	
8. A		18. B	
9. C		19. D	
10. C		20. A	

21. D
22. D
23. A
24. B
25. C

TEST 3

DIRECTIONS: Each question or incomplete statement is followed by several suggested answers or completions. Select the one that BEST answers the question or completes the statement. *PRINT THE LETTER OF THE CORRECT ANSWER IN THE SPACE AT THE RIGHT.*

1. When a primipara's normal first-born infant is brought to her for the first feeding, she says, *He's so little! I'm afraid I'll hurt him.*
Which of these responses would be MOST helpful from the standpoint of learning?
   A. You can practice taking care of the baby while you're here.
   B. Is there someone at home who can help you with the baby the first few weeks?
   C. You can watch me take care of the baby.
   D. The public health nurse can come to your home to show you how to take care of the baby.

1.___

Questions 2-4.

DIRECTIONS: Questions 2 through 4 are to be answered on the basis of the following information.

Ms. Marie DuPont, who was discharged two days ago from the postpartum unit, is visiting her newborn girl on the pediatric unit. Baby girl DuPont has a cleft lip and cleft palate.

2. The nurse should expect that because Ms. DuPont has an infant with an obvious physical defect, Ms. DuPont may
   A. have difficulty loving such an infant and responding warmly to it
   B. overtly express love for the infant because mother love is instinctive
   C. express mixed feelings for the infant that will require psychiatric treatment to overcome
   D. express guilt that will require her visits with the infant to be curtailed

2.___

3. Ms. DuPont is concerned about the likelihood of having other children with the same anomaly as her baby girl's. Ms. DuPont should be given which of the following information about her probability of having another child with a cleft palate?
   A. If this mother has close medical supervision during subsequent pregnancies, the anomaly is not likely to occur again.
   B. Since the anomaly is so rare, it is highly unlikely that a mother would have more than one child with such an anomaly.

3.___

C. There is little probability that future children of
this mother will have the same anomaly since there
is no genetic basis for its development.
D. A mother's having one child with this anomaly means
that there is a greater-than-average possibility of
her having other children with the same anomaly.

4. Children with cleft palates are MOST likely to have   4.___
A. abnormal dentition, speech impairments, and recurrent
otitis media
B. inadequate nutrition, poor muscle coordination, and
mental retardation
C. persistent infantile emotional pattern, regression
in speech development, and hearing deficit
D. accelerated caries formation, peer group maladjust-
ment, and maternal overprotection

Questions 5-10.

DIRECTIONS: Questions 5 through 10 are to be answered on the basis
of the following information.

John Stone, a 3½-year-old, was admitted to the hospital because
of a persistent bleeding from a minor laceration. His condition is
diagnosed as classic hemophilia (factor VIII deficiency).

5. Because of John's age, which of these aspects of hospi-   5.___
talization is likely to be MOST traumatic for him?
A. Being inhibited from running about freely
B. Being separated from his family
C. Being placed in an unfamiliar environment
D. Having his routines and rituals disrupted

6. John is an only child. His parents are concerned about   6.___
the possibility of their future offspring having hemophilia.
His parents should be told that
A. male offspring will have the hemophilic trait and
will either be carriers or will have the bleeding
tendency; female offspring will not be subject to
the condition
B. hemophilia is unlikely to occur in female offspring,
but they can be carriers; male offspring have a 50
percent chance of having the condition
C. the probability that hemophilia will occur in other
offspring is no greater than it is in the general
population
D. each of their offspring will have a 25 percent chance
of having hemophilia, a 50 percent chance of being a
carrier, and a 25 percent chance of being free of the
gene for hemophilia

7. Before his illness, John had achieved all of the following   7.___
   abilities.
   Which ability did he probably develop MOST recently?
   A. Throwing a large ball four to five feet
   B. Putting a spoon in his mouth without spilling the
      contents
   C. Speaking in sentences of three or four words
   D. Alternating his feet while walking upstairs

8. All of these measures should be considered in feeding   8.___
   John.
   Which one is MOST important in terms of the development
   needs of a 3½-year-old?
   A. Using colorful child-size cups and dishes for his
      food
   B. Having him sit at a table that is of a height appro-
      priate for his size
   C. Serving him small portions of food
   D. Letting him feed himself

9. In discussing dental prophylaxis for John with Mr. and   9.___
   Mrs. Stone, the nurse should tell them that dental visits
   should be
   A. scheduled only when definite symptoms occur
   B. preceded by the administration of antihemophilic
      globulin (AHG) factor VIII
   C. scheduled at regular intervals
   D. started when the deciduous teeth become loose

10. Which of these understandings about John should his   10.___
    parents be helped to gain?
    A. John's participation in active range-of-motion
       activities will help to prevent contractures.
    B. John's emotional development will be fostered by a
       warm, indulgent family, but some curtailment of his
       physical development may result.
    C. Overprotection may impede John's emotional and
       physical development.
    D. Children with John's condition tend to limit their
       own physical activity.

Questions 11-18.

DIRECTIONS: Questions 11 through 18 are to be answered on the basis
             of the following information.

Ms. Wendy Stevens, 18 years old, is admitted to the hospital with
a diagnosis of infectious hepatitis (Type A). Her orders include bed
rest and diagnostic studies.

11. On admission, Ms. Stevens should be expected to have
    which of these early symptoms of infectious hepatitis
    (Type A)?
    A. Loss of appetite
    B. Ecchymoses
    C. Shortness of breath on exertion
    D. Abdominal distension

11.___

12. Which of these factors in Ms. Stevens' history is MOST
    likely to be related to her diagnosis?
    A. Recent recovery from an upper respiratory infection
    B. Being bitten by an insect
    C. Contact with a person who was jaundiced
    D. Eating home-canned foods

12.___

13. The nurse should monitor the results of which of these
    tests that is used to assess Ms. Stevens' liver function?
    A. Serum transaminase   B. Protein-bound iodine
    C. Creatinine clearance   D. Glucose tolerance

13.___

14. All of the following precautionary measures are essential
    in Ms. Stevens' case EXCEPT
    A. serving food on disposable dishes
    B. wearing a face mask
    C. carrying out procedures for decontamination of urine
       and feces
    D. modifying procedures for discarding used syringes
       and needles

14.___

15. The CHIEF purpose of bed rest for Ms. Stevens is to
    A. minimize liver damage
    B. reduce the breakdown of fats for metabolic needs
    C. decrease the circulatory load to reduce cardiac
       effort
    D. control the spread of the disease

15.___

16. Members of Ms. Stevens' family who have been exposed to
    infectious hepatitis should be given
    A. penicillin
    B. sulfadiazine
    C. immune human serum globulin
    D. irradiated plasma

16.___

17. Ms. Stevens' condition improves.
    The nurse is planning Ms. Stevens' care during her
    convalescent period.
    The nurse should expect that Ms. Stevens will have the
    MOST difficulty with
    A. relieving pain
    B. regulating bowel elimination
    C. maintaining morale
    D. preventing respiratory complications

17.___

18. As a result of her having hepatitis, Ms. Stevens should   18.___
     be instructed NEVER to
          A. smoke   B. eat fried foods
          C. donate blood   D. exercise strenuously

Questions 19-25.

DIRECTIONS: Questions 19 through 25 are to be answered on the basis
             of the following information.

     Alison Wright, 19 months old, is diagnosed by the family doctor
as having acute laryngotracheobronchitis. Alison's temperature is
103°F. (39.4°C.) when Ms. Wright brings her to the hospital. This
is Alison's first hospital admission.

19. Two early symptoms that are MOST likely to occur in laryn- 19.___
     gotracheobronchitis are
          A. cough and inspiratory stridor
          B. elevated temperature and prostration
          C. Kussmaul respirations and bradycardia
          D. flushed face and labored expirations

20. Ms. Wright tells the nurse, who is filling out a habit   20.___
     record for Alison, that Alison has achieved bowel control.
     Which additional information would it be MOST important
     for the nurse to obtain from Ms. Wright at this time?
          A. The extent of Ms. Wright's understanding of the
             regressive effect of illness and hospitalization on
             bowel-training in children of Alison's age
          B. Alison's toileting routines at home
          C. The age at which Alison's bowel-training was started
          D. Whether Alison has indicated readiness for bladder-
             training

21. Alison is placed in a Croupette.   21.___
     Restraints are to be used on Alison because she continu-
     ally tries to get out of the Croupette.
     Because Alison requires the restraints, the nurse should
          A. tell Alison's mother that bilateral arm and leg
             restraints are necessary for toddlers
          B. inform Alison's mother that Alison will probably
             adjust better to restraints if she is left alone for
             a while after they are applied
          C. explain to Alison the need for the restraints in
             order to help her adjust to them
          D. watch Alison carefully after the restraints are
             applied to see whether she struggles to the point of
             negating the value of the therapy

22. Which of these symptoms in Alison could give the EARLIEST   22.___
     indication of increased respiratory difficulty?
          A. Generalized cyanosis
          B. Increased pulse rate
          C. Decreased respiratory rate
          D. Abdominal breathing

23. Alison is to receive a dose of aspirin in liquid form.   23.___
    In view of her condition and her age, it would be BEST
    to
    A. support Alison in a sitting position, hold the
       medicine glass with the medication to her lips, and
       tell her calmly and firmly to drink it
    B. turn Alison on her side, give her a straw, and tell
       her to suck the medication from the medicine glass
    C. hand Alison the medicine glass containing the drug
       and tell her to drink it, saying that it will taste
       like candy
    D. mix the medication in a 4-ounce glass of sweetened
       fruit juice, prop Alison up in a sitting position,
       give her the glass, and tell her in a positive tone
       to drink the juice

24. Alison's condition improves, and the Croupette is discon-   24.___
    tinued. Diet as tolerated is ordered for her.
    A nurse's aide reports to the nurse that although Alison
    seems hungry, she pushes the aide's hand away and will
    not eat when the aide tries to feed her.
    The nurse should communicate to the aide that most
    children of Alison's age
    A. eat better when seated at a table with adults
    B. prefer to feed themselves
    C. have finicky appetites
    D. have strong food preferences

25. A normal 19-month-old child can be expected to   25.___
    A. stand briefly on one foot without support and to
       put together simple jigsaw puzzles
    B. drink through a straw and to know his own sex
    C. manage finger foods and to understand *No, no*
    D. build a tower of 7 blocks and to open doors by
       turning knobs

KEY (CORRECT ANSWERS)

1. A		11. A	
2. A		12. C	
3. D		13. A	
4. A		14. B	
5. B		15. A	
6. B		16. C	
7. D		17. C	
8. D		18. C	
9. C		19. A	
10. C		20. B	

21.	D
22.	B
23.	A
24.	B
25.	C

EXAMINATION SECTION
TEST 1

1. At one year of age, an infant's weight should be APPROXI-MATELY _____ the birth weight.   1.___
   A. 50% more than   B. double
   C. triple   D. five times

2. A busy box is one of the MOST age-appropriate toys for an infant aged _____ months.   2.___
   A. 5   B. 15   C. 25   D. 35

3. All of the following statements about infant feeding (breast or formula) between ages 1 and 3 months are correct EXCEPT: 3.___
   A. An infant should be fed on demand, about every 2 to 5 hours
   B. The infant usually eats 4 to 5 oz. per feeding
   C. Burping should be encouraged after each 4 oz.
   D. The infant should be placed on the abdomen or the right side after feeding

4. In a 6 to 12 month-old infant, the habitual sucking on a bottle of milk or juice while lying down is the MOST common cause of _____ syndrome.   4.___
   A. respiratory distress   B. fetal alcohol
   C. bottle-mouth caries   D. none of the above

5. Since weight gain is considered a reliable indicator of infant health, the nurse needs to know that a 6 month-old infant normally weighs _____ the birth weight.   5.___
   A. the same as   B. double
   C. triple   D. quadruple

6. Mrs. Smith thinks that she might spoil her 3 month-old daughter, Bethy, by picking her up when she cries. The nurse's BEST response to Mrs. Smith's concerns would be: 6.___
   A. Cuddling and holding will not spoil Bethy; rather, it will strengthen the baby-mother bond
   B. If she isn't wet or soiled, just leave her alone and she will stop crying
   C. She should be hungry, try feeding her
   D. Give her some toy and leave her alone for 20 minutes. If she still hasn't stopped crying, then pick her up

7. When discussing with a new mother how to prevent injury   7.___
   in an infant, the BEST measure for the nurse to recommend
   is
   - A. placing safety gates across stairways once the infant
        begins to walk
   - B. keeping only medications out of the infant's reach
   - C. safe diapering practices (i.e., keeping a hand on
        the infant at all times)
   - D. avoid using a car seat until the infant is at least
        9 months old

8. Which of the following statements about introducing solid   8.___
   foods into an infant's diet is CORRECT?
   - A. Introduce solid foods when the infant is more than
        9 months old.
   - B. Mix the solid foods in the infant's bottle to ease
        the transition.
   - C. First introduce fruits and vegetables when the infant
        is 3 months old.
   - D. Introduce a single solid food at a time for a period
        of 4 to 7 days and so on.

9. Mrs. Merriwell mentions that since her 1 year old son,   9.___
   Frank, has started sitting so well by himself, she has
   loosened up on some of the child safety measures she
   used to institute.
   The nurse should be concerned about all of the following
   statements by Mrs. Merriwell EXCEPT:
   - A. He plays by himself in the bathtub, so it gives me
        a good chance to make some quick telephone calls
   - B. He sleeps so deeply during his naps that sometimes
        I leave him alone just to buy some necessary food
        stuff from the grocery store next door
   - C. I don't use the car seat for Frank because he can
        sit quite well in the regular seat belt
   - D. I still keep all the medicines and toxic substances
        in a locked cabinet

10. For best results, communication with an infant before   10.___
    any procedure is one of the most important factors.
    The nurse should NOT
    - A. explain the procedure, even if the infant cannot
         understand it well
    - B. allow a parent or close relative to be present
    - C. arrange for a primary nurse to perform all procedures
    - D. provide pictures of the procedure

11. The MOST accurate way of finding an infant's pulse rate   11.___
    is
    - A. listening to the heart rate apically for 1 full
         minute
    - B. palpating the apical pulse for 10 seconds, then
         multiplying the result by 6

    C. palpating the radial pulse for 1 full minute
    D. palpating the radial pulse for 10 seconds, then multiplying the result by 6

12. The MOST accurate technique for measuring an infant's height is to measure _____ height with the infant _____.   12.___
    A. recumbent; prone
    B. standing; held upright
    C. recumbent; supine
    D. recumbent; lying on his or her right side

13. All of the following statements about measuring an infant's blood pressure are correct EXCEPT: 13.___
    A. Use of a doppler instrument provides the most accurate results
    B. It is acceptable to record P (palpated) for the diastolic reading if it is undetectable by auscultation and record the systolic value in a young infant
    C. The blood pressure cuff should measure at least one-half of the infant's upper arm or thigh circumference
    D. Blood pressure measurement is not done until 10 months of age because it provides inaccurate results in younger infants

14. Regarding an infant's cultural background, it is TRUE that   14.___
    A. a culture may be defined as *a division of mankind possessing traits that are transmissible by descent and sufficient to characterize a distinct human type*
    B. a person's physical characteristics indicate his or her membership in a particular culture
    C. certain behavioral patterns are learned from ancestors and passed along to later generations
    D. heritage shows the particular cultural values that groups of people share

15. The MOST important variable influencing a child's growth is   15.___
    A. environmental influence   B. education
    C. nutrition   D. none of the above

16. Two-month-old Terry Franklin's mother brings him to a child clinic. The nurse explains to Mrs. Franklin that immunizations begin at this age.   16.___
During this visit, which of the following immunizations would Terry receive?
    A. Smallpox and tetanus toxoid
    B. Measles, mumps, and rubella
    C. Polio and diphtheria-pertussis-tetanus
    D. Typhoid and attenuated tuberculin bacillus

17. Breast engorgement following delivery NORMALLY occurs
_____ and lasts _____ days.
    A. 10 to 12 hours after delivery; 6
    B. on the 3rd postpartum day; 4
    C. on the 1st postpartum day; 4
    D. on the 2nd to 4th postpartum day; 1 to 2

17.____

18. The following nursing intervention that is EXTREMELY
important while administering nursing care to a patient
with aplastic anemia is to
    A. organize treatments so that they are all done at
       one time
    B. let the patient do as many activities of daily living
       as possible
    C. protect the patient from contamination
    D. protect yourself and the environment from contamina-
       tion

18.____

19. Three-year-old Frank Roosevelt has celiac disease. The
nurse is counseling Frank's parents about his diet.
The nurse should tell them to eliminate
    A. citrus fruits
    B. breads and cereals
    C. lean meat and poultry
    D. fresh green and leafy vegetables

19.____

20. In the case of a pregnant woman who is narcissistic, an
APPROPRIATE nursing intervention would be to
    A. concentrate, with all your health knowledge, on her
       comfort
    B. encourage her to be very concerned about herself
    C. tell her that she is acting silly
    D. divert her attention by focusing your health tech-
       niques on the baby

20.____

21. Four-year-old Kirk Douglas is admitted to the pediatric
unit with a diagnosis of nephrotic syndrome. The nurse
collects a urine specimen from Kirk.
The results of the urinalysis would indicate
    A. hematuria   B. albuminuria
    C. ketonuria   D. glucosuria

21.____

22. A nurse is going to administer an enema to a child who
is suffering from Hirschsprung's disease.
_____ should be utilized.
    A. Sodium phosphate   B. Soap suds
    C. Normal saline   D. Tap water

22.____

23. All of the following nursing interventions will help a
prospective father to accept his new role during pregnancy EXCEPT:
    A. Letting him verbalize his feelings about the pregnancy
    B. Explaining the psychological and physiological changes
       he can find in the mother

23.____

C. Encouraging him to think about what fatherhood will mean to him
D. Telling him that the mother will be emotionally supported by you, so he won't have to worry about her

24. Herald patch is MOST frequently associated with   24.___
    A. psoriasis   B. erythema infectiosum
    C. rubeola   D. pityriasis rosa

25. A Wilms tumor is MOST commonly metastasised to the   25.___
    A. brain   B. liver   C. vertebrae   D. lungs

KEY (CORRECT ANSWERS)

1. C	11. A		
2. A	12. C		
3. C	13. D		
4. C	14. C		
5. B	15. C		
6. B	16. C		
7. C	17. D		
8. D	18. C		
9. D	19. B		
10. D	20. A		

21. B
22. C
23. D
24. D
25. D

TEST 2

DIRECTIONS: Each question or incomplete statement is followed by several suggested answers or completions. Select the one that BEST answers the question or completes the statement. *PRINT THE LETTER OF THE CORRECT ANSWER IN THE SPACE AT THE RIGHT.*

1. Newborn Carl Lewis has been diagnosed with tracheoeso-   1.___
   phageal fistula.
   The PRIMARY objective of Carl's nursing care is to
   A. prevent upper respiratory tract infections
   B. maintain fluid and electrolyte balance
   C. prevent atelectasis and pneumothorax
   D. maintain a patent airway

2. Three-year-old Peter Rabbit is admitted to the pediatric   2.___
   unit with a diagnosis of possible intussusception.
   The nurse taking care of Peter would expect to observe
   _____ stools.
   A. constipated, black   B. soft, brown
   C. currant jelly   D. loose, green

3. Nine-year-old Rose Marry is suffering of carditis due to   3.___
   acute rheumatic fever. She has been placed on a low-
   sodium diet.
   Of the following, the MOST appropriate meal for Rose
   would be
   A. a grilled cheese sandwich, hot chocolate, tomato
      soup, and pound cake
   B. a hamburger, peaches, baked potato, and iced tea
   C. hot dogs, cookies, green salad, and milk
   D. a bacon, lettuce and tomato sandwich, fruit cocktail,
      and a cola beverage

4. Eight-year-old Mark Goodman has classic hemophilia. He   4.___
   falls in the playground near his house and injures his
   knee.
   When Mark arrives at the emergency room, the nurse will
   IMMEDIATELY
   A. administer an analgesic and wait until it is effec-
      tive before implementing further nursing care
   B. immobilize Mark's leg and apply an ice pack locally
   C. assess mobility by performing passive range of
      motion to Mark's knee
   D. elevate Mark's leg and apply warm compresses to the
      injured area

5. Nancy Skorpios has a new baby. She tells the nurse that   5.___
   her four-year-old son, Sam, is very jealous of his new
   sister.
   The nurse should recommend that Mrs. Skorpios
      A. buy something for Sam to play with
      B. talk about Sam's feelings with him
      C. plan some time each day to spend with Sam
      D. let Sam feed the new baby

6. Three-and-a-half year old Lorena Babbitt has nephrotic   6.___
   syndrome. She has proteinuria and generalized edema.
   The nursing intervention considered to be MOST important
   is
      A. monitoring blood pressure
      B. daily weighing
      C. frequent massage of extremities
      D. measuring intake and output every 12 hours

7. Ten-year-old Bruce Willis has juvenile rheumatoid   7.___
   arthritis. He is ready to be discharged from the hospital.
   Bruce loves to practice sports.
   Which of the following sports would now be APPROPRIATE for
   Bruce to participate in?
      A. Skiing   B. Hockey   C. Baseball   D. Swimming

8. Five-year-old Kato Kaelin is being prepared for repair   8.___
   of his inguinal hernia in the pediatric unit.
   To help Kato cope with the hospital experience, the nurse
   should provide him with
      A. a coloring book and crayons
      B. a pounding board
      C. singing bird dolls
      D. doctor and nurse puppets

9. Three-week-old Laura Palmer has a congenital dislocated   9.___
   hip.
   A clinical manifestation NORMALLY found in infants with
   this abnormality is limited _____ side.
      A. abduction of the leg on the affected
      B. extension of the knee on the unaffected
      C. flexion of the knee on the affected
      D. adduction of the leg on the unaffected

Questions 10-17.

DIRECTIONS: Questions 10 through 17 are to be answered on the
            basis of the following information.

   Two-year-old Anita Howard's mother brings her to the emergency
room with second- and third-degree burns of both hands. Mrs. Howard
says that Anita was burned when she accidentally turned on the hot
water faucet in the bathtub. Assessment of Anita also reveals
multiple bruises on her body. Child abuse is suspected.

10. Anita goes through an initial assessment by the nurse   10.___
    in the emergency room.
    Of the following findings, which one should be communi-
    cated to the physician IMMEDIATELY?
        A. Poor skin turgor, a blood pressure of 102/70, and a
           pulse rate of 92
        B. Cold and clammy skin, a pulse rate of 136, and a
           respiratory rate of 38
        C. Flushed face, a pulse rate of 100, and a respiratory
           rate of 26
        D. Pallor, slightly elevated temperature, and a blood
           pressure of 92/62

11. The APPROPRIATE nursing diagnosis related to Anita's   11.___
    third-degree burns would be alteration in skin integrity
    secondary to
        A. painless areas that appear to be pearly white and
           charred
        B. red areas that blanche
        C. red areas sensitive to temperature change
        D. painful red and blistered areas

12. Anita is now receiving intravenous fluids.   12.___
    The PRINCIPAL rationale for giving fluid therapy in burn
    victims is to
        A. administer antibodies   B. restore plasma volume
        C. improve liver function   D. correct alkalosis

13. Anita is admitted to the pediatric unit, and the nurse   13.___
    assigned to take care of Anita interviews Mrs. Howard
    to obtain a health history.
    Of the following statements, which describes the reaction
    of abusive parents to interview?
    Parents of abused children
        A. ask a lot about hospital procedures
        B. seem to be very guilty about the child's condition
        C. are mostly cooperative with child's health care staff
        D. often contradict themselves in describing the cause
           of the child's injury

14. Assessment of an abused child's parents MOST likely   14.___
    reveals that the parents
        A. have poor job histories
        B. were abused themselves as children
        C. are uneducated
        D. are very independent

15. The nurse is going to change Anita's dressing.   15.___
    The reaction of an abused child to painful procedures
    is USUALLY
        A. crying throughout the procedure
        B. striking out at the nurse
        C. assistance of the nurse during the procedure
        D. acceptance of pain without protest

16. Anita is now placed on a soft diet. Her serum shows low   16.___
    potassium.
    Of the following, an APPROPRIATE food for Anita would be
     A. apples   B. ice cream
     C. crackers   D. eggnog

17. The nurse taking care of Anita observes the mother-child   17.___
    interaction.
    The BEST nursing approach to establish rapport with
    Anita's mother would be to
    A. acknowledge parental strengths
    B. provide advice for discipline
    C. explain the child's developmental needs
    D. explain the child's progress in the hospital

Questions 18-25.

DIRECTIONS: Questions 18 through 25 are to be answered on the
                basis of the following information.

    Mark Anthony was born with a unilateral cleft lip and cleft
palate. He is transferred to the pediatric unit from the newborn
nursery for repair of his cleft lip.

18. During the admission procedure, Mr. and Mrs. Anthony are   18.___
    obviously upset over Mark's defect.
    The MOST appropriate intervention by the nurse at this
    time is to
    A. take Mark and his parents to a private room so that
       they can be alone
    B. encourage the parents to verbalize their feelings
       concerning their son's defects
    C. tell the parents that Mark's defect is not really a
       serious problem
    D. reassure the parents that surgical repair will
       completely correct the deformity

19. Mark's surgery is performed when he is just $2\frac{1}{2}$ months   19.___
    old.
    In the immediate postoperative care, Mark should be
    observed FREQUENTLY by the nurse for signs of
    A. dehydration   B. shock
    C. infection   D. respiratory distress

20. Mark is returned to his room in the pediatric unit.   20.___
    In which of the following positions should Mark be placed
    at this time?
    A. In a semi-Fowler's position
    B. On his abdomen
    C. In a supine position
    D. In a side-lying position

21. Mark is placed by his doctor on a clear liquid diet.
    Mark should be fed in a(n) _____ position, using a(n)
    _____ placed at the _____ of his mouth.
    A. upright; special cleft lip nipple; side
    B. supine; Asepto syringe; center
    C. upright; rubber-tipped medicine dropper; side
    D. side-lying; soft nipple; center

21.___

22. Mark's surgery has healed well, and he is now ready to
    be discharged.
    During the discharge, the nurse informs Mrs. Anthony
    about the future surgical plan for Mark by stating that
    the surgery will be done
    A. when Mark is between 1 and 2 years of age
    B. after Mark's third birthday
    C. before Mark is 8 months old
    D. the summer before Mark enters school

22.___

23. When Mark is 1 year and 8 months old, he is admitted to
    the hospital for repair of his cleft palate. Mrs. Anthony
    now has a 3-month-old infant and is unable to room-in with
    Mark.
    The behavior pattern MOST likely to be observed by the
    nurse after Mrs. Anthony leaves the hospital is that Mark
    A. holds up his arms to be picked up when the nurse
       enters the room
    B. stands in his crib crying *Mommy*
    C. lies quietly in his crib, clutching his teddy bear
    D. plays peek-a-boo in his crib

23.___

24. During the preoperative period, the nurse wants Mark to
    become familiar with the type of restraints that will be
    utilized in the postoperative period.
    The evening before surgery, _____ would be applied by the
    nurse for a short period of time.
    A. a Posey jacket   B. clove hitch restraints
    C. elbow restraints   D. a mummy restraint

24.___

25. Five days after surgery, Mark is placed on a full liquid
    diet.
    The nurse feeding Mark his breakfast should
    A. cleanse the suture line with hydrogen peroxide-
       moistened applicators before feeding
    B. irrigate Mark's mouth with sterile water after
       feeding
    C. allow Mark to feed cereal to himself with a small-
       size spoon
    D. allow Mark to drink with a straw to facilitate fluid
       intake

25.___

――――――

KEY (CORRECT ANSWERS)

1. D
2. C
3. B
4. B
5. C

6. B
7. D
8. D
9. A
10. C

11. D
12. B
13. D
14. B
15. A

16. B
17. C
18. B
19. D
20. D

21. C
22. A
23. B
24. C
25. B

EXAMINATION SECTION
TEST 1

DIRECTIONS: Each question or incomplete statement is followed by
several suggested answers or completions. Select the
one that BEST answers the question or completes the
statement. *PRINT THE LETTER OF THE CORRECT ANSWER IN
THE SPACE AT THE RIGHT.*

1. Normal reflexes during the neonatal period include   1.___
    A. moro   B. grasp
    C. stepping   D. all of the above

2. The milestone MOST likely to occur at 12 weeks of age is   2.___
    the infant's
    A. sustaining social contact
    B. laughing out loud
    C. rolling over
    D. sitting with pelvic support

3. A newborn infant CANNOT   3.___
    A. turn his head
    B. touch a surface with his nose
    C. lift his head to the plane of the body
    D. flex around his supporting hand

4. The age at which an infant starts to sustain his head in   4.___
    the plane of the body is APPROXIMATELY _____ month(s).
    A. one   B. two   C. three   D. four

5. At 4 months of age, an infant can do all of the following 5.___
    EXCEPT
    A. sit with a truncal support
    B. show displeasure if social contact is broken
    C. roll over
    D. none of the above

6. An infant starts using pincer movement at APPROXIMATELY   6.___
    _____ months of age.
    A. five   B. six   C. eight   D. nine

7. At what age can a child imitate a cross?   7.___
    _____ months.
    A. 18   B. 30
    C. 36   D. None of the above

8. Which of the following is a cognitive milestone achieved   8.___
    by a child at 28 weeks?
    A. Releasing one cube into a cup after demonstration
    B. Raking at a pallet
    C. Uncovering a hidden object
    D. Knowing one or more words and their meanings

9. A 3-month-old infant can do all of the following EXCEPT   9.___
   A. listen to music   B. creep-crawl
   C. fail to grasp   D. sustain social contact

10. Unassisted pincer movement develops at the age of _____   10.___
    months.
    A. four   B. six   C. eight   D. twelve

11. At 6 months of age, developmental milestones do NOT   11.___
    include the child's
    A. putting a pellet into a bottle
    B. releasing two cubes into a cup
    C. scribbling spontaneously
    D. enjoying a simple ball game

12. Which of the following is NOT a normal accomplishment of   12.___
    a child at 18 months of age?
    A. Learning to say *no*
    B. Listening to stories while looking at the pictures
    C. Identifying one or more body parts
    D. Kissing parent with a pucker

13. Normal milestones at 2 months of age include the infant's   13.___
    doing each of the following EXCEPT
    A. reaching at objects
    B. smiling on social contact
    C. attending to voices and coos
    D. following a moving object to 180° visually

14. A 15-month-old child can do all of the following EXCEPT   14.___
    A. walk alone
    B. crawl up stairs
    C. imitate a stroke of crayon
    D. make a tower of 3 cubes

15. During the second year of life, weight gain averages   15.___
    _____ kg per year.
    A. 1   B. 2.5   C. 3.5   D. 5

16. During the second year of life, height gain averages   16.___
    APPROXIMATELY _____ centimeters per year.
    A. 2   B. 6   C. 10   D. 15

17. At what age does a child usually reach double the length   17.___
    of his birth length?
    _____ year(s).
    A. 1   B. 2   C. 3   D. 4

18. A 15-month-old child can make a tower of _____ cubes.   18.___
    A. 3   B. 5   C. 7   D. 9

19. A 4-year-old child generally CANNOT   19.___
    A. throw a ball   B. climb well
    C. copy a triangle   D. hop on one foot

20. Which of the following is NOT considered a normal motor   20.___
    milestone for a child 3 years of age?
    A. Building a 10-cube tower
    B. Copying a circle
    C. Copying a square
    D. Attempting to draw a person

21. A normally developing 2-year-old child can do all of the   21.___
    following EXCEPT
    A. handle a spoon well
    B. alternate feet while going upstairs
    C. fold paper imitatively
    D. climb on furniture

22. At what age can a child with normal social and cognitive   22.___
    development know his or her own age and sex?
    At _____ months of age.
        A. 18   B. 24   C. 30   D. 36

23. A 3-year-old child can do all of the following EXCEPT   23.___
    A. alternate feet while going downstairs
    B. ride a tricycle
    C. hop on one foot
    D. repeat three numbers

24. Nuts, pitted fruits, and popcorn should not be given to a   24.___
    toddler PRIMARILY because they
    A. have almost no food value for a toddler
    B. can cause tooth cavities
    C. will affect the child's appetite
    D. are easily aspirated

25. All of the following statements describe toddlers' well-   25.___
    known sleeping patterns EXCEPT:
    A. Toddlers' sleep needs average 12 hours per day.
    B. A toddler typically discontinues daytime naps around
       age 3.
    C. A toddler typically sleeps through the night and has
       at least three daytime naps.
    D. A consistent bedtime ritual helps prepare a toddler
       for sleep.

26. The one of the following immunizations that is NOT   26.___
    necessary for a toddler to receive is
    A. MMR (measles, mumps, and rubella)
    B. DPT-4, OPV-3 (if not given earlier), PRP-D
    C. HBPV (hemophilus influenzae type B polysaccharide
       vaccine)
    D. DPT-5, OPV-4

27. Which of the following statements about toddlers' physical 27.___
    growth and development is NOT correct?
    A. Bow-leggedness typically persists through toddlerhood
       since the legs must bear the weight of the relatively
       large trunk.

B. Growth of about 3 inches per year and an average height of 34 inches at age 2 years is normal for toddlers.
C. Gain of about 4 to 6 lbs. per year and an average weight of 27 lbs. at age 2 years is normal for toddlers.
D. In toddlers, height and weight increase in a linear fashion.

28. All of the following information about toddlers' psycho-motor milestones is correct EXCEPT: 28.___
    A. Sensory changes increase as proximodistal sensations heighten.
    B. The toddler typically begins to walk by age 12 to 15 months, to run by age 2 years, and to walk backward and hop on one foot by age 3 years.
    C. By 24 months of age, a toddler usually achieves fairly good bowel and bladder control.
    D. The toddler usually cannot alternate feet when climbing stairs.

29. All of the following describe normal height and weight changes in children of 3 to 6 years of age EXCEPT: 29.___
    A. Gain of 6 to 8 lbs. per year
    B. Average height of 37 inches at age 3, 40½ inches at age 4, and 43 inches at age 5
    C. Growth of 2½ to 3 inches per year
    D. Average weight of 32 lbs. at age 3, 37 lbs. at age 4, and 41 lbs. at age 5

30. Which of the following is NOT a true fact about psycho-motor milestones of children age 3 to 6 years?   30.___
    A preschooler
    A. demonstrates increased skill in balancing; by age 4 or 5, he or she can balance on alternate feet with eyes closed
    B. alternates feet when climbing stairs, indicating increased balance and coordination
    C. can successfully perform jobs such as using scissors
    D. is still not skilled enough to tie his or her shoe-laces

KEY (CORRECT ANSWERS)

1. D	11. C	21. B
2. A	12. B	22. D
3. C	13. A	23. C
4. B	14. C	24. D
5. C	15. B	25. C
6. D	16. B	26. D
7. C	17. D	27. D
8. B	18. A	28. C
9. B	19. C	29. A
10. D	20. C	30. D

TEST 2

DIRECTIONS: Each question or incomplete statement is followed by several suggested answers or completions. Select the one that BEST answers the question or completes the statement. *PRINT THE LETTER OF THE CORRECT ANSWER IN THE SPACE AT THE RIGHT.*

1. Toys play a useful role in a child's development. All of the following factors should be taken into consideration while selecting a toy for a toddler EXCEPT
   A. expense
   B. durability
   C. safety
   D. weight

1.____

2. All of the following are appropriate and important components for disciplining a toddler EXCEPT
   A. distraction
   B. admonishment
   C. explanation
   D. praise

2.____

3. Which of the following statements MOST accurately describes the toilet training of a toddler?
   A. Bowel control is accomplished by 18 months.
   B. Daytime bladder control is achieved by 12 to 24 months.
   C. Nightime bladder control is achieved by 24 to 36 months.
   D. Toilet training is usually completed by 4½ years.

3.____

4. A toddler's daily nutritional needs from the four basic food groups do NOT include
   A. two servings from the meat group, 2 tablespoons per serving
   B. four servings from the fruit and vegetable group, 2 tablespoons per serving
   C. seven or more servings of breads and cereals, 1 slice of bread or 3/4 to 1 cup of cereal per serving
   D. 3 cups of milk or milk products

4.____

5. John and Peter, both 3 years of age, are fighting over a toy train.
   Which of the following interventions would be the MOST appropriate in this situation?
   A. Admonish them for fighting and tell them to share the train.
   B. Tell them to stop fighting and that there are enough toys to play with, and give Peter puzzles.
   C. Without saying anything, take the train away from the boys and place them in separate parts of the room, giving them some other toys to play with.
   D. Find another train and tell them that they can each have one.

5.____

6. Which of the following characteristics is NOT typical of   6.___
   a toddler's language development?
   A. Begins to use short sentences at 18 months to 2 years
   B. Can remember and repeat 3 numbers by 3 years
   C. Answers questions with multi-word sentences
   D. After knowing own name by 12 months, gives first name
      by 24 months and full name by 3 years

7. A child commonly experiences more fears during the pre-   7.___
   school period than at any other time.
   All of the following are good examples of preschoolers'
   common fears EXCEPT
   A. being left alone
   B. body mutilation
   C. small animals like rabbits, cats, etc.
   D. objects associated with painful experiences

8. In a conflict situation among preschoolers, which of the   8.___
   following disciplinary principles would be considered the
   BEST nursing intervention to help the child relieve inten-
   sity, regain control, and think about his or her behavior?
   A. Explaining to the child the negative aspects of the
      conflict
   B. Admonishing the child for the conflict
   C. Distracting the child by providing him with one of
      the toys he or she likes most
   D. Giving the child a short time-out of 1 minute per
      year of age

9. All of the following are findings of Freud's theory of   9.___
   psychosexual development of toddlers EXCEPT:
   A. The toddler experiences nothing else but a deep
      frustration as he or she gains control over con-
      taining and releasing bodily waste.
   B. In this stage, the child's focus shifts from the
      mouth to the anal area, with emphasis on bowel
      control as he or she gains neuromuscular control
      over the anal sphincter.
   C. In the *anal stage*, typically extending from age 8
      months to 4 years, the erogenous zone is the anus
      and buttocks, and sexual activity centers on expul-
      sion and retention of bodily waste.
   D. The conflict between *holding on* and *letting go*
      gradually resolves as bowel training progresses;
      resolution occurs once control is firmly established.

10. It is NOT true that a toddler of age 15 to 18 months   10.___
    A. does not have any signs of temper tantrums yet
    B. walks sideways and backwards
    C. imitates simple things
    D. pulls a toy while walking

11. Which of the following statements about toddlers' play activities is NOT correct? 11.___
   A. For a toddler, play is a major socializing medium.
   B. Play typically is parallel - beside rather than with another child.
   C. Push-pull toys help enhance walking skills.
   D. Because of a toddler's long attention span, he or she does not change toys often.

12. Of the following, the INCORRECT statement about toddlers' language and socialization patterns is: 12.___
   A. A toddler tends to ask many *what* questions
   B. A toddler typically begins to use longer sentences and has a vocabulary of about 500 words by age 2
   C. A toddler's social interaction is dominated by ritualism, negativism, and independence
   D. Confidence in separating from parents continues to grow

13. Common fears of toddlers include all of the following EXCEPT 13.___
   A. loss of parents, separation anxiety
   B. stranger anxiety
   C. musical toys' noises
   D. large animals

14. Discipline strategies are affected by a toddler's temperament.
   Which of the following disciplinary approaches would likely be the MOST effective for a *difficult* child? 14.___
   A. Sustained eye contact and a stern voice
   B. A friendly warning to curtail activities with structured time-out if necessary
   C. Time for gradual introduction to new situations
   D. A quick spanking with explanation for misbehavior

15. The toddler's feeling that commonly develops after a new baby is born, stemming from a sense of *dethronement* since he or she no longer is the sole focus of his parent's attention, is known as 15.___
   A. identification   B. mitleiden
   C. sibling rivalry   D. motivation

16. All of the following are considered as important interventions to prevent injuries in toddlers EXCEPT: 16.___
   A. Instruct parents to keep crib rails up, place gates across stairways, keep screens secure on all windows, and supervise the toddler at play
   B. Instruct parents never to forget about tightening the car safety belt while riding a toddler around in a car
   C. Teach parents to place all toxic substances up high and locked; secure safety caps on medications; and remove all small, easily aspirated objects from the child's environment
   D. Instruct parents to avoid using table covers to prevent spilling of hot foods or liquids by the child on himself or herself

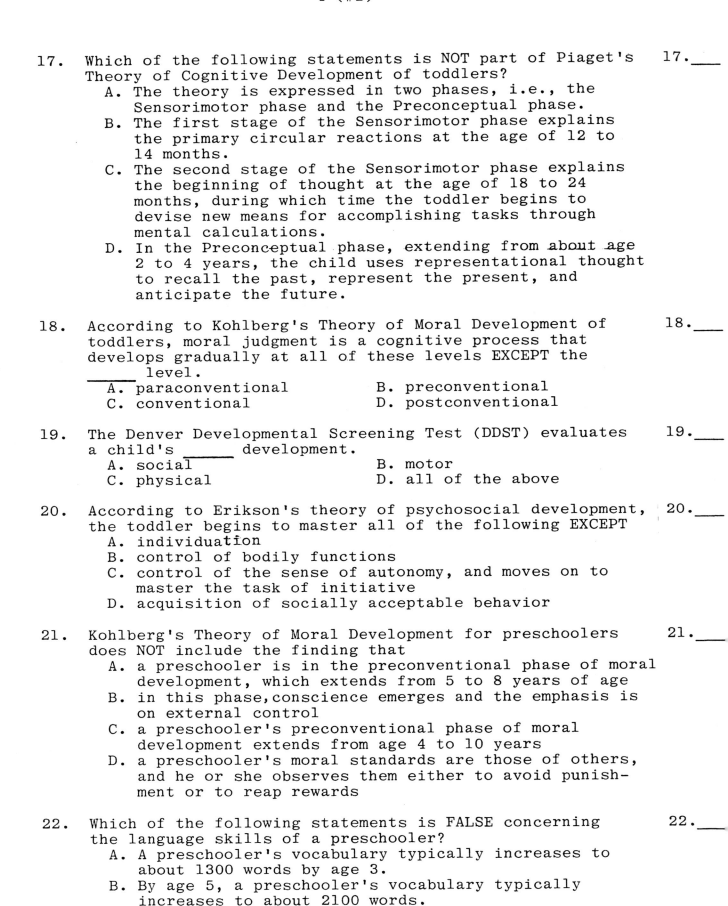

17. Which of the following statements is NOT part of Piaget's   17.___
    Theory of Cognitive Development of toddlers?
    A. The theory is expressed in two phases, i.e., the
       Sensorimotor phase and the Preconceptual phase.
    B. The first stage of the Sensorimotor phase explains
       the primary circular reactions at the age of 12 to
       14 months.
    C. The second stage of the Sensorimotor phase explains
       the beginning of thought at the age of 18 to 24
       months, during which time the toddler begins to
       devise new means for accomplishing tasks through
       mental calculations.
    D. In the Preconceptual phase, extending from about age
       2 to 4 years, the child uses representational thought
       to recall the past, represent the present, and
       anticipate the future.

18. According to Kohlberg's Theory of Moral Development of   18.___
    toddlers, moral judgment is a cognitive process that
    develops gradually at all of these levels EXCEPT the
    _____ level.
    A. paraconventional   B. preconventional
    C. conventional   D. postconventional

19. The Denver Developmental Screening Test (DDST) evaluates   19.___
    a child's _____ development.
    A. social   B. motor
    C. physical   D. all of the above

20. According to Erikson's theory of psychosocial development, 20.___
    the toddler begins to master all of the following EXCEPT
    A. individuation
    B. control of bodily functions
    C. control of the sense of autonomy, and moves on to
       master the task of initiative
    D. acquisition of socially acceptable behavior

21. Kohlberg's Theory of Moral Development for preschoolers   21.___
    does NOT include the finding that
    A. a preschooler is in the preconventional phase of moral
       development, which extends from 5 to 8 years of age
    B. in this phase, conscience emerges and the emphasis is
       on external control
    C. a preschooler's preconventional phase of moral
       development extends from age 4 to 10 years
    D. a preschooler's moral standards are those of others,
       and he or she observes them either to avoid punish-
       ment or to reap rewards

22. Which of the following statements is FALSE concerning   22.___
    the language skills of a preschooler?
    A. A preschooler's vocabulary typically increases to
       about 1300 words by age 3.
    B. By age 5, a preschooler's vocabulary typically
       increases to about 2100 words.

C. A preschooler may talk incessantly and ask many *why* questions.
D. By age 3, a child usually talks in three- or four-word sentences.

23. Which of the following is considered MOST appropriate to aid gross motor development of a preschooler?   23.___
    A. Dress-up clothes
    B. Paints, paper, and crayons
    C. Swimming
    D. Field trips to museums and parks

24. A preschooler needs regular interaction with agemates to help develop _____ skills.   24.___
    A. creative   B. imaginative
    C. motor   D. social

25. According to Erikson's Theory of Psychosocial Development, between 3 and 6 years of age, a child faces a psychosocial crisis which Erikson terms _____ vs. _____.   25.___
    A. definitive; initiative   B. initiative; terminative
    C. terminative; fear   D. initiative; guilt

26. According to Erikson's Theory, the development of a sense of guilt occurs when the child is made to feel that his or her imagination and activities are unacceptable. Guilt, anxiety, and fear result when the child's thoughts and actions clash with parents'   26.___
    A. guilt   B. fear
    C. anxiety   D. expectations

27. Freud terms his Theory of Psychosexual Development of Preschoolers all of the following EXCEPT the _____ stage.   27.___
    A. phallic   B. oedipal
    C. oediphallic   D. all of the above

28. In the phallic stage of Freud's theory, extending from about age 3 to 7, the child's pleasure centers on   28.___
    A. the attention given by the parents
    B. friendship with children of the opposite sex
    C. genitalia and masturbation
    D. all of the above

29. Piaget, who defines his Theory of Cognitive Development for preschoolers as a stage of preconceptual thoughts, classifies his theory in two phases, i.e., preconceptual phase and intuitive phase.   29.___
    He includes all of the following activities in the preconceptual phase, which extends from age 2 to 4, EXCEPT
    A. making simple classifications
    B. reasoning from specific to specific
    C. exhibiting egocentric thinking
    D. forming concepts that are complete and logical

30. According to the intuitive phase of Piaget's theory, which extends from age 4 to 7, it is NOT correct that a preschooler
    A. becomes capable of classifying, quantifying, and relating objects
    B. exhibits intuitive thought processes
    C. is aware of the principles behind classifying and relating objects
    D. uses many words appropriately but without a real knowledge of their meaning

30.___

_____

KEY (CORRECT ANSWERS)

1. A	11. D	21. A
2. B	12. B	22. A
3. A	13. C	23. C
4. C	14. B	24. D
5. D	15. C	25. D
6. C	16. B	26. D
7. C	17. B	27. C
8. D	18. A	28. C
9. A	19. D	29. D
10. A	20. C	30. C

_____

EXAMINATION SECTION

DIRECTIONS: Each question or incomplete statement is followed by
several suggested answers or completions. Select the
one that BEST answers the question or completes the
statement. PRINT THE LETTER OF THE CORRECT ANSWER IN
THE SPACE AT THE RIGHT.

1. *What* conceptual model of psychiatric care is PRIMARILY   1.___
    concerned with etiology, pathogenesis, signs and symptoms,
    differential diagnosis, treatment, and prognosis?
      A. Biological   B. Psychological
      C. Behavioral   D. Social
      E. Eclectic

2. During *what* phase of the life cycle is the problem   2.___
    of immaturity the greatest?
      A. Toddlerhood   B. Oedipal phase
      C. Latency   D. Adolescense
      E. Adulthood

3. *When* is couples group therapy indicated? *When*   3.___
      A. their relationship does not appear to be the problem
         of greatest priority
      B. the couple is not emotionally committed to working
         out their differences
      C. the problems are experienced both within and outside
         the marriage
      D. the problems are acute and ego-alien
      E. problems are long-standing and ego-syntonic

4. *What* is the *most usual* method of medical treatment   4.___
    of schizophrenia?
      A. Reserpine   B. Thioxanthenes
      C. Phenothiazine   D. Butyrophenones
      E. Meprobamate

5. *Which* of the following BEST describes how the nurse   5.___
    should deal with manic patients? *With*
      A. enthusiasm
      B. encouraging support
      C. a reassuring manner that reduces anxiety
      D. understanding
      E. quiet calmness

6. *Which* of the following is NOT a good technique for   6.___
    the nurse dealing with a patient with hysteria? The
    nurse should
      A. always refer to the condition by its proper name
      B. not accuse the patient of pretending to be sick
      C. not treat the patient as if the condition was
         an organic disorder
      D. have an optimistic attitude toward the patient's
         recovery
      E. encourage participation in ward activities

7. *Which* of the following defense mechanisms of the ego   7.____
   are *especially characteristic* of obsessional patients?
     I. Reaction formation
    II. Isolation
   III. Undoing
    IV. Projection
     V. Repression
   The CORRECT answer is:
     A. I, IV   B. I, II, III   C. II, III, V
     D. II, V   E. I, III, V

8. *Which* of the following is NOT a good interviewing   8.____
   technique?
     A. A direct approach should be used
     B. Double-edged questions should be avoided
     C. Asking irrelevant questions makes for a good opening
     D. The patient should be allowed to take the initiative
     E. The patient should be allowed to progress at his
        own pace

9. Nursing management of manipulative behavior involves   9.____
     A. not trying to control the behavior
     B. looking for the situation that has triggered the
        symptom
     C. understanding the meaning of the behavior and
        assessing how the patient understands it
     D. teaching the patient some of the social skills
        of how people develop relationships
     E. allotting as much time as possible to the patient
        in order to help him express his feelings

10. *Which* of the following techniques are *most effective*   10.____
    in interrupting children's hostile behavior in a
    treatment center?
      I. Verbal or physical limits
     II. Intervening technique
    III. Removing the cause of the hostility
     IV. Threatening the loss of privileges
      V. Ignoring the behavior
    The CORRECT answer is:
      A. I, III, V   B. I, II, III   C. I, IV, V
      D. II, III, V   E. I, III, IV

11. All of the following are behavior disorders in adults,   11.____
    termed oral behavior, EXCEPT
      A. impulsive greed
      B. clinging and demanding behavior
      C. cleanliness or dirtiness
      D. deep feelings of internal division
      E. distrust and reactive rage

12. All of the following are important guidelines for the nurse's notes EXCEPT:
    A. Avoid lengthy notes
    B. Use the patient's own words
    C. Avoid interpretations
    D. Answer the four "w's"
    E. Avoid the use of technical terminology

    12.___

13. *Which* of the following are factors indicating high risk or vulnerability to schizophrenia?
    I. Hyperactivity in the preschool age
    II. Unsocialized aggression among boys and overinhibited hyperconformity among girls during high school
    III. Presence of intimate peer relationships during early adolescense
    IV. Evidence of neuropathology under age 11
    V. Disorganized, disruptive families
    The CORRECT answer is:
    A. I, II, IV   B. II, IV, V   C. I, II, III
    D. I, III, V   E. All of the above

    13.___

14. *Which* of the following techniques should the nurse use in working with individual depressed patients?
    She *should*
    A. be aggressively cheerful
    B. indicate the patient's good prognosis
    C. push the patient toward making decisions
    D. always give elaborate encouragement
    E. try to convince the patient that his depression is unjustified by the reality of his life situation

    14.___

15. *How* does the nurse help the patient re-establish a level of good functioning that has been lost to the illness? Through
    A. exploratory work   B. direct advice
    C. support   D. comradeship bonds
    E. education

    15.___

16. *What* conceptual model of psychiatric care consists of clarifying the psychological meaning of events, feelings, and behaviors?
    A. Biological   B. Psychological
    C. Behavioral   D. Social
    E. Eclectic

    16.___

17. During *what* phase of the life cycle is the individual MOST vulnerable to despair?
    A. Oedipal phase   B. Latency
    C. Adolescence   D. Adulthood
    E. Older adulthood

    17.___

18. *Which* of the following is used to treat serious depres-   18.___
    sion when drug therapy has failed?
    A. Electroconvulsive therapy
    B. Insulin treatment
    C. Psychosurgery
    D. Hydrotherapy
    E. Hypnotic-sedative drugs

19. The psychiatric nurse's responsibility in dispensing   19.___
    medication is
    A. to know the reactions and side effects of the
       drug
    B. to regulate the dosage
    C. to determine a proper dosage schedule
    D. to keep the patient ignorant of the drugs he is
       receiving
    E. All of the above

20. *What* should the nurse's reaction be to a manic patient's   20.___
    loud jokes and crude pranks? She *should*
    A. react with studied prudishness
    B. acknowledge the hilarity
    C. chastise the patient
    D. put restraints on the patient
    E. react with silence, ignoring it

21. *Which* of the following defense mechanisms of the ego   21.___
    is *most pronounced* in paranoid conditions in which
    there is an actual break with reality?
    A. Displacement   B. Sublimation
    C. Isolation   D. Regression
    E. Projection

22. *Which* of the following verbal responses is the *most*   22.___
    useful to the therapeutic process? The _____ response.
    A. evaluative   B. reassuring
    C. probing   D. understanding
    E. hostile

23. *Which* of the following are qualities that distinguish   23.___
    the schizophrenic from the non-schizophrenic?
      I. A diminished capacity to experience pleasure
     II. A strong tendency to be dependent on others
    III. Awareness that there is a disturbance in mental
         functioning
     IV. A noteworthy impairment in social competence
      V. Partial loss of adaptation
    The CORRECT answer is:
    A. I, II, III   B. I, III, IV   C. I, IV, V
    D. I, II, V   E. II, III, IV

24. An overwhelming number of emotional problems in children   24.____
are related to
    I. faulty training and faulty life experiences
   II. surface conflicts between children and parents
  III. deeper conflicts within the child
  IV. a difficulty associated with physical handicaps
     and disorders
   V. difficulties associated with severe mental dis-
     orders
The CORRECT answer is:
  A. I, II   B. I, III   C. III, V
  D. II, IV   E. I, IV

25. Strong unconscious feelings of guilt and hostility   25.____
are *particularly common* in patients with
  A. obsessions   B. compulsion
  C. phobias   D. hysteria
  E. hypochondria.

26. Adults who withdraw into schizoid and depressive states   26.____
frequently fail to
  A. resolve the conflict of autonomy vs. shame and
     doubt
  B. resolve the oedipus complex
  C. master the task of industry
  D. develop basic trust during infancy
  E. establish an identity during adolescence

27. All of the following are defined as antipsychotic or   27.____
major tranquilizers EXCEPT
  A. Reserpine   B. Phenothiazines
  C. Tricyclics   D. Thioxanthenes
  E. Butyrophenones

28. The population felt to be of high risk or vulnerable   28.____
to schizophrenia are *usually* the children of
  A. disorganized, disruptive families
  B. homosexuals
  C. alcoholics
  D. manic depressives
  E. schizophrenics

29. *Which* of the following is *least likely* to make a suicide   29.____
attempt?
  A. The patient with a history of suicide attempts
  B. Members of the patient's family having a history
     of suicide attempts
  C. Patients who obsessively fear that they will commit
     suicide
  D. Patients who write suicide notes
  E. Patients who have access to suicidal agents

30. The nurse can communicate *more effectively* with small   30.____
    children by
       A. using simple sentences
       B. being specific
       C. being enthusiastic
       D. reflecting feeling tones
       E. all of the above

31. *What* conceptual mode of psychiatric care is more con-   31.____
    cerned with treating the overt systems (the learned
    behavior) and not the secondary manifestations of disease
    or unconscious conflict?
       A. Biological   B. Psychological
       C. Behavioral   D. Social
       E. Eclectic

32. The *most helpful* attitude a nurse should have during   32.____
    the therapeutic process is to be _____ the patient.
       A. reassuring to   B. supportive of
       C. sympathetic to   D. understanding of
       E. a friend to

33. *Which* is the BEST way to treat depression?   33.____
       A. The nurse helps the patient to bear the feelings
          he doesn't want to bear alone
       B. The nurse helps the patient resolve the feelings
          that brought on the depression
       C. The nurse encourages the patient to express negative
          feelings
       D. The nurse teaches the patient how to get the ego
          supplies he wants
       E. There is no single way to treat depression

34. *Which* of the following psychological disturbances are   34.____
    accompanied by the HIGHEST suicide rate?
       A. Pick's disease   B. Alzheimer's disease
       C. Huntington's chorea   D. Korsakoff's syndrome
       E. Senile dementia

35. *Which* of the following *should not be displayed* in   35.____
    explaining an anxiety state to the patient?
       A. Anxiousness
       B. Emotional tension
       C. Nervousness
       D. Wave of emotional tension
       E. Period of anxiousness

36. *What* occurs during the period of development called   36.____
    latency? The
       A. adolescent gains independence from the family
          and integrates new-found sexual maturity
       B. individual enters in an involved, reciprocal way
          with others sexually, occupationally, and socially
       C. child has a growing cognitive ability with the
          capacity to conceptualize and internalize relation-
          ships
       D. child enters into the first major social system
          outside the family
       E. child experiments with autonomy

37. *How should* the psychiatric nurse handle direct questions from the patient? The nurse should answer
   A. all questions to substantiate her professional credentials
   B. questions dealing with her personal life
   C. questions about the patient's illness
   D. questions about her behavior that the patient has observed
   E. all questions honestly

37.___

38. *What* is the main symptom of hebephrenic schizophrenia?
   A. The inappropriate affect of the person
   B. The total lack of any substantial relationships
   C. Abnormal and postural movements
   D. Delusions and extreme suspiciousness
   E. Undifferentiated symptoms

38.___

39. *What* causes neuroses?
   A. Depression
   B. Emotional turmoil
   C. Self-preoccupation
   D. Withdrawal
   E. Guilt

39.___

40. All of the following are good techniques for the nurse dealing with adolescents on psychiatric service EXCEPT:
   A. She should listen to complaints and criticisms with interest
   B. She should use some of the adolescent's jargon
   C. The relationship should develop at a rate the adolescent feels comfortable with
   D. A social relationship should be developed between nurse and patient
   E. Infractions of rules generally should be ignored

40.___

41. During what period is narcissim at its height? Between _____ years.
   A. 1-2
   B. 3-6
   C. 7-12
   D. 13-19
   E. 21-35

41.___

42. *Which* of the following is the *most effective* anti-depressant medication?
   A. Reserpine
   B. Tricyclics
   C. Thioxanthenes
   D. Miltown
   E. Paraldehyde

42.___

43. The role of the psychiatric nurse in the care and milieu management of a person who has a thought disorder *must be*
   A. supportive
   B. understanding
   C. sympathetic
   D. flexible
   E. rigid

43.___

44. *How should* a psychiatric nurse respond when a delusional   44.____
    patient fearfully tells her that people are waiting
    outside the hospital to kill him?
    A. "You don't have to worry because you are safe
       here."
    B. "You know as well as I do that no one is trying
       to kill you."
    C. "You should go to occupational therapy to take
       your mind off your fears."
    D. "You should rest now and, when you wake up, I'm
       certain you'll feel less afraid."
    E. "I understand how frightened you feel but when
       you are better you will see things in a different
       way."

45. *Which* of the following is a *proper* attitude toward   45.____
    a neurotic patient? The nurse *should*
    A. respond emotionally to the patient's behavior
    B. pass judgment on the patient
    C. express her own feelings and opinions
    D. place realistic limits on the patient's behavior
    E. not reassure the patient

46. *What* should the psychiatric nurse do when she notices   46.____
    herself becoming tense, rigid, and stilted and wishing
    that she felt more professional? She *should*
    A. worry less about trying too hard to follow the
       book and the prescribed rules, and concentrate
       on being natural
    B. assay the scope of her judgmental feelings and
       keep them in check so they do not interfere with
       the therapeutic process
    C. talk over her feelings with a staff member or
       supervisor
    D. take time to listen to the patient's requests
       and his perception of the situation
    E. realize that she is not expected to have all the
       answers to patients' situations and should consult
       with her colleagues

47. *What* is the *focus* of behavior therapy? The patient's   47.____
    A. thoughts
    B. overt behavior that is presenting the problem
    C. feelings
    D. behavior
    E. socialization problems

48. *What* is the *most prominent* symptom of senile dementia?   48.____
    A. An impaired time sense
    B. Disorientation
    C. Difficulty with abstract reasoning
    D. Impairment in the ability to retain and recall
       information
    E. Difficulty in identifying people

49. Psychiatric hospitalization is HIGHEST *among*   49.___
     A. single people
     B. married people
     C. widowed people
     D. divorced people
     E. Marital status has not proved to be a factor

50. *Which* of the following is TRUE of the organization   50.___
     of group psychotherapy?
     A. Divergent age, social and economic backgrounds
        should be represented
     B. Members should have similar problems
     C. Sexes should be separated into different groups
     D. Active and inactive members should be separated
        into different groups
     E. Members should be chosen at random

KEY (CORRECT ANSWERS)

1.	A	11.	C	21.	E	31.	C	41.	B
2.	C	12.	E	22.	D	32.	B	42.	B
3.	E	13.	B	23.	D	33.	E	43.	D
4.	C	14.	B	24.	A	34.	C	44.	E
5.	E	15.	C	25.	A	35.	C	45.	D
6.	A	16.	B	26.	D	36.	D	46.	A
7.	B	17.	E	27.	C	37.	D	47.	B
8.	C	18.	A	28.	E	38.	A	48.	D
9.	C	19.	A	29.	C	39.	B	49.	D
10.	B	20.	E	30.	E	40.	D	50.	B

EXAMINATION SECTION

TEST 1

DIRECTIONS: Each question or incomplete statement is followed by several suggested answers or completions. Select the one that BEST answers the question or completes the statement. *PRINT THE LETTER OF THE CORRECT ANSWER IN THE SPACE AT THE RIGHT.*

Questions 1-9.

DIRECTIONS: Questions 1 through 9 are to be answered on the basis of the following information.

Ms. Evelyn Hart, a 75-year-old widow, is admitted to a psychiatric hospital. Her son, who brings her, says that she has been confused and wandered away from home. Also, she has become increasingly careless about her appearance.

1. With a chronic brain syndrome such as Ms. Hart's, the personality changes are MOST often manifested as
   A. an exaggeration of previous traits
   B. overt pleas for assistance
   C. suspicion and reticence
   D. marked resistance and negativism

1.___

2. During the early period following Ms. Hart's admission, the nursing procedure that would be BEST for her is
   A. carrying out activities in the same order each day
   B. insisting that she focus her conversation on present events
   C. providing a variety of novel experiences
   D. rotating staff assignments so that she will become acquainted with each member of the nursing staff

2.___

3. When Ms. Hart's son comes to visit her the day after admission, Ms. Hart refuses to talk to him. The son goes to the nurse and says, *My mother won't talk to me. Why is she acting like this? I had to do something with her. I couldn't keep her with us. Oh, what a mess!* Which of these responses by the nurse would be MOST appropriate initially?
   A. You feel guilty about having your mother here.
   B. Your mother is having a little difficulty adjusting to the hospital.
   C. This is a difficult situation for you and your mother.
   D. I'm sure you did the best you could under the circumstances.

3.___

4. Ms. Hart's son asks the nurse whether he should come to   4.___
   see his mother again on the following day in view of
   her reaction to his first visit.
   Which of these responses would be BEST?
      A. Advising the son to wait until his mother gives some
         indication that she is ready to see him
      B. Suggesting that the son come back the next day since
         his continuing interest is important to his mother
      C. Telling the son that his mother will not miss him
         if he doesn't visit because she will become attached
         to staff members
      D. Informing the son that it is important for his mother
         to have visitors and suggesting that he ask one of
         her friends to visit her

5. The nurse finds Ms. Hart standing near the lavatory door.   5.___
   She has wet herself - as she does occasionally - because
   she does not allow herself sufficient time to reach the
   bathroom. Ms. Hart looks ashamed and turns her head
   away from the nurse.
   Which of these responses by the nurse would be BEST?
      A. Asking, *Can you tell me why you wait so long, Ms.
         Hart?*
      B. Saying, *I know that this is upsetting to you, Ms.
         Hart. Come with me and I'll get a change of clothes
         for you*
      C. Asking, *Can you think of any way in which we can
         help you to manage your bathroom trips, Ms. Hart?*
      D. Sending Ms. Hart to her room to change her clothing

6. At about 3 P.M. one day, Ms. Hart comes to the nurse and   6.___
   says, *I haven't had a thing to eat all day.* The nurse
   knows that Ms. Hart did have lunch.
   Which of these understandings by the nurse should be
   BASIC to a response?
      A. Confabulation is used by elderly patients as a means
         of relieving anxiety.
      B. Hunger is symbolic of a feeling of deprivation.
      C. Retrospective falsification is a mechanism commonly
         used by elderly persons who are unhappy.
      D. Loss of memory for recent events is characteristic
         of patients with senile dementia.

7. Ms. Hart is to be encouraged to increase her intake of   7.___
   protein.
   The addition of which of these foods to 100 cc. of milk
   will provide the GREATEST amount of protein?
      A. 50 cc. light cream and 2 tablespoons corn syrup
      B. 30 grams powdered skim milk and 1 egg
      C. 1 small scoop (90 grams) vanilla ice cream and
         1 tablespoon chocolate syrup
      D. 2 egg yolks and 1 tablespoon sugar

8. One day when another patient, Mr. Simon, is about to go   8.___
    to the canteen, Ms. Hart says to him, *Bring me a candy
    bar.* Mr. Simon replies, *Okay, give me the twenty-five
    cents for it.* Ms. Hart struggles with the idea, taking
    out a quarter and holding it but not giving it to Mr.
    Simon. Mr. Simon goes off impatiently, and Ms. Hart
    looks forlorn.
    Which of these responses by the nurse would probably be
    MOST useful to Ms. Hart?
    A. Ms. Hart, when we get things from the canteen, we
       have to pay for them. Do you want to buy candy?
    B. It was hard for you to decide whether or not to give
       Mr. Simon the money for the candy. Let's go to the
       canteen together.
    C. I know you are upset about Mr. Simon's going off,
       but he did have a right to ask you for the money
       for the candy.
    D. You feel you annoyed Mr. Simon. Would you like to
       talk about it?

9. Ms. Hart tells stories over and over about her childhood.   9.___
    One day she keeps talking about holidays and how she used
    to make cookies for visiting children.
    Which of the responses by the nurse would be BEST?
    A. That must have been a lot of fun, Ms. Hart. Will
       you help us make popcorn balls for the unit party?
    B. I can understand that those things were important
       to you, Ms. Hart. Now we can talk about something
       that is going on in the unit.
    C. Things are different now, Ms. Hart. What does your
       family serve as party refreshments nowadays?
    D. Those were the good old days. Did you ever go on a
       hayride?

Questions 10-17.

DIRECTIONS: Questions 10 through 17 are to be answered on the basis
             of the following information.

     Mr. David Tripp, 28 years old, is brought from his place of work
to the emergency department of a local general hospital by the police.
He had been threatening his supervisor, who had criticized his work.
During the admission procedure, he says, *They're all in on the plot
to lock me up so I can't protect the world from them.*

10. During the early period of Mr. Tripp's hospitalization,   10.___
    which of these plans of care would probably be BEST for
    him?
    A. Encourage him to enter into simple group activities.
    B. Establish a daily routine that will help him become
       oriented to this new environment.
    C. Plan to cope with his slowness in carrying out his
       daily schedule.
    D. Assign the same members of the nursing team to care
       for him each day.

11. Mr. Tripp is on chlorpromazine hydrochloride (Thorazine)   11.___
    100 mg. t.i.d. and 200 mg. at h.s.
    The CHIEF purpose of chlorpromazine for Mr. Tripp is to
        A. relieve his anxiety
        B. control his aggression
        C. decrease his psychotic symptoms
        D. alleviate his depression

12. Mr. Tripp is walking into the dayroom when a male patient   12.___
    runs toward him screaming, *Let me out! Let me out!* A
    nurse's aide is following the screaming patient and is
    talking soothingly to him. Mr. Tripp seems panic-stricken
    and turns to flee.
    Which of these initial responses to Mr. Tripp by the
    nurse would be BEST?
        A. Don't go, Mr. Tripp. That patient won't hurt you.
           He is frightened.
        B. It is upsetting to hear someone scream. The aide
           will help that patient. I will stay with you for a
           while, Mr. Tripp.
        C. Don't be upset, Mr. Tripp. That patient is sicker
           than you are. It's all right for you to go to your
           room if you like.
        D. This is nothing to be disturbed about, Mr. Tripp.
           It is part of that patient's illness.

13. One afternoon, Mr. Tripp is sitting in a small lounge   13.___
    watching a TV news program. During a biographical sketch
    of a criminal, Mr. Tripp begins to shout frantically,
    No, I am not one! You've no right to say that!
    Mr. Tripp's response to the program is MOST clearly an
    example of
        A. an idea of reference   B. an obsession
        C. confabulation   D. negativism

14. Mr. Tripp seems to value his regular sessions with the   14.___
    nurse, but on one occasion he becomes agitated and
    suddenly gets up and starts to mumble and pace back and
    forth.
    Which of these actions by the nurse would be BEST when
    Mr. Tripp does this?
        A. Sit quietly, while remaining attentive to him.
        B. Join him and pace with him.
        C. Leave the room until he calms down.
        D. Get a male nurse's aide to come and stand by and
           observe Mr. Tripp.

15. Mr. Tripp, who has read widely in the field of psychology, 15.___
    quotes fluently from various authorities with whose works
    the nurse is only vaguely acquainted.
    Which of these actions by the nurse in this situation
    would probably be BEST?
        A. Make an attempt to learn more about psychology in
           order to be able to converse with Mr. Tripp.

    B. Point out to Mr. Tripp that such theoretical knowledge is of little value unless it is applied in daily life.
    C. Listen attentively, in a relaxed manner, without attempting to compete with Mr. Tripp.
    D. Ask Mr. Tripp if he understands why he feels the need to give evidence of his knowledge of psychology.

16. Mr. Tripp is much improved and is to go home for a weekend.   16.___
    Since he is taking chlorpromazine hydrochloride (Thorazine), he should be given information regarding side-effects such as
    A. loss of pubic hair and weight gain
    B. agranulocytosis and nausea
    C. gastrointestinal bleeding and gynecomastia
    D. susceptibility to sunburn and potentation of alcohol

17. One day Mr. Tripp remarks to the nurse, *Now that I can*   17.___
concentrate more, I can probably hold down a job when I'm discharged from the hospital.
    Which of these responses by the nurse would probably be MOST appropriate?
    A. Don't you expect to go back to your old job, Mr. Tripp?
    B. You have improved, Mr. Tripp, but you must be careful not to take on too much.
    C. Have you thought of something you might like to do, Mr. Tripp?
    D. There are agencies that will find work for you when you are ready, Mr. Tripp.

Questions 18-25.

DIRECTIONS: Questions 18 through 25 are to be answered on the basis of the following information.

    Ms. Nancy Balm, a 20-year-old former music student, is admitted to a psychiatric hospital. Six months after entering school, she was dismissed for engaging in drug parties and sexual orgies in the dormitory. She has also been involved in the theft of a car and in several minor traffic violations. Ms. Balm has grown up in a permissive atmosphere with few controls.

18. After a few days, it is noted that Ms. Balm frequently   18.___
seeks the attention of one of the female nurses; Ms. Balm calls her by her first name, offers to help her with her work, and frequently tells her that she is the nicest person on the unit.
    Based on Ms. Balm's history, it is probably MOST justifiable to say that she
    A. has developed the capacity to be concerned about other people
    B. is asking for help from this nurse

C. is attempting to use this nurse for her own purposes
D. genuinely likes this nurse

19. Ms. Balm is on a locked unit. A new nurse on the unit
is about to leave and is holding the key. Ms. Balm
approaches, saying eagerly, *Let me turn the key and
unlock the door. The other nurses let me.*
Which response by the nurse would be MOST appropriate?
A. Going to the nurse in charge to ask if Ms. Balm's
request should be granted
B. Telling Ms. Balm in a friendly way that this is not
permissible
C. Letting Ms. Balm turn the key in the lock but keeping close to her while she does it
D. Asking Ms. Balm why she feels that it is important
for her to turn the key

19.____

20. One day Ms. Balm talks with the nurse about the events
that led up to her hospitalization. She volunteers the
information that she had stolen a car.
Considering the kind of illness she has, which additional comment that she might make would probably BEST
indicate her basic attitude?
A. I wanted a new sportscar, and that one was just what
I had been looking for, so I took it.
B. For a long time, I had wanted to steal a car but
had been able to control my desire, but finally it
overpowered me.
C. I knew it was wrong to steal a car, but my friend
dared me to.
D. Once I had driven away in the car, I was sorry I had
taken it.

20.____

21. At unit parties, Ms. Balm frequently dances with an
elderly man who has chronic brain syndrome. She is
courteous to him, though somewhat condescending. The
elderly patient receives the attention happily.
It would be CORRECT for staff members to make which of
these evaluations about this situation?
A. Ms. Balm should not be permitted to dance with the
elderly patient.
B. Personnel should let Ms. Balm know that they are
aware she is using this means to get approval.
C. The elderly patient will terminate their relationship if he ceases to obtain pleasure from it.
D. The activity need not be interrupted as long as
both Ms. Balm and the elderly patient receive
satisfaction from it.

21.____

22. A young male nurse who works with Ms. Balm has been
going to the unit in the evening to see her. When
questioned about this, the nurse states that he is fond
of Ms. Balm.
It would be ESSENTIAL for the nurse to recognize that
A. his emotional involvement with Ms. Balm may interfere
with his therapeutic effectiveness

22.____

B. Ms. Balm's emotional involvement with him may interfere with her progress
C. hospital policy prohibits romantic relationships between patients and nurses
D. Ms. Balm may prove so demanding that he will drop the relationship, thus traumatizing her

23. When Ms. Balm's parents come to see her, they berate her for disgracing them, but they demand special privileges for her from the staff.
It is probably MOST justified to say that they
  A. are unable to express their love directly to their daughter
  B. feel protective toward their daughter
  C. feel that a permissive environment would be better for their daughter
  D. have conflicting feelings about their daughter

23.___

24. Several patients are in the dayroom singing with a piano accompaniment. Ms. Balm enters and interrupts the group by turning on the television set.
In addition to turning off the television set, which of these responses by the nurse would be MOST appropriate?
  A. Ask Ms. Balm if she would like to lead the group singing.
  B. Tell Ms. Balm that she cannot use the television while the group is singing and offer her a choice of some other activities.
  C. Tell Ms. Balm that she can watch television later.
  D. Tell Ms. Balm that she cannot stay in the dayroom if she continues to disturb the group.

24.___

25. Several weeks after Ms. Balm's admission, a group of patients who have written a play for a hospital party ask her to read the script because they know she had a story printed in the hospital newspaper. Ms. Balm agrees to do so and makes several good suggestions to the group, but does not try to assume control of the project.
It is MOST justifiable to say that she is
  A. expressing a need to be liked
  B. indifferent to this project
  C. using a new method of manipulating the group
  D. showing improvement

25.___

KEY (CORRECT ANSWERS)

1. A	6. D	11. C	16. D	21. D
2. A	7. B	12. B	17. C	22. A
3. C	8. B	13. A	18. C	23. D
4. B	9. A	14. A	19. B	24. B
5. B	10. D	15. C	20. A	25. D

TEST 2

DIRECTIONS: Each question or incomplete statement is followed by several suggested answers or completions. Select the one that BEST answers the question or completes the statement. *PRINT THE LETTER OF THE CORRECT ANSWER IN THE SPACE AT THE RIGHT.*

Questions 1-9.

DIRECTIONS: Questions 1 through 9 are to be answered on the basis of the following information.

Andrew Miles, 18 years old and living away from home for the first time, is a freshman in college. He is admitted to the hospital because he has been having episodes in which he runs about, screams, and then drops to the floor and lies motionless for a few minutes, after which he gets up, mumbles *I'm sorry*, and behaves normally. His school record has been satisfactory, but his contacts with his peer group have decreased greatly because of these episodes. On the basis of diagnostic studies, it has been determined that Mr. Miles' illness is schizophrenia, catatonic type.

1. Stereotyped behavior such as that shown by Mr. Miles can   1.___
    be BEST explained as a(n)
    A. way of assuring predictability
    B. device to gain help and treatment
    C. means of increasing interpersonal distance
    D. attempt to control inner and outer forces

2. The behavior demonstrated by patients such as Mr. Miles   2.___
    is USUALLY thought to be indicative of
    A. damage to the cortex of the brain
    B. an expression of intrapersonal conflict
    C. a deficiency of vitamin B complex in the diet
    D. a disturbance in intellectual functioning

3. Upon Mr. Miles' admission, his needs would BEST be met   3.___
    by a plan that provides
    A. an introduction to each member of the staff
    B. a climate that makes few demands on him
    C. minimal sensory stimulation
    D. time for him to reflect on his problems without
       interference

4. The day after Mr. Miles' admission, a nurse, Ms. Caan,   4.___
    is assigned to stay with him for a period every day in
    order to establish a therapeutic nurse-patient relation-
    ship.
    In carrying out this assignment, it is ESSENTIAL for this
    nurse to understand that Mr. Miles will probably
       A. be extremely sensitive to the feeling tones of others

    B. be unaware of the nurse's presence
    C. be hostile and verbally abusive
    D. talk if the nurse introduces topics that are of
       interest to him

5. Which of these insights that Mr. Miles might gain would
   be MOST basic to his improvement?
    A. Introjection of parental standards in childhood
       contributed to my personality.
    B. I am a person of worth and value.
    C. My behavior interferes with the development of good
       relationships.
    D. I require more reassurance than most people do.

6. One day a nurse finds Mr. Miles and another young male
   patient having an argument in the lounge. The other
   patient says, *Don't criticize me, you phony. You and
   your fits!* The other patient is pressing the argument,
   and Mr. Miles has run behind a chair.
   Which of these measures by the nurse would probably be
   BEST?
    A. Attempting to find out who started the argument
    B. Firmly directing each patient to go to his room
    C. Engaging the attention of the dominant patient
    D. Explaining to the other patient that Mr. Miles
       cannot control his spells

7. Mr. Miles now carries on brief conversations with Ms.
   Caan. During one such conversation, he seems relaxed
   and affable initially but soon begins to shift his
   position frequently, grasping the arms of his chair
   so tightly that his fingers blanch. Ms. Caan remarks
   to Mr. Miles that he seems tense, to which he replies
   Yes.
   Which of these responses by the nurse at this time
   would demonstrate the BEST understanding?
    A. I'm beginning to feel tense too, Mr. Miles.
    B. I wonder if I have said something wrong, Mr. Miles.
    C. Do women usually make you feel nervous, Mr. Miles.
    D. At what point in our talk did you begin to feel
       uneasy, Mr. Miles?

8. When Ms. Caan tells Mr. Miles that she will be off duty
   for two days, he says flatly, *So what. It doesn't matter.*
   It is MOST accurate to say that Mr. Miles is
    A. incapable of manifesting emotion
    B. confident of his ability to manage without the nurse
    C. controlling expression of his feelings
    D. apathetic toward the nurse

5.___

6.___

7.___

8.___

9. Family therapy is recommended for Mr. Miles.   9.___
    When explaining the purpose of this type of therapy to
    Mr. Miles' family, which of the following information
    would it be important to convey to them?
    A. Family members can reinforce the therapist's recom-
       mendations between sessions.
    B. Family members need advice in dealing with the
       identified patient's behavior.
    C. Joint treatment permits equal participation, elimi-
       nating anxieties that might otherwise lead to ter-
       mination of treatment.
    D. Joint treatment alters family interaction, facili-
       tating change in the behavior of the identified
       patient.

Questions 10-16.

DIRECTIONS: Questions 10 through 16 are to be answered on the basis
              of the following information.

    Fifty-year-old Mr. Jack Dunn, accompanied by his wife, is brought
to the emergency room by the police. He has been despondent because
he was not promoted in his job. After calling his son to say goodbye,
insisting that he was going to end it all, he locked himself in the
bathroom, and the police were called to get him out. Mr. Dunn is
admitted to the psychiatric unit.

10. Which of these interpretations of Mr. Dunn's behavior   10.___
    should serve as the basis for formulating his nursing
    care plan?
    He
    A. wants to punish those around him
    B. is trying to manipulate his environment
    C. is attempting to get attention and sympathy
    D. is looking for relief from helplessness and hope-
       lessness

11. Which of these statements ACCURATELY assesses Mr. Dunn's 11.___
    potential for suicide?
    His
    A. sex and present stress suggest a high risk, but the
       likelihood of suicide is low in his age group
    B. threat suggests that the risk of suicide is minor
    C. age, sex, and present stress suggest a high risk of
       suicide
    D. sex suggests a low risk since suicide occurs 30 times
       more often in females than in males

12. Which of these occurrences would be MOST likely to result 12.___
    in an INCREASE in Mr. Dunn's suicidal thoughts?
    His
    A. expressing hostility overtly before he is able to
       tolerate doing so
    B. entrance into a deeply retarded phase of depression

    C. being required to perform work in the kitchen
    D. being allowed to talk about his morbid ideas

13. During a staff conference concerning Mr. Dunn's care,   13.___
a young nursing student says, *Even though I know that
Mr. Dunn's condition requires time to respond to therapy,
I feel discouraged when I'm with him. No matter what I
do, he talks about his failures and makes no attempt to
help himself.*
The interpretation of the student's reaction to Mr.
Dunn's behavior that is probably MOST justifiable is
that the
    A. student's difficulty arises from an attitude of
       hopelessness toward older persons
    B. student feels that Mr. Dunn's condition is not
       remediable unless he is willing to help himself
    C. student has set up a failure situation that is
       detrimental to therapeutic usefulness to Mr. Dunn
    D. student's self-concept as a helping person is
       being threatened

14. A nurse finds Mr. Dunn cutting his wrist with a razor   14.___
blade.
Which of these actions should the nurse take?
    A. Shout *Stop!* and then say, *Tell me what caused your
       despair.*
    B. Say, *Think of what it would do to your family!*
    C. Grab Mr. Dunn's arm to stop him and say, *I'm going
       to stay with you.*
    D. Say, *Why, Mr. Dunn! You've just begun to feel better
       and now look what you've done.*

15. Mr. Dunn seems improved and is sent home on a trial visit. 15.___
He is then admitted to the intensive care unit for treat-
ment for a self-inflicted gunshot wound in the chest.
When he is somewhat improved, Mr. Dunn remarks, *Everyone
here must think I'm some kind of freak.*
Which of these responses would be MOST appropriate?
    A. None of us thinks that you are a freak.
    B. You feel that others are judging you.
    C. I understand that you were upset when this happened.
    D. What made you so desperate that you did a thing like
       this?

16. Mr. Dunn has improved and is discharged.   16.___
A few days after Mr. Dunn returns to work, while he is
talking with a co-worker, a number of things go wrong
in the office. Mr. Dunn slams a book on the table and
says, *Dammit!* The co-worker who is present is aware
that Mr. Dunn has been mentally ill.
Which of these actions on the part of the co-worker
would be BEST?
    A. Wait for Mr. Dunn to cool off and then resume the
       discussion.
    B. Suggest that Mr. Dunn go home and remain there
       until he calms down.

    C. Urge Mr. Dunn to take his tranquilizers.
    D. Talk with Mr. Dunn about his particular need for controlling outbursts.

Questions 17-25.

DIRECTIONS: Questions 17 through 25 are to be answered on the basis of the following information.

    Ms. Julia Warren, 53 years old and with no previous history of mental illness, is admitted to a private psychiatric hospital because of symptoms, including pacing, wringing her hands, moaning, beating her forehead, and saying, *I'm a terrible woman.* She has been unable to do her job as a bookkeeper and has had to have members of her family stay with her day and night.

17. The extent of the nurse's orientation of Ms. Warren to the hospital environment should be based CHIEFLY upon Ms. Warren's   17.___
    A. willingness to stay with the nurse
    B. ability to concentrate
    C. persistence in making demands on other patients
    D. acceptance of the need for hospitalization

18. During the acute phase of Ms. Warren's illness, it is ESSENTIAL that the nurse have the ability to   18.___
    A. minimize stimuli in Ms. Warren's environment
    B. interest Ms. Warren in a variety of activities
    C. accept Ms. Warren's self-accusations
    D. strengthen Ms. Warren's intellectual defenses

19. Ms. Warren shows typical distress upon being informed of her impending electric convulsive therapy.
Which understanding by the nurse would BEST serve as the basis for preparing Ms. Warren psychologically for it?   19.___
    A. Misinformation may be contributing to her anxiety.
    B. Emphasizing the safety of the procedure will reduce her fear.
    C. Knowing that most people have the same response is usually comforting.
    D. A high level of anxiety renders an individual more receptive to information given by helping persons.

20. Depressions of the type Ms. Warren has usually respond well to electric convulsive therapy, but the consequent memory loss is quite disturbing.
The nurse can be MOST helpful to the patient who has such a loss of memory by   20.___
    A. engaging the patient in diversional activities
    B. reporting the problem to the physician
    C. explaining to the patient that other patients receiving this therapy also have this problem
    D. reassuring the patient repeatedly that this is an expected and temporary reaction

21. Which of the following defense mechanisms is MOST likely
    to be used by a person who is as depressed as Ms. Warren?
    A. Turning against the self
    B. Projection
    C. Rationalization
    D. Displacement of instinctual aims

21.___

22. When Ms. Warren learns that occupational therapy has
    been ordered for her, she scoffs at the idea, saying
    it is silly.
    If Ms. Warren were to think all of the following
    thoughts regarding occupational therapy, which one would
    be MOST acceptable to her?
    A. This is enjoyable.
    B. I'm helping to pay for my care.
    C. This keeps me from thinking about my failures.
    D. I didn't know that I was so creative.

22.___

23. Ms. Warren is assigned to group therapy.
    Which of these ideas would it be MOST desirable for
    each participant to gain?
    A. Each person's opinion is respected.
    B. Verbalization will help each individual to gain
       insight.
    C. Each member has a responsibility to other members
       of the group.
    D. The group work consists of analyzing each other's
       motivations.

23.___

24. Ms. Warren improves and goes out with her husband for
    the afternoon. That evening, a nurse finds Ms. Warren
    sitting by herself in the dayroom.
    Which of these comments by the nurse would probably be
    BEST?
    A. Why are you so preoccupied, Ms. Warren?
    B. You look tired, Ms. Warren. Was your afternoon too
       much for you?
    C. You seem very quiet, Ms. Warren.
    D. You looked happier yesterday, Ms. Warren.

24.___

25. Ms. Warren is discharged.
    The day Ms. Warren goes back to work, Bob, a customer
    she has known for many years, comes in and says, *Hello
    there, Julia. Good to see you back! Your boss told me
    that you were sick. What was wrong with you?*
    Which of these replies by Ms. Warren would indicate that
    she accepted her illness and has recovered?
    A. I was kind of mixed up for a while, Bob, but I'm
       all right now.
    B. I just didn't feel good, Bob. Old age coming on, I
       guess.
    C. I was just down in the dumps, Bob, but my doctor
       insisted that I go to the hospital. You know how
       they are.
    D. I'm glad to be back. What can I do for you, Bob?

25.___

KEY (CORRECT ANSWERS)

1. D		11. C
2. B		12. A
3. B		13. D
4. A		14. C
5. B		15. B
6. C		16. A
7. D		17. B
8. C		18. C
9. D		19. A
10. D		20. D

21. A
22. B
23. A
24. C
25. A

———

TEST 3

DIRECTIONS: Each question or incomplete statement is followed by several suggested answers or completions. Select the one that BEST answers the question or completes the statement. *PRINT THE LETTER OF THE CORRECT ANSWER IN THE SPACE AT THE RIGHT.*

Questions 1-7.

DIRECTIONS: Questions 1 through 7 are to be answered on the basis of the following information.

When Mark Levine, 5½ years old, goes to school for the first time, he screams and seems terrified when he sees the drinking fountain near his classroom door. Mark's mother tells the school nurse that he has an intense fear of drinking fountains.

1. The understanding of Mark's fear of fountains that is   1.___
   MOST justifiable is that it
   A. is a symptom common in dyslexic children
   B. is not subject to his conscious control
   C. stems from his lack of understanding of plumbing
   D. results from having learned that his symptoms have a
      manipulative potential

2. Behavior therapy will be used in treating Mark's symptoms.   2.___
   His plan of care will include
   A. authoritative instruction
   B. increased cultural orientation
   C. direct interpretations
   D. systematic desensitization

3. Mark's behavior reflects his need to control anxiety by   3.___
   A. refusing to recognize the source of his anxiety
   B. making a conscious effort to avoid situations that
      cause anxiety
   C. substituting a neutral object as the target of his
      negative feelings
   D. acting in a manner opposite to his underlying need

4. Parents should be instructed that a child's mental health   4.___
   will BEST be promoted if the love he receives from his
   parents
   A. is related to the child's behavior
   B. is unconditional
   C. makes externally imposed discipline unnecessary
   D. is reinforced by unchanging physical demonstrations

5. Ms. Levine calls the community mental health clinic and
tells the nurse that Mark has suddenly become terrified
of getting into the family car, refuses to do so, and
is in the yard screaming uncontrollably.
What would it be BEST for the nurse to tell Ms. Levine
to do FIRST?
   A. Hold Mark snugly and talk softly to him.
   B. Give Mark a warm bath and put him to bed.
   C. Bring Mark to the clinic as soon as possible.
   D. Remind Mark that he has never before been afraid
      of automobiles.

5.___

6. Mark is having play therapy.
The choice of play therapy for children of Mark's age
should PROBABLY be based upon their inability to
   A. overcome inhibitors about revealing family conflicts
      and behaviors
   B. differentiate between reality and fantasy
   C. recognize the difference between right and wrong
   D. adequately describe feelings and experience

6.___

7. On a rainy day, after Mark's play-therapy session, Ms.
Levine hands Mark his overshoes and says, *Put them on.
It's pouring outside.* Mark answers defiantly, *No, they're
too hard to put on. I can't.* Then he sits down on a
bench and pouts. Ms. Levine looks at the nurse in a
perplexed way, saying nothing.
Which of these responses by the nurse would probably be
BEST?
   A. Say to Ms. Levine, *Maybe the overshoes are too small
      to Mark.*
   B. Sit on the bench with Mark and say calmly, *It's
      raining. You start pulling your overshoes on, and
      I'll help you with the hard part.*
   C. Hand Mark his overshoes and say to him in a matter-
      of-fact way, *If you will put the first one one, I'll
      put on the second one for you.*
   D. Say to Mark, firmly but kindly, *You are trying to
      test your mother's authority. This behavior will not
      be tolerated. Put your overshoes on right now.*

7.___

Questions 8-14.

DIRECTIONS: Questions 8 through 14 are to be answered on the basis
of the following information.

Ms. Eileen Gray, 33 years old, is admitted to the psychiatric
hospital with a diagnosis of obsessive-compulsive reaction. Her
chief fear is that her excreta may harm others on the unit. As a
result, she spends hours in the bathroom washing not only her hands,
arms, vulva, and anal area, but also the walls, toilet, and toilet
stall. In the process, she discards wet paper towels in every
direction and leaves puddles of water everywhere.

8. Ms. Gray's symptoms are MOST clearly an example of   8.___
   A. sublimation of anxiety-producing fantasies and day-
      dreams
   B. compensation for an imaginary object loss
   C. a symbolic expression of conflict and guilt feelings
   D. an infantile maneuver to avoid intimacy

9. On the unit, Ms. Gray carries out her elaborate washing   9.___
   routine several times a day. She says to the nurse, *I
   guess all this seems awfully silly to you.*
   It is MOST justifiable to say that she
   A. is asking the nurse to keep her from performing
      these unreasonable acts
   B. really believes her acts are completely rational,
      and she is testing the nurse
   C. is indicating an appreciation of the unreasonable-
      ness of her behavior
   D. is deliberately putting the nurse in a difficult
      position

10. The nurse should understand that the probable effect of   10.___
    permitting Ms. Gray to perform her washing routines will
    be to
    A. confirm a basic delusion
    B. help Ms. Gray to perceive how illogical her behavior
       is
    C. create distrust of the nurse, who ought to symbolize
       reality
    D. temporarily reduce Ms. Gray's anxiety

11. Ms. Gray is unable to get to the dining room in time   11.___
    for breakfast because of her washing rituals.
    During the early period of her hospitalization, it would
    be MOST appropriate to
    A. wake Ms. Gray early enough so that she can perform
       her rituals in time to get to breakfast
    B. firmly insist that Ms. Gray interrupt her rituals
       at breakfast time
    C. explain to Ms. Gray that her rituals are not helping
       her to get well
    D. give Ms. Gray a choice between completing her rituals
       or going to breakfast

12. During a nursing team conference, staff members voice   12.___
    frustration concerning Ms. Gray's constant questions
    such as *Shall I go to lunch or finish cleaning my room?*
    and *Should I go to O.T. or mend my coat?*
    In order to deal effectively with this behavior, team
    members should know that Ms. Gray's
    A. dependence upon staff is a symptom that needs to be
       interrupted by firm limit-setting
    B. inability to make decisions reflects her basic
       anxiety about failure

C. indecisiveness is meant to test the staff's acceptance of her

D. relentless need to seek attention represents a developmental arrest at the autistic (prototaxic) level

13. Ms. Gray is being treated by psychotherapy. The physician tells the nurse to expect her to be upset at times when she returns from her session with him and to let her be upset.
By this directive, the physician MOST probably wants to
A. put Ms. Gray under stress so that she will become more responsive to suggestions
B. teach Ms. Gray to be satisfied with advice from only one person
C. help Ms. Gray become aware of her feelings
D. make Ms. Gray independent, which would not be possible if she were to develop alliances with members of the nursing staff

13.___

14. Ms. Gray is given her first pass to spend the night at home. As the time approaches for her to leave the hospital, she seems increasingly tense and says, *Maybe I shouldn't stay home all night. Maybe I should just stay for dinner and then come back here.* When the nurse responds nondirectively, Ms. Gray answers, *I'm just sort of anxious about things in general. It's nothing specific.*
Which of these responses by the nurse would probably be BEST?
A. Everyone is scared of his first overnight pass. You'll find that it will be easier than you expect.
B. It's understandable that you are concerned about your first night at home. Would it help if you make the decision after you've been home for a while and see how things are going?
C. I know how you feel, but the staff think that you are well enough to stay home overnight. Won't you try to do so?
D. It's important for you to try to remain at home overnight. If you are able to do it, it will be a measure of your improvement.

14.___

Questions 15-25.

DIRECTIONS: Questions 15 through 25 are to be answered on the basis of the following information.

Ms. Kathy Collins, 47 years old, has been hospitalized several times over a period of years because of episodes of elation and depression. She lives with her mother and sister. She is well known to the nursing staff. While she is again being admitted, she is chainsmoking cigarettes, walking back and forth, and talking loudly and gaily about her romantic successes.

15. Which of these greetings by the nurse who is admitting   15.___
Ms. Collins would probably be MOST appropriate?
    A. We're sorry you had to come back, Ms. Collins, but
        we are glad to see you.
    B. Good morning, Ms. Collins. Your doctor called to
        say you were coming. I will show you to your room.
    C. Hello, Ms. Collins. You're cheerful this morning.
    D. It's good to see you again, Ms. Collins. You don't
        seem to mind coming back to the hospital.

16. The nurse who will care for Ms. Collins each day should   16.___
expect to make use of which of these interventions?
    A. Distracting and redirecting
    B. Orienting and reminding
    C. Explaining and praising
    D. Evoking anger and encouraging insight

17. Ms. Collins is an overactive patient with a mood dis-   17.___
turbance rather than a thought disorder.
Because of this type of illness, the nursing care plan
should include measures that respond to the fact that
she is
    A. disoriented
    B. easily stimulated by what is going on around her
    C. preoccupied with a single idea
    D. likely to be panicked by physical contact

18. Which of these nursing goals is likely to require the   18.___
MOST attention while Ms. Collins is acutely ill?
    A. Orientation to time, place, and person
    B. Establishment of a sense of self-esteem
    C. Promotion of adequate rest
    D. Prevention of circulatory stasis

19. Ms. Collins and her roommate are in their room. While   19.___
passing by, a registered nurse hears them arguing. Ms.
Collins says, *You're a slob. How can anybody live in
this mess!* The roommate answers, *What right do you
have to say that?* and starts to cry.
Which of these interventions by the nurse would be
appropriate?
    A. Enter the room and say to Ms. Collins, *You have
        upset your roommate. She's crying.*
    B. Enter and say, *It sounds as if you are both upset.*
    C. Stand in the doorway and say, *It's part of your
        therapy to learn how to get along together.*
    D. Take the roommate aside and explain to her that Ms.
        Collins can be expected to be difficult for a few
        days.

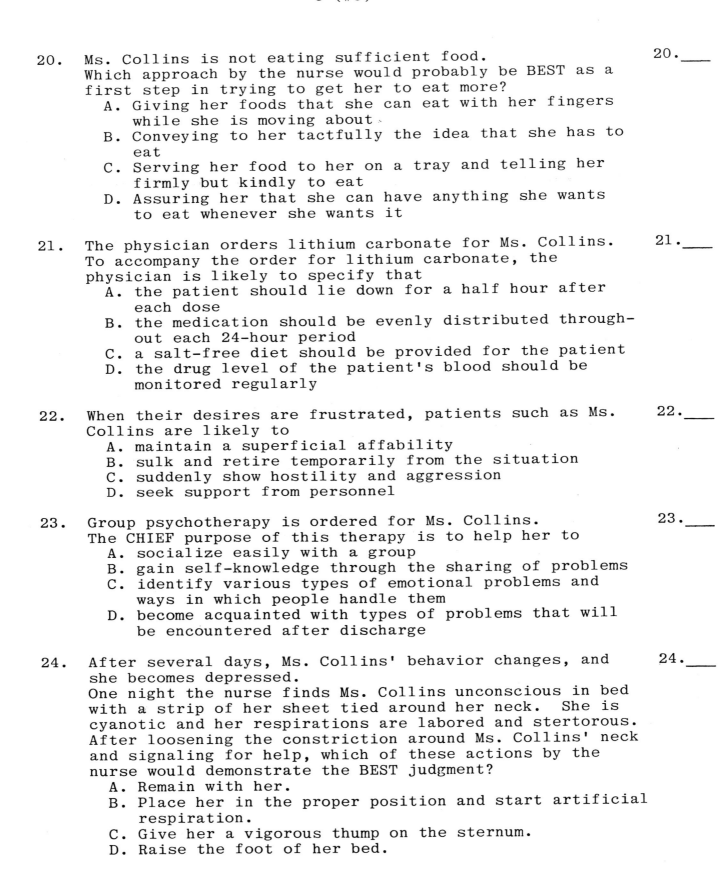

20. Ms. Collins is not eating sufficient food.   20.___
    Which approach by the nurse would probably be BEST as a
    first step in trying to get her to eat more?
        A. Giving her foods that she can eat with her fingers
           while she is moving about
        B. Conveying to her tactfully the idea that she has to
           eat
        C. Serving her food to her on a tray and telling her
           firmly but kindly to eat
        D. Assuring her that she can have anything she wants
           to eat whenever she wants it

21. The physician orders lithium carbonate for Ms. Collins.   21.___
    To accompany the order for lithium carbonate, the
    physician is likely to specify that
        A. the patient should lie down for a half hour after
           each dose
        B. the medication should be evenly distributed through-
           out each 24-hour period
        C. a salt-free diet should be provided for the patient
        D. the drug level of the patient's blood should be
           monitored regularly

22. When their desires are frustrated, patients such as Ms.   22.___
    Collins are likely to
        A. maintain a superficial affability
        B. sulk and retire temporarily from the situation
        C. suddenly show hostility and aggression
        D. seek support from personnel

23. Group psychotherapy is ordered for Ms. Collins.   23.___
    The CHIEF purpose of this therapy is to help her to
        A. socialize easily with a group
        B. gain self-knowledge through the sharing of problems
        C. identify various types of emotional problems and
           ways in which people handle them
        D. become acquainted with types of problems that will
           be encountered after discharge

24. After several days, Ms. Collins' behavior changes, and   24.___
    she becomes depressed.
    One night the nurse finds Ms. Collins unconscious in bed
    with a strip of her sheet tied around her neck. She is
    cyanotic and her respirations are labored and stertorous.
    After loosening the constriction around Ms. Collins' neck
    and signaling for help, which of these actions by the
    nurse would demonstrate the BEST judgment?
        A. Remain with her.
        B. Place her in the proper position and start artificial
           respiration.
        C. Give her a vigorous thump on the sternum.
        D. Raise the foot of her bed.

25. Ms. Collins is gradually improving, and the team talks of   25.___
    plans for her discharge.
    On a visit to the unit, Ms. Collins' mother and sister
    tell the nurse that Ms. Collins doesn't seem much better,
    and they are very hesitant about having her return home
    because of the previous problems they've had with her.
    Which of these actions should INITIALLY be taken by the
    nurse?
    A. Suggest that the family find a place where Ms.
       Collins can live by herself after discharge.
    B. Elaborate on Ms. Collins' hospital regimen and the
       normality of her present behavior.
    C. Assure the relatives that Ms. Collins is better and
       refer them to the physician if they have further
       questions.
    D. Listen to Ms. Collins' relatives and suggest that
       they make an appointment with the family counselor.

———————

KEY (CORRECT ANSWERS)

1. B		11. A	
2. D		12. B	
3. C		13. C	
4. B		14. B	
5. A		15. B	
6. D		16. A	
7. B		17. B	
8. C		18. C	
9. C		19. B	
10. D		20. A	

21. D
22. C
23. B
24. A
25. D

———————

EXAMINATION SECTION
TEST 1

DIRECTIONS: Each question or incomplete statement is followed by several suggested answers or completions. Select the one that BEST answers the question or completes the statement. *PRINT THE LETTER OF THE CORRECT ANSWER IN THE SPACE AT THE RIGHT.*

1. Major depression is defined as a severe episodic depressive   1.___
   disorder or uniform depression.
   Which of the following may be present nearly every day for
   at least two weeks to fulfill the diagnostic criteria of
   major depression?
   A. Dysphoric mood with sadness, unhappiness, or irrita-
      bility with possible complete loss of interest or
      pleasure in activities and pastimes that were
      previously enjoyable
   B. Loss of sexual drive, appetite, weight, energy, and
      sleep, with diminished ability to think and concen-
      trate
   C. Feeling of worthlessness or excessive guilt with
      recurrent thoughts of death and recurrent suicidal
      ideation
   D. All of the above

2. In the case of major depression, nursing intervention to   2.___
   take care of a patient include all of the following EXCEPT:
   A. Checking the patient regularly for any suicidal
      ideation and removing potentially harmful articles
   B. Starting with antipsychotic medication and closely
      looking for side effects
   C. Encouraging change to more positive topics if self-
      deprecating thoughts persist
   D. Assisting with dressing, hygiene, and feeding

3. Electroconvulsive therapy may be included in the treatment   3.___
   plan for major depression in refractory cases and when
   side effects of antidepressants must be avoided.
   A nurse treating a patient with ECT would NOT necessarily
   A. remove all hairpins and dentures and ensure loose
      clothing
   B. continue with the antidepressants during the course
      of ECT
   C. check vitals before and after the procedure
   D. reorient and reassure that any memory loss is
      temporary

4. Dysthymia was previously known as depressive neurosis.   4.___
   All of the following statements about dysthymia are true
   EXCEPT:
   A. Symptoms and signs should be present for at least 8
      months to fulfill the diagnostic criteria

B. Onset generally occurs in 20's-30's and is more common and chronic in women
C. Symptoms include poor appetite, overeating, sleep disturbances, low self-esteem, poor concentration, difficulty making decisions, and a feeling of hopelessness
D. Recurrent thoughts of suicide and death are often present

5. Melancholia is a type of depression characterized by loss of interest in almost all activities. DSM-III-R diagnostic criteria for melancholia do NOT include   5.___
   A. absence of reactivity of mood, that is, inability to feel better even when something good happens
   B. depression worse in evening
   C. awakening early in morning, at least two hours before waking times
   D. psychomotor retardation or agitation

6. A manic episode consists of a group of characteristic symptoms accompanying an abnormal mood that is predominantly euphoric, expansive, or irritable. DSM-III-R diagnostic criteria for manic episodes include all of the following EXCEPT   6.___
   A. rapid shifts to anger or even short-lived spells of depression
   B. increased psychomotor activity and restlessness with flight of ideas and racing thoughts
   C. most of the symptoms present most of the time for at least six weeks
   D. mood disturbances sufficiently severe to cause marked impairment in occupational functioning or in usual social activities

7. While managing a manic episode, a nurse would NOT   7.___
   A. provide a quiet environment and decrease stimuli
   B. argue with patient about his disruptive behavior
   C. while administering medication as advised, observe for side effects, monitor lithium blood levels, and maintain fluid and salt intake
   D. assist dressing and bathing

8. Delusional disorder, previously known as paranoid disorder, is a condition in which the primary, if not sole, manifestation is a delusion that is fixed and unshakable. DSM III-R diagnostic criteria for delusional disorder include all of the following EXCEPT: 8.___
   A. Apart from delusion, behavior not obviously odd or bizarre
   B. Signs and symptoms present for at least one year
   C. If a major depression or manic syndrome has been present, the total duration of all episodes of mood syndrome has been brief relative to total duration of delusional disturbance
   D. Auditory or visual hallucinations, if present, are not prominent

9. In the management planning of a patient with a delusional   9.___
   disorder, the nursing goals would include that the patient
   will
   A. develop a trusting relationship with the nurse
   B. decrease the frequency of delusional content in his
      speech
   C. ingest medications and nutrition and socialize with
      the nurse and others
   D. all of the above

10. All of the following should be included in the classifica-   10.___
    tion of *paranoid disorder* EXCEPT _____ disorder.
    A. schizophreniform
    B. chronic paranoid
    C. shared paranoid (folie a deux)
    D. acute paranoid

11. A nurse taking care of a patient with a delusional dis-   11.___
    order would generally NOT
    A. present reality to the patient but accept his needs
       for delusions
    B. give liquid form of medication so that patient can
       swallow easily, and give clear and concise information
       about medications
    C. respect patient's privacy, but offer self and
       encourage interaction
    D. none of the above

12. In brief reactive psychosis, symptoms develop immediately   12.___
    following a recognizable psychosocial stress that would
    be expected to produce emotional distress in most patients.
    Diagnostic criteria for brief reactive psychosis include
    all of the following EXCEPT:
    A. All the symptoms present for at least 4 months
    B. Loosening of association. Delusion and hallucination
       may be present indicating impaired reality testing.
    C. Rapid shifts from one intense effect to another
    D. Absence of prodromal symptoms of schizophrenia and
       failure to meet diagnostic criteria for schizotypal
       personality disorder

13. A part of schizophrenic illness in which the patient   13.___
    believes that important people in the environment have
    been taken away and duplicates have been substituted
    for them is known as
    A. Cotard's syndrome   B. Capgras syndrome
    C. autoscopic psychosis   D. atypical psychosis

14. Freud used the term *neurosis* descriptively to indicate   14.___
    unpleasant symptoms with intact reality testing.
    These neurotic disorders are groups of symptoms having
    all of the following characteristics EXCEPT:

A. They are distressing to the person and regarded as unacceptable and ego-dystonic
B. Symptoms tend to be recurring, unless effective treatment is obtained
C. There is a demonstrable organic etiology involved
D. Symptoms are not limited to temporary reaction to external stress

15. An anxiety disorder is a pathologic state characterized by a feeling of dread accompanied by somatic signs indicative of a hyperactive autonomic nervous system. NOT included in the diagnostic criteria for generalized anxiety disorder is that

    15.___

A. the diagnosis can and should be made in patients under 18 years of age
B. it is characterized by the presence of persistent free-floating anxiety of at least one month's duration
C. this condition interferes with effectiveness in living, achievement of desired realistic goals and satisfaction or emotional comfort
D. symptoms associated with other neurotic disorders, such as phobias and obsessions, are minimal or absent

16. Phobic disorder is a state of anxiety about a specific situation or object.
Which of the following are diagnostic criteria for simple phobias?

    16.___

A. Persistent fear of a circumscribed stimulus other than fear of having a panic attack
B. Avoidant behavior which significantly interferes with the person's normal routine, social activities, or relationships with others
C. Exposure to a specific stimulus invariably provoking an anxiety response
D. All of the above

17. Obsessive-compulsive disorders are types of anxiety disorders in which there exist persistent needs to repeat thoughts or behaviors.
Obsessive-compulsive disorders include

    17.___

A. recurrent and persistent ideas, thoughts, impulses or images that are experienced, at least initially, as intrusive and senseless
B. attempts to ignore or suppress such thoughts or impulse or to neutralize them with some other thought or action
C. repetitive, purposeful, and intentional behaviors that are performed in response to an obsession or according to certain rules or in stereotyped fashion
D. all of the above

18. In post-traumatic stress disorder, persistent symptoms of   18.___
    increased arousal, which were not present before the
    trauma, include all of the following EXCEPT
        A. difficulty concentrating
        B. person becomes more sleepy all the time
        C. irritability or outbursts of anger
        D. hypervigilance and exaggerated startle response

19. After post-traumatic stress disorder, there is persistent   19.___
    avoidance of stimuli associated with trauma or numbing
    of general responsiveness.
    This avoidant behavior includes
        A. psychogenic amnesia, which is the inability to recall
           an important aspect of the trauma
        B. a sense of foreshortened future and feeling of
           detachment from others
        C. markedly diminished interest in significant activities
           which are specific to the certain age group through
           which the person is passing at time of trauma
        D. all of the above

20. The INCORRECT statement about persistent re-experiencing   20.___
    of the traumatic event in a patient of post-traumatic
    stress distress is that _____ occur(s).
        A. recurrent distressing dreams of the event
        B. signs and symptoms present for at least two years
        C. intense psychological distress at exposure to events
           that symbolize or resemble an aspect of the traumatic
           event
        D. sudden acting or feeling as if the traumatic event
           were recurring

21. Considering the psychodynamics of anxiety disorders,   21.___
    the one of the following defense mechanisms which may be
    used by a patient of simple phobia is
        A. reaction formation
        B. regression or repression
        C. displacement and symbolization
        D. denial and undoing

22. Many psychological, medical, and neurologic disorders   22.___
    have anxiety as a major component.
    The differential diagnosis of anxiety disorders includes
    all of the following EXCEPT
        A. schizophrenia and atypical psychosis
        B. organic anxiety syndrome
        C. depression and substance abuse
        D. none of the above

23. Discussing the course and prognosis of a panic disorder,   23.___
    the nurse should NOT tell the patient at the time of
    discharge that

A. it tends to recur daily or 2-3 times per week
B. without treatment prognosis it worsens and ultimately leads to death
C. it takes a chronic course with remissions and exacerbation
D. prognosis is excellent with therapy

24. Common medical conditions mimicking the presentation of anxiety disorder include all of the following EXCEPT   24.___
    A. hyperventilation syndromes
    B. hypoglycemia and carcinoid syndromes
    C. hypothyroidism
    D. angina pectoris or myocardial infarction

25. Hysterical neurosis is characterized by involuntary   25.___
    alteration or limitation of physical function as a result of psychologic conflict or need.
    Its differential diagnosis does NOT include
    A. paralysis, ataxia, and blindness
    B. mimic malingering, as these patients are aware that they are faking symptoms and have insight into what they are doing
    C. pseudoseizures and hysterical pain
    D. sensory loss and deafness

26. Multiple personality disorders are distinct and separate   26.___
    personalities within the same person.
    Which of the following statements about multiple personality disorders is NOT true?
    A. There may be sudden transition from one personality to another with amnesia for other personalities.
    B. It is more common in females and first degree relatives.
    C. Almost complete recovery is possible.
    D. Severe sexual and psychologic abuse in childhood is considered in etiology.

27. Depersonalization disorder involves persistent, recurrent   27.___
    episodes of feeling detached from one's self and body to the extent of feeling mechanical or being in a dream.
    All of the following characterize this disorder EXCEPT
    A. distortion in sense of time and space
    B. reality testing completely lost
    C. extremities experienced as too large or too small and other persons seem robot-like
    D. dizziness, depressive and obsessive ruminations, anxiety, and somatic preoccupations

28. In the therapy management of simple phobic disorder, the   28.___
    treatment of choice is
    A. systematic desensitization
    B. minor tranquilizer drug therapy
    C. aversive conditioning
    D. supportive therapies and environmental manipulation

29. Wilson's disease is included in the etiology of organic   29.___
mental disorder.
Which of the following statements about Wilson's disease
is NOT correct?
    A. It is a hereditary disorder transmitted as an auto-
somal dominant gene.
    B. Because of the inability to excrete copper, there is
copper deposition in the liver, brain, eye, and other
organs.
    C. Atrophy of lenticular nuclei causes involuntary
choreiform movement or ataxia.
    D. If the disease is not treated, there will be relent-
less organ damage, progressive dementia, and
eventual death.

30. The single MOST important indicator of social status in   30.___
the United States is
    A. locality of residence   B. occupation
    C. wealth   D. education

KEY (CORRECT ANSWERS)

1. D	11. D	21. C
2. B	12. A	22. D
3. B	13. B	23. B
4. A	14. C	24. C
5. B	15. A	25. B
6. C	16. D	26. C
7. B	17. D	27. B
8. B	18. B	28. A
9. D	19. D	29. A
10. A	20. B	30. B

TEST 2

DIRECTIONS: Each question or incomplete statement is followed by several suggested answers or completions. Select the one that BEST answers the question or completes the statement. *PRINT THE LETTER OF THE CORRECT ANSWER IN THE SPACE AT THE RIGHT.*

1. Systematic desensitization is a method for overcoming neurotic anxiety and overlearned fear responses. In systematic desensitization,
   A. the person should be trained in deep muscle relaxation
   B. a hierarchical list of anxiety evoking situations is constructed from no anxiety to maximum anxiety
   C. as progress through the hierarchy is achieved, the therapist instructs the patient to actually enter into the real life situations
   D. all of the above

   1.___

2. General guidelines in the nursing care of a patient with anxiety-related disorders include
   A. assessing both subjective and objective symptoms of anxiety and noting symptom changes before and after treatment
   B. spending time with the patient in order to ensure verbal and physical release from anxiety
   C. being alert for signs of increased dependency or overuse of medication and also teaching the patient about drug interaction
   D. all of the above

   2.___

3. Panic disorder consists of discrete episodes of extreme anxiety, occurring at least 3 times in as many weeks, against a background of milder anxiety and nervousness. Nursing intervention in panic disorder includes all of the following EXCEPT
   A. moving patient from a more confined quiet space to a large open area
   B. if physical restraint is necessary, remaining with the patient
   C. assuring the patient that you are in immediate control of the situation, but avoiding false reassurance
   D. assisting the patient to express his perception of what is happening

   3.___

4. Generalized anxiety disorder is characterized by the presence of persistent free floating anxiety of at least one month's duration. Nursing care of a patient with this disorder includes all of the following EXCEPT
   A. providing a calm, comfortable environment
   B. never asking the patient to explore the situation, as it may aggravate his condition

   4.___

    C. accepting and showing understanding of the patient's
       feelings
    D. helping the patient to develop new coping mechanisms

5. Taking care of a patient with phobic disorder, a nurse   5.___
    would NOT be expected to provide
        A. activities that help the patient to feel safer but
           do not allow him to become totally withdrawn
        B. a critical environment with negative reinforcement
        C. safety and comfort measures as necessary
        D. adequate fluid and food intake

6. Obsessive compulsive behavior is a type of neurotic dis-   6.___
    order.
    Nursing care of such a patient does NOT include
        A. using a warm, caring approach indicating acceptance
           of patient and awareness and empathy for his behavior
        B. helping patient to explore ways of setting limits on
           his own behavior
        C. keeping frequent changes in the environment around
           the patient, especially in his room
        D. showing the patient your interest and concern,
           reinforcing his self-worth

7. A nurse taking care of a patient with somatization dis-   7.___
    order should
        A. use a consistent, firm approach and spend a minimal
           amount of time discussing symptoms
        B. utilize biofeedback and relaxation techniques
        C. help patient to verbalize anxiety and intervene if
           suicidal potential appears high
        D. all of the above

8. A schizophrenic patient has communication impairment   8.___
    related to anxiety and autistic withdrawal.
    Nursing intervention in such a case involves all of
    the following EXCEPT:
        A. Share thoughts and perceptions regarding one-to-one
           relationship to develop an effective nurse-patient
           interaction
        B. Even if unsure of patient's message, pretend to under-
           stand what she may be saying
        C. Use clarification techniques to encourage patient to
           communicate more clearly
        D. Validate understanding of message by rephrasing it

9. A schizophrenic patient has thought disorders and hallu-   9.___
    cinations related to excessive anxiety and possibly
    neurohormonal transmission dysfunction.
    It is NOT the responsibility of the nurse to
        A. administer lithium for these symptoms
        B. provide consistent reassurance and assistance in
           testing and interpreting reality and environment

C. promote simple, supervised, reality-based activities to focus patient's attention and activity
D. communicate in clear, simple, and concrete terms

10. Nursing interventions in a schizophrenic patient with   10.___
poor hygiene and grooming secondary to behavioral
disorganization and regression include
    A. assessing for any additional causes of poor hygiene,
       e.g., fears related to showering
    B. assisting and providing reassurance as needed to
       assure hygiene and appearance
    C. positively reinforcing self-care action
    D. all of the above

11. Antisocial personality disorder involves continuous and   11.___
uninhibited acting out of selfish impulses in which the
rights of others are violated.
Predisposing factors of this disorder include all of the
following EXCEPT
    A. violence or abuse by parents or others
    B. illegitimacy
    C. lack of consistent discipline
    D. none of the above

12. Seductive behavior is seen as an expression of sexuality,   12.___
but more broadly it is a behavior to gain another's
attention.
Nursing intervention in such a patient includes
    A. refusing to accept the behavior and being judgmental
       of the patient
    B. avoiding setting limits and rules
    C. encouraging the patient to express his seductive
       behavior
    D. allowing nurse-patient relationship to progress freely,
       without any set expectations

13. In narcissistic behavior, there is a sense of self-   13.___
importance or uniqueness with inability to feel empathy
for others. Narcissistic patients always require
constant attention and admiration.
Nursing care of such a patient includes
    A. setting firm limits with manipulative behavior
    B. exploring feelings motivating behavior and maintaining
       a non-judgmental approach
    C. both of the above
    D. none of the above

14. The characteristic feature of passive-aggressive persona-   14.___
lity disorder is resistance to demands for adequate
performance in both occupational and social functioning.
An attending nurse would NOT
    A. strongly discourage patient from expressing his feelings
       and beliefs about the response of others towards
       himself

B. give patient specific, concrete feedback on behavior
C. assist patient to identify alternate means to meet needs and enlist support from others in encouraging new behavior
D. present patient with the expectation that he responds to feedback or input from others at the time it is given

15. Nursing intervention to a patient with helpless or dependent behavior (in which passivity associated with lack of self-confidence and indecisiveness are prominent features) include all of the following EXCEPT   15.___
    A. providing a safe environment and encouraging as much independent care as possible
    B. trying to make all decisions on part of patient
    C. encouraging problem-solving behavior by exploring available choices in a situation
    D. encouraging patient to express the feelings he is having at the time of behavior

16. A 19 year-old girl was raped.   16.___
    Nursing intervention to take care of a victim of rape include which of the following?
    A. Providing for medical treatment with support during examination as well as follow-up in case of pregnancy, infection, or venereal disease
    B. Evaluating for homicidal or suicidal feelings because of intense anger and guilt victims commonly feel
    C. Engaging in social support. Helping victim to plan a way to tell members of support system
    D. All of the above

17. A couple that had been married for 7 years gets a divorce.   17.___
    Nursing counseling in this case includes all of the following EXCEPT
    A. allowing for expression of guilt generated as a result of failure or feeling of relief that marriage is ended
    B. assisting client to find ways to meet needs with spouse absent
    C. identifying multiple losses perceived by client, for example, financially, as role changes from spouse to single, and socially, as social network frequently changes
    D. none of the above

18. Nursing intervention in dealing with a infertile couple   18.___
    includes all of the following EXCEPT:
    A. Never involve the couple in support groups, as they may be ashamed of each other and won't follow the advice properly
    B. Discuss threats to self-esteem, as they commonly see self as defective and view infertility as punishment for being bad

    C. Discuss how infertility may affect sexuality and relationship with partner

    D. None of the above

19. Which of the following is a requirement for hospice nursing?   19.___

    A. Thorough knowledge of anatomy, physiology, and pharmacology and great skills in physical examination as well as procedures like catheterization, colostomy, and traction care

    B. Skills in using psychological principles in both one-to-one and group situations

    C. Great sensitivity in human relationships and knowledge of measures to comfort the dying in their last hours

    D. All of the above

20. While interviewing a patient to obtain sexual information, a nurse should NOT   20.___

    A. maintain an attitude that is frank, open, warm, objective, and empathic

    B. obtain information when others are present or take copious notes

    C. have a prepared introduction to state purpose of interview and use appropriate vocabulary

    D. identify attitudes, values, beliefs, and feelings

21. In the comparison of physical responses in psychogenic vs. grand mal seizures, all of the following favor psychogenic seizures EXCEPT   21.___

    A. respiration more rapid than normal

    B. pupils fixed and dilated

    C. no incontinence of urine

    D. muscular contractions irregular and random

22. The advantage of group therapies stem from one major factor, i.e., the presence of many people rather than a solitary therapist, who participate in the therapeutic experience.   22.___

Advantages include

    A. stimuli from multiple sources, enabling distortions in interpersonal relationships to be revealed so that they can be examined and resolved

    B. an interpersonal testing ground that enables members to try out old and new ways of being in an environment structured for that purpose

    C. multiple sources of feedback

    D. all of the above

23. The depressed elderly are more prone to commit suicide than any other age group in the United States.   23.___

Of the following groups of elders, the ones at the LEAST risk of suicide are those who

    A. have chronic pain and terminal illness

    B. are married males

    C. are from lower socioeconomic classes

    D. are lonely and isolated in an urban setting

24. Chronic use of sedatives and hypnotics by elderly people   24.___
    has not been shown to improve quality of sleep and can
    lead to dangerous side effects.
    Nurses teach elderly people all of the following guide-
    lines to improve sleep EXCEPT:
    A. Increase physical activity, particularly in the late
       afternoon and early evening hours
    B. Have a light bedtime snack containing calcium
       combined with sugar
    C. Sleep in an overly warm room as opposed to a cool
       room
    D. Spend as little time as possible in the bedroom
       during the daytime

25. The elderly rarely report abuse themselves out of fear of   25.___
    disbelief or institutionalization.
    Evaluation of a patient seeking treatment in the emergency
    room should include looking for
    A. falls and injuries, particularly bruises on face,
       arms, legs, and buttocks
    B. extended periods of neglect or restraint evidenced by
       contracture pressure, sores, and long, curved finger-
       nails and toenails
    C. malnutrition and deprivation of life-sustaining
       medications
    D. all of the above

26. Before rape victims are assessed or treated, they need to   26.___
    be informed of their rights, which include all of the
    following EXCEPT
    A. a rape crisis advocate accompanying them to the
       hospital and their personal physician notified
    B. nobody allowed to be present during questioning and
       examination
    C. confidentiality maintained by all staff
    D. detailed explanation and consent for all tests and
       procedures

27. Resistance inevitably surfaces in the course of one-to-   27.___
    one work, and mostly begins when the patient addresses
    self-defeating thoughts, feelings, and behaviors.
    Resistance can be expressed by
    A. forgetting events
    B. expressing antagonism towards the nurse
    C. falling in love with the nurse
    D. all of the above

28. *Acting out* is a particularly destructive form of resistance 28.___
    in which a patient puts into action a memory that has been
    forgotten or repressed.
    Nursing intervention regarding acting out includes all of
    the following EXCEPT
    A. bringing acting out to the attention of the patient
    B. decreasing frequency of contact
    C. looking for evidence of transference phenomenon
       towards the nurse
    D. none of the above

29. Malpractice has been defined as the treatment of a patient 29.__
in a manner contrary to accepted rules and with injurious
results to the patient.
The elements constituting a cause of action based on
negligence do NOT include
   A. physician has not fulfilled his legal duty or obligation to conform to a reasonable standard of care
   B. loss or damage has resulted to the person or property
of another
   C. there has been no reasonably close causal connection
between the substandard conduct involved and resulting
injury
   D. physician has failed to adhere to the standard
required

30. Testamentary capacity is defined as mental competency 30.__
for making a will.
In order to make a valid will, the testator must be able
to comply with all of the following EXCEPT
   A. know the nature of the act he or she is about to
perform
   B. know the names, identities, and relationships with
the persons who are to be beneficiaries
   C. appreciate the relations of these factors to one
another
   D. none of the above

KEY (CORRECT ANSWERS)

1. D	11. D	21. B
2. D	12. C	22. D
3. A	13. C	23. B
4. B	14. A	24. C
5. B	15. B	25. D
6. C	16. D	26. B
7. D	17. D	27. D
8. B	18. A	28. B
9. A	19. D	29. C
10. D	20. B	30. D

EXAMINATION SECTION
TEST 1

DIRECTIONS: Each question or incomplete statement is followed by
several suggested answers or completions. Select the
one that BEST answers the question or completes the
statement. *PRINT THE LETTER OF THE CORRECT ANSWER IN
THE SPACE AT THE RIGHT.*

Questions 1-6.

DIRECTIONS: Questions 1 through 6 are to be answered on the
basis of the following information.

The nursing staff on a medical unit meets every week to discuss
problem areas they are encountering while giving nursing care. The
areas of discussion are (1) the nursing process and (2) emotional
needs of clients.

1.   The first staff meeting covers the best nursing approach   1.___
to meet the clients' emotional needs.
Which basic factor should be determined FIRST by the staff?
      A. Why the clients behave as they do
      B. Which nursing approach has been effective or needs
         changing
      C. Which clients have symptoms of increased anxiety
      D. What dependent needs of the client the nurse can meet

2.   The staff discusses methods of data collection by the   2.___
nurse.
Which would be the MOST significant in making a nursing
care plan?
      A. The nursing report on the client's problems
      B. The physical/emotional history supplied by the
         client's family
      C. Reviewing the client's chart
      D. Interviewing the client immediately on admission

3.   The staff agrees that the BASIC principle of planning   3.___
nursing care is to
      A. accept the client as he or she is
      B. meet the client's needs
      C. believe the client will improve
      D. know the client as a person

4.   The staff also stresses that, at the initial interview with   4.___
the client, the nurse should use open-ended questions to
collect data.
Which question would be a good example?
      A. Are there any questions you want to ask?
      B. Tell me something about yourself.
      C. Can you give me any information?
      D. Were you brought to the hospital by your family?

5. The nursing staff discusses evaluation of nursing care.   5.___
    Which evaluation should be identified as a *halo* evaluation?
    The client('s)
      A. has learned some control
      B. behavior is to demand attention
      C. continues to be negative
      D. care plan has been effective

6. The staff identifies the best time for the nurse to record   6.___
    the observed behavior of a client.
    That time is
      A. when the behavior has become a problem
      B. at the end of every shift
      C. immediately after contact with the client
      D. after conferring with other staff members

7. Many people with mental disorders have poor self-images,   7.___
    which they need to improve in order to recover.
    All of the following factors contribute to self-image
    EXCEPT
      A. body image
      B. personally judging others
      C. relationships within the family
      D. interpersonal relationships outside of the family

8. The MOST important feeling for the nurse to convey to the   8.___
    client in order for the client to accept the nurse is one
    of
      A. respect for the client   B. willingness to help
      C. professional competence   D. no-nonsense demands

9. A patient being treated for an aggressive personality   9.___
    disorder insists that the last time he was in the clinic
    he was given lithium, which helped him, and he demands
    that the nurse get him some immediately.
    The nurse's BEST reply to this demand would be:
      A. We never administer drugs to people in your condition
      B. I will go get some for you if you calm down
      C. You don't need lithium
      D. Be patient, and I'll talk to your doctor about whether
         lithium would be appropriate for you

10. All of the following principles of psychiatric-mental   10.___
    health nursing help form the basis of the therapeutic
    use of self EXCEPT:
      A. Be aware of your own feelings and responses and main-
         tain objectivity while being aware of your own needs
      B. Accept clients as they are, be nonjudgmental, and
         recognize that emotions influence behaviors
      C. Use sympathy, not empathy, and observe a client's
         behaviors to analyze needs and problems
      D. Avoid verbal reprimands, physical force, giving
         advice, or imposing your own values on clients.
         Also assess clients in the context of their social
         and cultural group.

Questions 11-20.

DIRECTIONS: Questions 11 through 20 are to be answered on the
basis of the following information.

Pete Jones, the mental health nurse specialist, conducts group
therapy sessions for the outpatient clinic.

11. During group formation, Mr. Jones should SPECIFICALLY   11.___
     select a group of clients that is no more than _____ in
     number and has homogeneity of _____.
     A. 6; goals
     B. 4; age and sex
     C. 14; ability and willingness
     D. 10; problems and needs

12. Mr. Jones has selected his group, and they meet daily from   12.___
     2 to 3 P.M. It is a closed group and does not allow any
     interruptions.
     During the period that it takes the group to become
     acquainted, what kind of behavior would Mr. Jones expect
     from the group?
     A. Open and positive interaction, rather than projection
        of their feelings
     B. Conflict, lack of unity, testing, and politeness
        toward each other
     C. Trust and acceptance of each other and the therapist
     D. Discussion centering on the mental health unit and
        their expectations

13. Mr. Jones explains to the group that its main function is   13.___
     sharing feelings and behaviors among the members. The
     group is often a substitute for, or is compared to, one's
     own family.
     What does the group accomplish for each member through
     this identification process?
     The group
     A. gives the client hope in himself and makes him
        realize that others are available for comfort and
        acceptance
     B. teaches the client new skills in socialization that
        will be more acceptable to his family
     C. assists the client in replacing negative past
        experiences with a new set of positive group experi-
        ences
     D. helps the client feel that he is being helpful and
        interested in the well-being of others

14. Mr. Jones' group therapy is based on interventive-explora-   14.___
     tory therapy.
     When he defines this type of therapy to his group, what
     should he say?
     A. You will verbally express your emotional problems
        with individual and group relationships.

B. The main focus of this group is the support of existing coping mechanisms.
C. The emphasis is on social interaction, which encourages control.
D. This is an intellectual and emotional exchange of things that you value.

15. Mr. Jones observes that one of the clients monopolizes the group discussion.
What action should Mr. Jones take?
   A. Accept the client's behavior as his/her way of coping
   B. Allow the group members to intervene if they are able to
   C. Interrupt and ask the client to limit the discussion
   D. Ask another client if this discussion is relevant

15.___

16. One of the clients in the group is verbally aggressive toward another client.
What should Mr. Jones do INITIALLY?
   A. Set up individual therapy to explore the hostile client's feelings
   B. Ask the aggressive client to leave the group until control is gained
   C. Set an example by being uninvolved with the aggressor
   D. Sit still, observe, and avoid taking sides with either client

16.___

17. Mr. Jones and the group feel that they are not progressing.
What should the group do?
   A. Explore the reasons for the lack of group productivity
   B. Establish other goals that will be more compatible to the group
   C. Disband because the members are not compatible
   D. Accept new members into the group to provide more feedback

17.___

18. After a group session, one of the clients says, *Today I felt we were really a group.*
When Mr. Jones asks that client to identify the reason for this feeling, which response demonstrates ACCURATELY that the group was cohesive?
   A. We have learned to speak directly to each other rather than to the whole group.
   B. We have been able to discuss similarities of thoughts and conflicts.
   C. We have not been so hostile or anxious with each other.
   D. As individuals, each one has identified ways of fulfilling his or her goal.

18.___

19. During one of the group sessions, Mrs. Elena tells Mr. Jones that he is one of the smartest men she has ever known and feels she has learned so much from him.
How should Mr. Jones respond?

19.___

A. That is very nice of you, but we are not here to discuss me.
B. We are not here to give compliments to any one member.
C. You seem anxious, share your feelings with us.
D. The purpose of the group is to learn more about each other.

20. The group has reached its goal and is now talking about termination.
Which action by the group members shows that they are ready to terminate the group?
A. Members no longer feel abandoned, rejected, or forsaken.
B. Feelings are expressed that members of the group will keep in touch.
C. Each member learns to handle his or her own feelings of loss without support.
D. There is effective coping with feelings of loss and separation anxiety.

20.___

KEY (CORRECT ANSWERS)

1.	C	11.	D
2.	D	12.	B
3.	A	13.	C
4.	B	14.	A
5.	C	15.	B
6.	C	16.	D
7.	B	17.	A
8.	A	18.	B
9.	D	19.	C
10.	C	20.	D

TEST 2

DIRECTIONS: Each question or incomplete statement is followed by several suggested answers or completions. Select the one that BEST answers the question or completes the statement. *PRINT THE LETTER OF THE CORRECT ANSWER IN THE SPACE AT THE RIGHT.*

Questions 1-6.

DIRECTIONS: Questions 1 through 6 are to be answered on the basis of the following information.

Ms. Cohen is a nurse working in a crisis center with a volunteer group.

1. One of the volunteers asks, *What is a crisis?*   1.____
   The nurse should reply that a crisis is a situation in which the person or family
      A. is too subjectively involved to realize when there is a problem
      B. constantly looks to others to resolve certain conflicts
      C. has difficulty with growth and development periods
      D. has had no experience in knowing how to deal with a problem

2. Ms. Cohen tells the volunteers that those working with   2.____
   people in crisis should recognize that one of the first reactions to crisis is the use of defense mechanisms. They should know that these defenses at the time of a crisis
      A. are useful in helping clients protect themselves
      B. are irrelevant, as they are part of the basic personality
      C. should be interrupted to prevent further damage
      D. are an indication that the client is coping well

3. Ms. Cohen explains to the group that people in crisis often   3.____
   use isolation as a defense. Ms. Cohen asks, *Which behavior should be assessed as isolation?*
   The person
      A. blames others for causing the problem
      B. minimizes the seriousness of the problem
      C. accepts the problem intellectually but not emotionally
      D. puts excess energy in another area to neutralize the problem

4. Ms. Cohen instructs the volunteers that when people in   4.____
   crisis first come to the center to seek information about their problem, only specific questions should be answered, with no details given at this time.
   Why is this approach taken?

    A. The person may be mentally incompetent and may lose control.
    B. A nurse or doctor should give specific information.
    C. The person may be overwhelmed with excessive information.
    D. The person is not interested in detailed information.

5. Ms. Cohen states that when a person is in crisis, the   5.___
   BEST support group would be
    A. the volunteers in the community
    B. close family and friends understanding the problem
    C. other people who have similar problems
    D. the professional working in the crisis center

6. One of the volunteers asks, *Why is the crisis intervention*   6.___
   limited from 1 to 6 weeks?
   Ms. Cohen replies that a person can stand the disequilibrium only for a limited time, and during this time will
    A. more likely accept intervention to help with coping
    B. return to a familiar pattern of behavior
    C. require long-term counseling after this period
    D. refuse help from any other support group

Questions 7-11.

DIRECTIONS: Questions 7 through 11 are to be answered on the basis of the following information.

   Lauren Oland, age 14, was brought to the crisis center by a policeman. She had been raped by a friend of the family.

7. Which nursing action should have TOP priority?   7.___
    A. Explain to her that she will be safe here.
    B. Get a detailed description of the attack.
    C. Have a calm and accepting approach.
    D. Treat her physical wounds.

8. Lauren Oland sobs, *My family will kill me if they find out.* 8.___
   Which response by the nurse would be MOST appropriate?
    A. You are underage so your family will have to be informed.
    B. Your family is your best support at this time.
    C. Don't you think that they would rather kill the man?
    D. Tell me how your family reacts during stressful times.

9. After Lauren calms down and accepts Ms. Cohen, she confides, *I feel so dirty. I will never feel clean again.*   9.___
   How should the nurse reply?
    A. This is a normal feeling after what has happened to you.
    B. Are you saying you feel guilty? Let's talk about that feeling.
    C. I can understand; I would feel the same way.
    D. You shouldn't think of yourself as dirty; it wasn't your fault.

10. Lauren tells the nurse, *I feel like my love life is over.*   10.___
    No decent boy will ever look at me again.
    To help Lauren assess the situation, how should the nurse
    reply?
       A. I know it is difficult, but you are strong.
       B. You are not to blame so you shouldn't punish yourself.
       C. What was your relationship with boys before?
       D. You are a pretty girl; you will have many boyfriends.

11. Lauren tells Ms. Cohen that she will not testify against   11.___
    the family friend because then everyone will know about
    her.
    Which reply by the nurse would BEST help Lauren with this
    plan of action?
       A. How do you think you will feel if you do nothing?
       B. It will be a closed court, so no one will know.
       C. This is difficult, but I'm sure you will make the
          right choice.
       D. You have an obligation to protect other women from
          this man.

Questions 12-15.

DIRECTIONS: Questions 12 through 15 are to be answered on the
              basis of the following information.

     Kirt Russel, a volunteer, answers the hotline. The caller, a
female, tells Kirt that she plans on killing herself.

12. How should Kirt reply?   12.___
       A. Are you alone? Is there someone else that I can
          talk to?
       B. How do you plan on killing yourself?
       C. You have called the right number to prevent that from
          happening.
       D. What is your name, address, and telephone number?

13. What is the BEST approach for Kirt to take while talking   13.___
    to the *suicide caller*?
       A. Neutral, not condoning or condemning
       B. Distracting the caller from talking about suicide
       C. One of concern and support
       D. Acting as the conscience of the caller

14. The caller identifies herself as Barbra and states that   14.___
    she is going to poison herself.
    What should Kirt then say?
       A. Have you thought of the agony of such a death?
       B. What kind of poison are you going to take?
       C. Tell me if you've ever had these feelings before.
       D. Give me the name of your doctor.

15. Kirt keeps Barbra on the phone, pleading with her not to   15.___
    hang up, but to keep talking to him.
    Kirt's purpose in doing this is to
      A. give her time to gain her equilibrium and reconsider
         her actions
      B. let her know that someone cares enough to talk to her
      C. keep her mind off her problems and the thought of
         suicide
      D. keep her occupied until an emergency team arrives

Questions 16-20.

DIRECTIONS: Questions 16 through 20 are to be answered on the
               basis of the following information.

    Doreen Darby is a 16 year-old high school student with a history
of poor social contact. Always an introvert, for the past month
Doreen has refused to go to school, spent her time in bed, and taken
nourishment only when spoon-fed. Her family took her to the
emergency room of the general hospital when she reported that voices
had told her she was *no good and should stay away from others*.

16. The nurse in the emergency room identifies Doreen's   16.___
    behavior as depersonalization.
    This term is BEST described as
      A. pathological narcissism
      B. inability to empathize with others
      C. experiencing the world as dreamlike
      D. absence of a moral code

17. The staff is planning Doreen's immediate care.   17.___
    The MOST suitable choice at this time would be
      A. weekly visits to the psychiatric clinic for medical
         therapy and psychotherapy
      B. a small psychiatric unit for 24 hour-a-day treatment
      C. attendance at the day hospital and home with her
         family at night
      D. in her home, with her family, under the supervision
         of a psychiatrist

18. Doreen is assessed as having low self-esteem.   18.___
    Which characteristic BEST defines this problem?
      A. Social withdrawal   B. Flat faces
      C. Alienation from self   D. Feelings of persecution

19. The nursing staff plans an intensive therapeutic approach   19.___
    for Doreen.
    Such an approach is CRUCIAL for Doreen because
      A. she will be missing her family, which is her primary
         support group
      B. she is acutely ill and is completely out of contact
         with reality

    C. the staff must thoroughly evaluate Doreen's physical, social, and emotional condition
    D. it is critical for her to learn to trust those in her environment

20. Doreen has learned to relate to her primary nurse but refuses to get involved in any of the activities with others on the unit.
    Which approach by her primary nurse would be the MOST therapeutic for Doreen?
    A. Telling Doreen she is expected at assigned activities
    B. Becoming involved in activities with Doreen
    C. Observing Doreen with others
    D. Waiting until Doreen asks to attend the activities

20.___

Questions 21-25.

DIRECTIONS: Questions 21 through 25 are to be answered on the basis of the following information.

Mrs. Agnes Smith comes to the crisis center with her two small daughters, ages 3 and 4. She has numerous contusions on her face and body. She tells the nurse, *I've been beaten by my husband for the last time. I want to leave him but have no place to go. Maybe when he sobers up, I can go back - if he will go on the wagon.*

21. Which analysis by the nurse takes PRIORITY?
    A. Recognize that the client is correct in wanting to leave her husband
    B. Know the effect the problem will have on the client
    C. Use own past experience to help the client understand her problem
    D. Understand the implications of the problem from the client's viewpoint

21.___

22. During the assessment period, which question should the nurse ask Mrs. Smith?
    A. Why can't you plan to live with your family?
    B. Does your husband earn enough to support two households?
    C. How often does your husband beat you?
    D. You say you want to go yet stay. Are there any alternatives we can discuss?

22.___

23. Mrs. Smith has identified her problem as being too dependent on her husband.
    What plan would BEST help her resolve this problem?
    A. Learn to have a better self-image
    B. Talk to her husband about her need to be independent
    C. Find a new home for herself and her children
    D. Go to school or get a job

23.___

24. The children and Mrs. Smith have made contact with friends   24.___
    and will be temporarily staying with them.
    The nurse understands that this is important for the family
    at this time because
    A. the tension in their own home is too great
    B. in a neutral environment Mrs. Smith can better plan
       for the future
    C. they will be safer there than in their own home
    D. both the abuser and abused need time apart

25. Mrs. Smith plans to go to group therapy.   25.___
    Which group would be MOST beneficial at this time?
    A. Abusers Anonymous
    B. Family therapy
    C. Parents without partners
    D. Al-Anon

KEY (CORRECT ANSWERS)

1. D
2. A
3. C
4. C
5. B

6. A
7. C
8. D
9. B
10. C

11. A
12. D
13. C
14. B
15. D

16. C
17. B
18. A
19. D
20. B

21. D
22. D
23. A
24. C
25. B

LISTENING COMPREHENSION
EXAMINATION SECTION

TEST 1

DIRECTIONS: In this part a passage will be read orally to you.
It is NOT written out in the test booklet so you
will have to listen carefully. After the reading of the
passage, you will answer the questions that follow.
Each question or incomplete statement is followed by
several suggested answers or completions. Select the
one that BEST answers the question or completes the
statement. *PRINT THE LETTER OF THE CORRECT ANSWER
IN THE SPACE AT THE RIGHT.*

Listening Passage

(The following speech was delivered by Ronald Roskens at com-
mencement exercises at the University of Nebraska, 1981.)

Thoureau tells us that dreams are the touchstones of our
characters. As educated individuals we should understand that
the impediments to realizing our aspirations often lie within
ourselves. If we are content merely to accept what comes to
us and to fashion a life which permits no challenges — medioc-
rity, or even failure, will be our lot. We will have killed our
own dreams, and no matter how much we might have succeeded in the
eyes of others, our accomplishments will not have approached the
potential which lies within us.

Each of us is human, and the essence of that humanity is that
we have, and will persistently exercise, the capacity to make mistakes, to be less than perfect. Human weaknesses are inevitably
magnified when subjected to the harsh glare of public scrutiny.
The shortcomings of one public official trigger a disregard for
all elements of government. One practitioner fails, and an entire
profession falls into disrepute.

The Hebrew prayerbook *Ethics of the Fathers* tells us:
    "There are seven marks of an uncultured man, and
    seven of a wise man. The wise man does not speak
    before him who is greater than he in wisdom; and
    does not break in upon the speech of his fellow;
    he is not hasty to answer; he questions according
    to the subject matter, and answers to the point;
    he speaks upon the first thing first, and upon the
    last last; regarding that which he has not under-
    stood he says, I do not understand it, and he
    acknowledges the truth. The reverse of all this
    is to be found in an uncultured man." (End of quote.)

Do you sense the seeds of such wisdom in yourselves? If you do,
the University has passed this final examination. If you do not, I
hope that you will have found at this University the foundation of
such wisdom, and may take comfort in the fact that "learning
never ends."

Whatever your answer, you will find that your time at the
University has profoundly influenced you. You will, for the rest
of your lives, play out your experiences here, even as we continue
to reach out to you through your memories and in your skills.

Who is wise? All of us — if we continue to care about learning and learn about caring. For that is the essence of wisdom.

1. According to the speaker, we are frequently kept from 1._____
   reaching our goals by
   A. our own attitudes
   B. the lack of opportunity
   C. the frustrations of daily life
   D. the lack of education

2. According to this speech, a person's dreams can be 2._____
   destroyed only by
   A. society   B. passiveness
   C. wealth   D. pressure

3. The speaker says that it is in the nature of humans to 3._____
   A. be too ambitious   B. make errors
   C. distrust public officials D. despair too easily

4. The speaker states that human weaknesses are inevitably 4._____
   magnified when they are
   A. questioned   B. acknowledged
   C. publicized   D. despised

5. According to the speaker, the effect of one practitioner's 5._____
   wrongdoings is to
   A. discredit the entire profession
   B. weaken the government
   C. lead to reform of social institutions
   D. encourage others to commit wrongs

6. The Hebrew prayerbook states that if a man is wise, he 6._____
   will never
   A. dispute an older person's opinion
   B. speak until spoken to
   C. leave the least important thing until last
   D. speak before someone wiser than he

7. When the Hebrew prayerbook says that a wise man "speaks 7._____
   upon the first things first, and upon the last last," it
   means that a wise man
   A. states simple things first
   B. saves the best for last
   C. knows the proper value of things
   D. waits for his turn to speak

8. According to the Hebrew prayerbook, the opposite of a 8._____
   wise man is
   A. an uneducated man   B. an uncultured man
   C. a simple man   D. an insensitive man

9. The speaker says that the University can continue to be 9._____
   valuable in life if one
   A. does well on final examinations

B. returns to renew the experience
C. accepts the truth
D. remembers and uses what he has learned

10. The speaker says that the essence of wisdom is a combina- 10.____
tion of
A. learning and caring
B. education and experience
C. character and ambition
D. culture and truth

_____

KEY (CORRECT ANSWERS)

1.	A		6.	D
2.	B		7.	C
3.	B		8.	B
4.	C		9.	D
5.	A		10.	A

_____

TEST 2

DIRECTIONS: In this part a passage will be read orally to you. It is NOT written out in the test booklet so you will have to listen carefully. After the reading of the passage, you will answer the questions that follow. Each question or incomplete statement is followed by several suggested answers or completions. Select the one that BEST answers the question or completes the statement. *PRINT THE LETTER OF THE CORRECT ANSWER IN THE SPACE AT THE RIGHT.*

Listening Passage

(The following speech to a graduating class has been adapted from "Finding America" by George Hartzog.)

History mocks those who suggest that the past is wholly dreadful and ignoble.

It is from beachheads secured at great personal sacrifice by individuals and generations gone before that society has been able to find the higher ground. Each of our lives has been enriched by the works of a Gandhi, a Rembrandt, and a Woody Guthrie.

We must preserve the independence of the youthful spirit and the continuing values of the past. For every future is shaped by the past. Only in knowing the past may we judge wisely what is obsolete and what is not, what to discard and what to preserve.

Aristotle observed that youth has a long time before it and a short past behind: on the first day of one's life one has nothing at all to remember and can only look forward. By contrast, he added, the elderly live by memory rather than hope; for what is left to them of life is little compared with the long past.

The capacity to love and to cherish ideals with intransigent commitment is a marvelous trait of youth. On the other hand, the wisdom and earthbound experience that come with age are necessary balance wheels on the soaring fantasy, the untested ideas and the despair of youth.

As you set out to revise and rebuild the Establishment into which you are about to enter, I suggest that you do not deny your birthright; nor reject the proud heritage which is rightfully yours.

Today is your opportunity for greatness!
Go then. Build your houses of tomorrow.
In them may you experience a new quality of life.

1. Which phrase *most nearly* expresses the MAIN idea of this   1.____
   speech?
   A. A perspective of the past   B. The generation gap
   C. The ignoble past   D. Aristotle's legacy

2. An underlying principle of the speech seems to be that   2.____
   A. youth is more valuable than age
   B. knowledge is cumulative
   C. the present is identical to the past
   D. Greek philosophers had the answers

3. One specific benefit of the past which is referred to in   3.____
   the speech is
   - A. land acquisition
   - B. the invention of printing
   - C. artistic creation
   - D. judicial precedent

4. According to this speech, the value of the past is MOST   4.____
   beneficial in
   - A. justifying old people's existence
   - B. giving a sense of roots
   - C. making reasonable judgments
   - D. retaining everything that has been created

5. By quoting Aristotle, the author demonstrates his own   5.____
   belief that
   - A. philosophy is the goal of age
   - B. old people are wise
   - C. young people are romantic
   - D. the past enriches the present

6. According to Aristotle, the CHIEF asset of youth is   6.____
   - A. hope   B. strength
   - C. experience   C. the past

7. According to the speaker, the experiences of youth could   7.____
   be BEST described as
   - A. new and tranquil   B. extreme and varied
   - C. bright and wise   D. restrained and optimistic

8. The speaker indicates that the BEST approach to life for   8.____
   his audience is a
   - A. concentration on the past
   - B. reversal of the past
   - C. blending of the past and present
   - D. concentration on the future

9. The ideas in the speech are developed basically through   9.____
   the technique of
   - A. comparing qualities   B. quoting authorities
   - C. understanding suggestions   D. logical deductions

10. The overall tone of this speech can be BEST described as   10.____
    - A. despondent   B. cynical
    - C. cautious   D. optimistic

KEY (CORRECT ANSWERS)

1.	A	6.	A
2.	B	7.	B
3.	C	8.	C
4.	C	9.	A
5.	D	10.	D

TEST 3

Listening Passage

(The following speech by Ray Billington has been adapted from "Cowboys, Indians, and the Land of Promise," *Representative American Speeches*, 1975-1976.)

The persuasive influence of the frontier image is nowhere better exhibited than by the cultists of other nations who try to recapture life in that never-never land of the past. In Paris, western addicts buy "outfits" at a store near the Arch of Triumph called the Western House and spend weekends at Camp Indian clad in Comanche headdresses.

All are responding to the image of the American West projected by twentieth-century films, novels, and television programs: a sun-drenched land of distant horizons, peopled largely by scowling bad men in black shirts, villainous Indians, and those Galahads of the Plains, the cowboys, glamorous in hip-hugging Levis and embroidered shirts, a pair of Colt revolvers worn low about the waist. A land, too, of the shoot-out, individual justice, and sudden death at the hand of lynch mobs. A few months ago an Israeli army psychologist, pleased that his country's soldiers did not use their guns when on leave, expressed delight that "There is no shooting like in the Wild West."

That such an image should be popular today is easy to understand. To empathize with a make-believe land of masculinity and self-realization is to forget momentarily the monotony of a standardized machine civilization, to escape the uncertainties of a turbulent world, and to recapture an unregimented past. The vogue of a "Western" cult demonstrates a universal urge to lessen the controls necessary in today's societies.

1. By his word choice, the speaker suggests that the French   1.____
   buy cowboy outfits in order to
      A. enjoy a fantasy world
      B. express strong anti-Indian feelings
      C. have a better concept of the American West
      D. relive their own past glory

2. Which are the major sources of the popular frontier image? 2.____
      A. American myths   B. Mass media
      C. Travel brochures   D. Historical accounts

3. In this speech, the depiction of sinister characters is   3.____
   best described as
   A. accurate   B. conflicting
   C. stereotyped   D. vague

4. According to this speech, most Indians in Western stories   4.____
   are portrayed as
   A. bad   B. passive
   C. glamorous   D. oppressed

5. The speaker compares the position of the cowboy to that   5.____
   of
   A. a TV programmer   B. an Israeli soldier
   C. a famous actor   D. a chivalrous knight

6. According to the projected image of the Old West, justice   6.____
   was handled by
   A. the sheriff   B. each person
   C. the good guys   D. no one

7. According to the speaker, the main reason for the allure   7.____
   of this Western imagery is that the
   A. past provides relief from the present
   B. present is very similar to the past
   C. past serves as a model for the present
   D. achievement of the present outweighs that of the past

8. Throughout this description of the West, a recurring   8.____
   difference from modern day life that is expressed is the
   A. cowboy's knowledge of self-defense
   B. chance to fight evil
   C. individual's control of his life
   D. opportunity to become famous

9. This speech suggests that the projected image of the West   9.____
   is best described as
   A. realistic   B. understated
   C. changing   D. romantic

10. According to this speech, the largest group that accepts 10.____
    the projected image of the West is
    A. modern ranchers   B. movie viewers
    C. the American public   D. people around the world

————

KEY (CORRECT ANSWERS)

1.	A	6.	B
2.	B	7.	A
3.	C	8.	C
4.	A	9.	D
5.	D	10.	D

————

TEST 4

DIRECTIONS: In this part a passage will be read orally to you. It is NOT written out in the test booklet so you will have to listen carefully. After the reading of the passage, you will answer the questions that follow. Each question or incomplete statement is followed by several suggested answers or completions. Select the one that BEST answers the question or completes the statement. *PRINT THE LETTER OF THE CORRECT ANSWER IN THE SPACE AT THE RIGHT.*

Listening Passage

(The following speech has been adapted from *At Wit's End* by Erma Bombeck.)

The end of summer is to me like New Year's Eve. I sense an end to something carefree and uninhibited, sandy and warm, cold and melting, barefoot and tanned. And yet I look forward with great expectation to a beginning of schedules and appointments, bookbinders with little tabs, freshly sharpened pencils, crisp winds, efficiency, and routine.

I am sadly aware of a great rushing of time as I lengthen skirts and discard sweaters that hit above the wristbones. Time is moving and I want to stop it for just a while so that I may snatch a quiet moment and tell my children what it is I want for them.

The moment never comes, of course. I must compete with Captain Kangaroo, a baseball game, a record, a playmate, a cartoon or a new bike in the next block. So I must keep these thoughts inside.

Too fast....you're moving too fast. Don't be in such a hurry. You're going to own your own sports car before you've tried to build one out of orange crates and four baby buggy wheels. You're going to explore the world before you've explored the wonders of your own back yard.

Don't shed your childhood like a good coat that's gotten a little small for you. A full-term childhood is necessary as are all phases of your growth. Childhood is a time for absorbing ideas, knowledge, and people like a giant sponge. Childhood is a time when "competition" is a baseball game and "responsibility" is a paper route.

I want to teach you so much that you must know to find happiness within yourself. Yet, I don't know where to begin or how.

If I could only be sure all the lessons are sinking in and are being understood. How can I tell you about disappointments? You'll have them you know. And they'll be painful, they'll hurt, they'll shatter your ego, lay your confidence in yourself bare, and sometimes cripple your initiative. But people don't die from them. They just emerge stronger. I want you to hear the thunder, so you can appreciate the calm. I want you to fall on your face in the dirt once in a while, so you will know the pride of being able to stand tall.

1. To the speaker, the end of summer represents   1.____
   A. the end of a routine
   B. a new beginning
   C. a continuation of her schedule
   D. an end to childhood

2. To the speaker, summer appears to represent   2.____
   A. growth   B. responsibility
   C. efficiency   D. freedom

3. To the speaker, fall appears to represent   3.____
   A. peace   B. competition
   C. routine   D. maturity

4. The speaker's thoughts are not said aloud to her children   4.____
   because she
   A. finds no time in their busy schedule
   B. realizes it would make no difference
   C. fears rejection
   D. has too much to say

5. Which statement best expresses the speaker's advice to   5.____
   her audience?
   A. Do not think of the future.
   B. Try to avoid disappointments.
   C. Listen to experienced people.
   D. Enjoy the present.

6. The speaker compares childhood to a coat because they   6.____
   both can be
   A. altered to fit   B. put aside
   C. stored   D. worn

7. According to the speaker, the positive aspect of disap-   7.____
   pointments is that they
   A. are short-lived   B. build character
   C. reveal true friends   D. make people humble

8. The speaker's feelings about her own ability to help her   8.____
   children can best be described as
   A. uncertain   B. unrealistic
   C. sophisticated   D. matter-of-fact

9. What is the main idea of the speech?   9.____
   A. Children need some pain in order to become strong.
   B. Only adults appreciate life.
   C. People should learn to appreciate all stages of life.
   D. Competition and responsibility are only for adults.

10. A characteristic of the speaker's style in this speech is 10.____
    that she
    A. depends on humor to make her point
    B. makes the same point in different ways
    C. uses sentimental appeal to please her audience
    D. uses irony to emphasize her theme

KEY (CORRECT ANSWERS)

1.	B		6.	B
2.	D		7.	B
3.	C		8.	A
4.	A		9.	C
5.	D		10.	B

———

TEST 5

DIRECTIONS: In this part a passage will be read orally to you.
It is NOT written out in the test booklet so you
will have to listen carefully. After the reading of the
passage, you will answer the questions that follow.
Each question or incomplete statement is followed by
several suggested answers or completions. Select the
one that BEST answers the question or completes the
statement. *PRINT THE LETTER OF THE CORRECT ANSWER IN
THE SPACE AT THE RIGHT.*

Listening Passage

(The following passage is adapted from "America and the
Americans" by John Steinbeck.)

The American dream does not die. The dreams of a people
either create folk literature or find their way into it; and folk
literature, again, is always based on something that happened. Our
most persistent folk tales concern cowboys, gunslinging sheriffs
and Indian-fighters. These folk figures did exist and this dream
persists. Businessmen in Texas wear the high-heeled boots though
they ride in air-conditioned cars and have forgotten the reason
for the high heel. Our children play cowboy and Indian. And in
these moral tales, virtue does not arise out of reason or orderly
process of law — it is imposed by violence and maintained by the
threat of violence. Are these stories permanent because we know
within ourselves that only the threat of violence makes it possible
for us to live together in peace?

Something happened in America to create the Americans. Now
we face the danger which in the past has been most destructive to
the human: success, plenty, comfort, and ever-increasing leisure.
No dynamic people has ever survived these dangers. I wonder about
the tomorrow of my people, which is a young people. My questioning
is compounded of some fear, more hope, and great confidence.

I have named the destroyers of nations: comfort, plenty and
security — out of which grows boredom, in which rebellion against
the world as it is, and myself as I am, is submerged in listless
self-satisfaction. A dying people tolerates the present, rejects
the future and finds its satisfactions in past greatness and half-
remembered glory. A dying people arms itself with defense weapons
against change. It is in the American negation of these symptoms
of extinction that my hope and confidence lie. We are not satisfied.
Our restlessness, perhaps inherited from the hungry immigrants of
our ancestry, is still with us.

How will the Americans act and react to a new set of circumstances for which new rules must be made? We know from our past
some of the things we will do. We will make mistakes; we always
have. But from our beginning, our social direction is clear. We
have tried to become one people out of many. We have failed sometimes, taken wrong paths, paused for renewals; but we have never
slipped back — never.

1. Although not completely attained, the American dream seems to be
   A. outlived   B. persistent
   C. realistic   D. democratic
                                                  1._____

2. According to his passage, which statement about folk heroes is most likely true?
   A. They are based on fact.
   B. They are created in someone's imagination
   C. They are only an American dream.
   D. They are created as a way for Americans to escape reality.
                                                  2._____

3. The speaker cites the wearing of high heeled boots by Texas businessmen as evidence of their
   A. ability to buy whatever they want
   B. interest in the work of the cowboy
   C. belief in the dream of folk heroes
   D. desire to return to the past
                                                  3._____

4. According to the speaker, folk tales indicate that Americans generally do the right thing because of their
   A. belief in law and order
   B. moral convictions
   C. fear of violence
   D. confidence in the future
                                                  4._____

5. The speaker implies that success, plenty, and comfort should be regarded with
   A. amazement   B. confidence
   C. toleration   D. suspicion
                                                  5._____

6. The speaker believes that a self-satisified nation will
   A. eventually perish   B. be more comfortable
   C. become revolutionary   D. invent myths
                                                  6._____

7. According to the speaker, one valuable quality America inherited from its immigrants is
   A. belief in myths   B. belief in hard work
   C. restlessness   D. stability
                                                  7._____

8. Past experience suggests that one of the reactions Americans will have to new situations will be to
   A. give up the American dream   B. make some mistakes
   C. resist any change   D. relive past glories
                                                  8._____

KEY (CORRECT ANSWERS)

1.	B	5.	D
2.	A	6.	A
3.	C	7.	C
4.	C	8.	B

READING COMPREHENSION
UNDERSTANDING AND INTERPRETING WRITTEN MATERIAL
EXAMINATION SECTION

DIRECTIONS: Each question or incomplete statement is followed by several suggested answers or completions. Select the one that BEST answers the question or completes the statement. *PRINT THE LETTER OF THE CORRECT ANSWER IN THE SPACE AT THE RIGHT.*

TEST 1

Skiing has recently become one of the more popular sports in the United States. Because of its popularity, thousands of winter vacationers are flying north rather than south. In many areas, reservations are required months ahead of time.

I discovered the accommodation shortage through an unfortunate experience. On a sunny Saturday morning, I set out from Denver for the beckoning slopes of Aspen, Colorado. After passing signs for other ski areas, I finally reached my destination. Naturally, I lost no time in heading for the nearest tow. After a stimulating afternoon of miscalculated stem turns, I was famished. Well, one thing led to another, and it must have been eight o'clock before I concerned myself with a bed for my bruised and aching bones.

It took precisely one phone call to ascertain the lack of lodgings in the Aspen area. I had but one recourse. My auto and I started the treacherous jaunt over the pass and back towards Denver. Along the way, I went begging for a bed. Finally, a jolly tavernkeeper took pity, and for only thirty dollars a night allowed me the privilege of staying in a musty, dirty, bathless room above his tavern.

1. The author's problem would have been avoided if he had 1.____
   A. not tired himself out skiing
   B. taken a bus instead of driving
   C. looked for food as soon as he arrived
   D. arranged for accommodations well ahead of his trip
   E. answer cannot be determined from the information given

TEST 2

Helen Keller was born in 1880 in Tuscumbia, Alabama. When she was two years old, she lost her sight and hearing as the result of an illness. In 1886, she became the pupil of Anne Sullivan, who taught Helen to *see* with her fingertips, to *hear* with her feet and hands, and to communicate with other people. Miss Sullivan succeeded in arousing Helen's curiosity and interest by spelling the names of objects into her hand. At the end of three years, Helen had mastered the manual and the braille alphabet and could read and write.

2. When did Helen Keller lose her sight and hearing? 2.____
   A. 1880   B. 1882   C. 1886   D. 1890   E. 1900

TEST 3

Sammy got to school ten minutes after the school bell had rung. He was breathing hard and had a black eye. His face was dirty and scratched. One leg of his pants was torn.

Tommy was late to school, too; however, he was only five minutes late. Like Sammy, he was breathing hard, but he was happy and smiling.

3. Sammy and Tommy had been fighting.   3.___
   Who probably won?
      A. Sammy   B. Tommy
      C. Cannot tell from story   D. The teacher
      E. The school

—

TEST 4

This is like a game to see if you can tell what the nonsense word in the paragraph stands for. The nonsense word is just a silly word for something that you know very well. Read the paragraph and see if you can tell what the underlined nonsense word stands for.

You can wash your hands and face in <u>zup</u>. You can even take a bath in it. When people swim, they are in the <u>zup</u>. Everyone drinks <u>zup</u>.

4. <u>Zup</u> is PROBABLY   4.___
      A. milk   B. pop   C. soap   D. water   E. soup

—

TEST 5

After two weeks of unusually high-speed travel, we reached Xeno, a small planet whose population, though never before visited by Earthmen, was listed as *friendly* in the INTERSTELLAR GAZETTEER.

On stepping lightly (after all, the gravity of Xeno is scarcely more than twice that of our own moon) from our spacecraft, we saw that *friendly* was an understatement. We were immediately surrounded by Frangibles of various colors, mostly pinkish or orange, who held out their *hands* to us. Imagine our surprise when their *hands* actually merged with ours as we tried to shake them!

Then, before we could stop them (how could we have stopped them?) two particularly pink Frangibles simply stepped right into two eminent scientists among our party, who immediately lit up with the

same pink glow. While occupied in this way, the scientists
reported afterwards they suddenly discovered they *knew* a great deal
about Frangibles and life on Xeno.

Apparently, Frangibles could take themselves apart atomically
and enter right into any other substance. They communicated by
thought waves, occasionally merging *heads* for greater clarity. Two
Frangibles who were in love with each other would spend most of their
time merged into one; they were a bluish-green color unless they
were having a lover's quarrel, when they turned gray.

5. In order to find out about an object which interested   5.___
   him, what would a Frangible MOST likely do?
   A. Take it apart
   B. Enter into it
   C. Study it scientifically
   D. Ask earth scientists about it
   E. Wait to see if it would change color

TEST 6

This is like a game to see if you can tell what the nonsense
word in the paragraph stands for. The nonsense word is just a silly
word for something that you know very well. Read the paragraph and
see if you can tell what the underlined nonsense word stands for.

Have you ever smelled a <u>mart</u>? They smell very good. Bees like
<u>marts</u>. They come in many colors. <u>Marts</u> grow in the earth, and they
usually bloom in the spring.

6. <u>Marts</u> are PROBABLY   6.___
   A. bugs   B. flowers   C. perfume
   D. pies   E. cherries

TEST 7

Christmas was only a few days away. The wind was strong and
cold. The walks were covered with snow. The downtown streets were
crowded with people. Their faces were hidden by many packages as
they went in one store after another. They all tried to move faster
as they looked at the clock.

7. When did the story PROBABLY happen?   7.___
   A. November 28   B. December 1   C. December 21
   D. December 25   E. December 28

TEST 8

THE WAYFARER

The wayfarer,
Perceiving the pathway to truth,
Was struck with astonishment.
It was thickly grown with weeds.
Ha, he said,
I see that no one has passed here
In a long time.
Later he saw that each weed
Was a singular knife,
Well, he mumbled at last,
Doubtless there are other roads.

8. *I see that no one has passed here*   8.__
    In a long time.
    What do the above lines from the poem mean?
    A. The way of truth is popular.
    B. People are fascinated by the truth.
    C. Truth comes and goes like the wind.
    D. The truth is difficult to recognize.
    E. Few people are searching for the truth.

————

TEST 9

Any attempt to label an entire generation is unrewarding, and
yet the generation which went through the last war, or at least could
get a drink easily once it was over, seems to possess a uniform,
general quality which demands an adjective. It was John Kerouac, the
author of a fine, neglected novel, THE TOWN AND THE CITY, who finally
came up with it. It was several years ago, when the face was harder
to recognize, but he had a sharp, sympathetic eye, and one day he
said, *You know, this is really a beat generation.* The origins of
the word *beat* are obscure, but the meaning is only too clear to most
Americans. More than mere weariness, it implies the feeling of havin
been used, of being raw. It involves a sort of nakedness of mind, an
ultimately, of soul; a feeling of being reduced to the bedrock of
consciousness. In short, it means being undramatically pushed up
against the wall of oneself. A man is beat whenever he goes for
broke and waters the sum of his resources on a single number; and
the young generation has done that continually from early youth.

9. What does the writer suggest when he mentions a *fine,*   9.__
    neglected novel?
    A. Kerouac had the right idea about the war
    B. Kerouac had a clear understanding of the new post-war
       generation
    C. Kerouac had not received the recognition of THE TOWN
       AND THE CITY that was deserved
    D. Kerouac had the wrong idea about the war.
    E. All of the above

TEST 10

One spring, Farmer Brown had an unusually good field of wheat. Whenever he saw any birds in this field, he got his gun and shot as many of them as he could. In the middle of the summer, he found that his wheat was being ruined by insects. With no birds to feed on them, the insects had multiplied very fast. What Farmer Brown did not understand was this: A bird is not simply an animal that eats food the farmer may want for himself. Instead, it is one of many links in the complex surroundings, or environment, in which we live.

How much grain a farmer can raise on an acre of ground depends on many factors. All of these factors can be divided into two big groups. Such things as the richness of the soil, the amount of rainfall, the amount of sunlight, and the temperature belong together in one of these groups. This group may be called nonliving factors. The second group may be called living factors. The living factors in any plant's environment are animals and other plants. Wheat, for example, may be damaged by wheat rust, a tiny plant that feeds on wheat, or it may be eaten by plant-eating animals such as birds or grasshoppers...

It is easy to see that the relations of plants and animals to their environment are very complex, and that any change in the environment is likely to bring about a whole series of changes.

10. What does the passage suggest a good farmer should under- 10.___
     stand about nature?
     A. Insects are harmful to plants
     B. Birds are not harmful to plants
     C. Wheat may be damaged by both animals and other plants
     D. The amount of wheat he can raise depends on two
        factors: birds and insects
     E. A change in one factor of plants' surroundings may
        cause other factors to change

11. What important idea about nature does the writer want us 11.___
     to understand?
     A. Farmer Brown was worried about the heavy rainfall
     B. Nobody needs to have such destructive birds around
     C. Farmer Brown did not want the temperature to change
     D. All insects need not only wheat rust but grasshoppers
     E. All living things are dependent on other living things

TEST 11

For a 12-year-old, I've been around a lot because my father's in the Army. I have been to New York and to Paris. When I was nine, my parents took me to Rome. I didn't like Europe very much because the people don't speak the same language I do. When I am older, my mother says I can travel by myself. I think I will like that. Ever since I was 13, I have wanted to go to Canada.

12. Why can't everything this person said be TRUE?   12.__
    A. 12-year-olds can't travel alone
    B. No one can travel that much in 12 years
    C. There is a conflict in the ages used in the passage
    D. 9-year-olds can't travel alone
    E. He is a liar

TEST 12

Between April and October, the Persian Gulf is dotted with the small boats of pearl divers. Some seventy-five thousand of them are busy diving down and bringing up pearl-bearing oysters. These oysters are not the kind we eat. The edible oyster produces pearls of little or no value. You may have heard tales of divers who discovered pearls and sold them for great sums of money. These stories are entertaining but not accurate.

13. The Persian Gulf has many   13.__
    A. large boats of pearl divers
    B. pearl divers who eat oysters
    C. edible oysters that produce pearls
    D. non-edible oysters that produce pearls
    E. edible oysters that do not produce pearls

TEST 13

Art says that the polar ice cap is melting at the rate of 3% per year. Bert says that this isn't true because the polar ice cap is really melting at the rate of 7% per year.

14. We know for certain that   14.__
    A. Art is wrong
    B. Bert is wrong
    C. they are both wrong
    D. they both might be right
    E. they can't both be right

TEST 14

FORTUNE AND MEN'S EYES

Shakespeare

```
 1.  When, in disgrace with fortune and men's eyes,
 2.  I all alone beweep my outcast state,
 3.  And trouble deaf heaven with my bootless cries,
 4.  And look upon myself and curse my fate,
 5.  Wishing me like to one more rich in hope,
 6.  Featured like him, like him with friends possessed
 7.  Desiring this man's art, and that man's scope,
 8.  With what I most enjoy contented least;
 9.  Yet in these thoughts myself almost despising,
10.  Haply I think on thee; and then my state,
11.  Like to the lark at break of day arising
12.  From sullen earth, sings hymns at heaven's gate;
13.  For thy sweet love remembered, such wealth brings
14.  That then I scorn to change my state with kings.
```

15. What saves this man from wishing to be different than he   15.____
    is?
    A. Such wealth brings
    B. Hymns at heaven's gate
    C. The lark at break of day
    D. Thy sweet love remembered
    E. Change my state with kings

           ____

TEST 15

My name is Gregory Gotrocks, and I live in Peoria, Illinois. I
sell tractors. In June 1952, the Gotrocks Tractor Company (my dad
happens to be the president) sent me to Nepal-Tibet to check on our
sales office there.

Business was slow, and I had a lot of time to kill. I decided
to see Mt. Everest so that I could tell everyone back in Peoria that
I had seen it.

It was beautiful; I was spellbound. I simply had to see what
the view looked like from the top. So I started up the northwest
slope. Everyone know that this is the best route to take. It took
me three long hours to reach the top, but the climb was well worth it.

16. Gregory Gotrocks went to see Mt. Everest so that he could   16.____
    A. see some friends
    B. sell some tractors
    C. take a picture of it
    D. plant a flag at its base
    E. entertain his friends back home

           ____

TEST 16

Suburbanites are not irresponsible. Indeed, what is striking about the young couples' march along the abyss is the earnestness and precision with which they go about it. They are extremely budget-conscious. They can rattle off most of their monthly payments down to the last penny; one might say that even their impulse buying is deliberately planned. They are conscientious in meeting obligations and rarely do they fall delinquent in their accounts.

They are exponents of what could be called budgetism. This does not mean that they actually keep formal budgets - quite the contrary. The beauty of budgetism is that one doesn't have to keep a budget at all. It's done automatically. In the new middle-class rhythms of life, obligations are homogenized, for the overriding aim is to have oneself precommitted to regular, unvarying monthly payments on all the major items.

Americans used to be divided into three sizable groups: those who thought of money obligations in terms of the week, of the month, and of the year. Many people remain at both ends of the scale; but with the widening of the middle class, the mortgage payments are firmly geared to a thirty-day cycle, and any dissonant peaks and valleys are anathema. Just as young couples are now paying winter fuel bills in equal monthly fractions through the year, so they seek to spread out all the other heavy seasonal obligations they can anticipate. If vendors will not oblige by accepting equal monthly installments, the purchasers will smooth out the load themselves by floating loans.

It is, suburbanites cheerfully explain, a matter of psychology. They don't trust themselves. In self-entrapment is security. They try to budget so tightly that there is no unappropriated funds, for they know these would burn a hole in their pocket. Not merely out of greed for goods, then, do they commit themselves; it is protection they want, too. And though it would be extreme to say that they go into debt to be secure, carefully chartered debt does give them a certain peace of mind - and in suburbia this is more coveted than luxury itself.

17. What is the *abyss* along which the young couples are   17.___
    marching?
    A. Nuclear war   B. Unemployment
    C. Mental breakdown   D. Financial disaster
    E. Catastrophic illness

18. What conclusion does the author reach concerning carefully   18.___
    chartered debt among young couples in the United States
    today?
    It
    A. is a symbol of love
    B. brings marital happiness
    C. helps them to feel secure
    D. enables them to acquire wealth
    E. provides them with material goods

TEST 17

Read the verse and fill in the space beside the object described in the verse.

You see me when I'm right or wrong;
My face I never hide.
My hands move slowly round and round
And o'er me minutes glide.

19.   A. ___ Book   B. ___ Clock   C. ___ Record   19.___
      D. ___ Table   E. ___ Lock

TEST 18

Until about thirty years ago, the village of Nayon seems to have been a self-sufficient agricultural community with a mixture of native and sixteenth century Spanish customs. Lands were abandoned when too badly eroded. The balance between population and resources allowed a minimum subsistence. A few traders exchanged goods between Quito and the villages in the tropical barrancas, all within a radius of ten miles. Houses had dirt floors, thatched roofs, and pole walls that were sometimes plastered with mud. Guinea pigs ran freely about each house and were the main meat source. Most of the population spoke no Spanish. Men wore long hair and concerned themselves chiefly with farming.

The completion of the Guayaquil-Quito railway in 1908 brought the first real contacts with industrial civilization to the high inter-Andean valley. From this event gradually flowed not only technological changes but new ideas and social institutions. Feudal social relationships no longer seemed right and immutable; medicine and public health improved; elementary education became more common; urban Quito began to expand; and finally, and perhaps least important so far, modern industries began to appear, although even now on a most modest scale.

In 1948-49, the date of our visit, only two men wore their hair long; and only two old-style houses remained. If guinea pigs were kept, they were penned; their flesh was now a luxury food, and beef the most common meat. Houses were of adobe or fired brick, usually with tile roofs, and often contained five or six rooms, some of which had plank or brick floors. Most of the population spoke Spanish. There was no resident priest, but an appointed government official and a policeman represented authority. A six-teacher school provided education. Clothing was becoming citified; for men it often included overalls for work and a tailored suit, white shirt, necktie, and felt hat for trips to Quito. Attendance at church was low, and many festivals had been abandoned. Volleyball or soccer was played weekly in the plaza by young men who sometimes wore shorts, blazers, and berets. There were few shops, for most purchases were made in Quito, and from there came most of the food, so that there was a far more varied diet than twenty-five years ago. There were piped water and sporadic health services; in addition, most families patronized Quito doctors' in emergencies.

The crops and their uses had undergone change. Maize, or Indian corn, was still the primary crop, but very little was harvested as grain. Almost all was sold in Quito as green corn to eat boiled on the cob, and a considerable amount of the corn eaten as grain in Nayon was imported. Beans, which do poorly here, were grown on a small scale for household consumption. Though some squash was eaten, most was exported. Sweet potatoes, tomatoes, cabbage, onions, peppers and, at lower elevations, sweet yucca, and arrowroot were grown extensively for export; indeed, so export-minded was the community that it was almost impossible to buy locally grown produce in the village. People couldn't be bothered with retail scales.

20. Why was there primitiveness and self-containment in Nayon before 1910?   20.___
    A. Social mores   B. Cultural tradition
    C. Biological instincts   D. Geographical factors
    E. Religious regulations

21. By 1948, the village of Nayon was   21.___
    A. a self-sufficient village
    B. out of touch with the outside world
    C. a small dependent portion of a larger economic unit
    D. a rapidly growing and sound social and cultural unit
    E. a metropolis

22. Why was Nayon originally separated from its neighbors?   22.___
    A. Rich arable land
    B. Long meandering streams
    C. Artificial political barriers
    D. Broad stretches of arid desert
    E. Deep rugged gorges traversed by rock trails

TEST 19

Read the verse and fill in the space beside the object described in the verse.

    I have two eyes and when I'm worn
    I give the wearer four.
    I'm strong or weak or thick or thin -
    Need I say much more?

23. A.___ Clock   B. ___ Eyeglasses C.___Piano   23.
    D.___ Thermometer E. ___ I don't know

TEST 20

Scarlet fever begins with fever, chills, headache, and sore throat. A doctor diagnoses the illness as scarlet fever when a characteristic rash erupts on the skin. This rash appears on the neck and chest in three to five days after the onset of the illness and spreads rapidly over the body. Sometimes the skin on the palm of the hands and soles of the feet shreds in flakes. Scarlet fever is usually treated with penicillin and, in severe cases, a convalescent serum. The disease may be accompanied by infections of the ear and throat, inflammation of the kidneys, pneumonia, and inflammation of the heart.

24. How does the author tell us that scarlet fever may be a serious disease?   24.____
   A. He tells how many people die of it.
   B. He tells that he once had the disease.
   C. He tells that hands and feet may fall off.
   D. He tells how other infections may come with scarlet fever.
   E. None of the above

TEST 21

Read the verse and fill in the space beside the object described in the verse.

I have no wings but often fly:
I come in colors many.
From varied nationalities
Respect I get a-plenty.

25. A.____ Deck of cards   B. ____ Eyeglasses   C. ____ Flag   25.____
    D.____ Needles   E. ____ None of the above

KEY (CORRECT ANSWERS)

1. D	6. B	11. E	16. E	21. C
2. B	7. C	12. C	17. D	22. E
3. B	8. E	13. D	18. C	23. B
4. D	9. C	14. E	19. B	24. D
5. B	10. E	15. D	20. D	25. C

WORD MEANING

COMMENTARY

DESCRIPTION OF THE TEST

On many examinations, you will have questions about the meaning of words, or vocabulary.

In this type of question you have to state what a word or phrase means. (A phrase is a group of words.) This word or phrase is in CAPITAL letters in a sentence. You are also given for each question five other words or groups of words -- lettered A,B,C,D, and E -- as possible answers. One of thes words or groups of words means the same as the word or group of words in CAPITAL letters. Only one is right. You are to pick out the one that is right and select the letter of your answer.

HINTS FOR ANSWERING WORD-MEANING QUESTIONS

Read each question carefully.

Choose the best answer of the five choices even though it is not the word you might use yourself.

Answer first those that you know. Then do the others.

If you know that some of the suggested answers are not right, pay no more attention to them.

Be sure that you have selected an answer for every question, even if you have to guess.

———

SAMPLE QUESTIONS

DIRECTIONS: For the following questions, select the word or group of words lettered A,B,C,D, or E that means MOST NEARLY the same as the word in capital letters. Indicate the letter of the CORRECT answer for each question.

SAMPLE QUESTIONS 1 AND 2

1. The letter was SHORT.   SHORT means *MOST NEARLY*
    A. tall   B. wide   C. brief   D. heavy   E. dark
    EXPLANATION
    SHORT is a word you have used to describe something that is small, or not long, or little,etc. Therefore you would not have to spend much time figuring out the right answer. You would choose C. brief.

2. The young man is VIGOROUS.   VIGOROUS means *MOST NEARLY*
    A. serious   B. reliable C. courageous D. strong E. talented
    EXPLANATION
    VIGOROUS is a word that you have probably used yourself or read somewhere. It carries with it the idea of being active,full of pep, etc. Which one of the five choices comes closest to meaning that? Certainly not A. serious, B. reliable, or E. talented; C. courageous -- maybe, D. strong-- maybe. But between courageous or strong, you would have to agree that strong is the better choice. Therefore, you would choose D.

———

DIRECTIONS FOR THIS SECTION:
  For the following questions, select the word or group of words lettered A,B,C,D, or E that means MOST NEARLY the same as the word in
capital letters. *PRINT THE LETTER OF THE CORRECT ANSWER IN THE SPACE
AT THE RIGHT.*

TEST 1

1. To SULK means MOST NEARLY to   1. ...
    A. cry   B. annoy   C. lament   D. be sullen
    E. scorn
2. To FLOUNDER means MOST NEARLY to   2. ...
    A. investigate B. label C. struggle D. consent E. escape
3. PARLEY means MOST NEARLY   3. ...
    A. discussion B. thoroughfare C. salon D. surrender
    E. division
4. MAESTRO means MOST NEARLY   4. ...
    A. official B. ancestor C. teacher D. watchman E. alien
5. MEANDERING means MOST NEARLY   5. ...
    A. cruel B. adjusting C. winding D. smooth E. combining
6. GNARLED means MOST NEARLY   6. ...
    A. angry B. bitter C. twisted D. ancient E. embroidered
7. TEMPERANCE means MOST NEARLY   7. ...
    A. moderation B. climate C. carelessness
    D. disagreeableness   E. rigidity
8. A PRECARIOUS position is one that is   8. ...
    A. foresighted B. careful C. modest D. headstrong
    E. uncertain
9. COVETOUS means MOST NEARLY   9. ...
    A. undisciplined B. grasping C. timid D. insincere
    E. secretive
10. PRIVATION means MOST NEARLY   10. ...
    A. reward B. superiority in rank   C. hardship
    D. suitability of behavior   E. solitude

———

TEST 2

1. To INFILTRATE means MOST NEARLY to   1. ...
    A. pass through B. stop C. consider D. challenge openly
    E. meet secretly
2. REVOCATION means MOST NEARLY   2. ...
    A. certificate B. repeal C. animation D. license E. plea
3. LOQUACIOUS means MOST NEARLY   3. ...
    A. grim B. stern C. talkative D. lighthearted
    E. liberty-loving
4. APERTURE means MOST NEARLY   4. ...
    A. basement B. opening C. phantom D. protective coloring
    E. light refreshment
5. A PUNGENT odor is one that is   5. ...
    A. biting B. smooth C. quarrelsome D. wrong E. proud
6. To CORROBORATE means MOST NEARLY to   6. ...
    A. deny B. elaborate C. confirm D. gnaw E. state

2

7. BENEVOLENCE means MOST NEARLY   7. ...
    A. good fortune   B. well-being   C. inheritance   D. violence
    E. charitableness
8. PETULANT means MOST NEARLY   8. ...
    A. rotten   B. fretful   C. unrelated   D. weird   E. throbbing
9. DERELICT means MOST NEARLY   9. ...
    A. abandoned   B. widowed   C. faithful   D. insincere
    E. hysterical
10. INCISIVE means MOST NEARLY   10. ...
    A. stimulating   B. accidental   C. brief   D. penetrating
    E. final

TEST 3

1. To LAUD means MOST NEARLY to   1. ...
    A. praise   B. cleanse   C. replace   D. squander
    E. frown upon
2. To TAUNT means MOST NEARLY to   2. ...
    A. jeer at   B. tighten   C. rescue   D. interest   E. ward off
3. DEITY means MOST NEARLY   3. ...
    A. renown   B. divinity   C. delicacy   D. destiny   E. futility
4. GRAVITY means MOST NEARLY   4. ...
    A. displeasure   B. thankfulness   C. suffering   D. roughness
    E. seriousness
5. A CONTEMPTUOUS author is one that is   5. ...
    A. thoughtful   B. soiled   C. dishonorable   D. scornful
    E. self-satisfied
6. To WAIVE means MOST NEARLY to   6. ...
    A. exercise   B. swing   C. claim   D. give up   E. wear out
7. To ASPIRE means MOST NEARLY to   7. ...
    A. fade away   B. excite   C. desire earnestly
    D. breathe heavily   E. roughen
8. PERTINENT means MOST NEARLY   8. ...
    A. related   B. saucy   C. quick   D. impatient   E. excited
9. DEVASTATION means MOST NEARLY   9. ...
    A. desolation   B. displeasure   C. dishonor   D. neglect
    E. religious fervor
10. IMMINENT means MOST NEARLY   10. ...
    A. sudden   B. important   C. delayed   D. threatening
    E. forceful

TEST 4

1. CONTROVERSIAL means MOST NEARLY   1. ...
    A. faultfinding   B. pleasant   C. debatable   D. ugly
    E. talkative
2. GHASTLY means MOST NEARLY   2. ...
    A. hasty   B. furious   C. breathless   D. deathlike
    E. spiritual
3. A BELLIGERENT attitude is one that is   3. ...
    A. worldly   B. warlike   C. loudmouthed   D. furious
    E. artistic

3

4. PROFICIENCY means MOST NEARLY   4. ...
   A. wisdom   B. oversupply   C. expertness   D. advancement
   E. sincerity
5. COMPASSION means MOST NEARLY   5. ...
   A. rage   B. strength of character   C. forcefulness
   D. sympathy   E. uniformity
6. DISSENSION means MOST NEARLY   6. ...
   A. treatise   B. pretense   C. fear   D. lineage   E. discord
7. To INTIMATE means MOST NEARLY to   7. ...
   A. charm   B. hint   C. disguise   D. frighten   E. hum
8. To BERATE means MOST NEARLY to   8. ...
   A. classify   B. scold   C. underestimate   D. take one's time
   E. evaluate
9. DEARTH means MOST NEARLY   9. ...
   A. scarcity   B. width   C. affection   D. wealth   E. warmth
10. To MEDITATE means MOST NEARLY to   10. ...
   A. rest   B. stare   C. doze   D. make peace   E. reflect

TEST 5

1. BONDAGE means MOST NEARLY   1. ...
   A. poverty   B. redemption   C. slavery   D. retirement
   E. complaint
2. AGILITY means MOST NEARLY   2. ...
   A. wisdom   B. nimbleness   C. agreeable   D. simplicity
   E. excitement
3. To ABDICATE means MOST NEARLY to   3. ...
   A. achieve   B. protest   C. renounce   D. demand   E. steal
4. To STIFLE means MOST NEARLY to   4. ...
   A. talk nonsense   B. sidestep   C. depress   D. smother
   E. stick
5. EDICT means MOST NEARLY   5. ...
   A. abbreviation   B. lie   C. carbon copy   D. correction
   E. decree
6. AMITY means MOST NEARLY   6. ...
   A. ill will   B. hope   C. pity   D. friendship   E. pleasure
7. COERCION means MOST NEARLY   7. ...
   A. force   B. disgust   C. suspicion   D. pleasure   E. criticism
8. To ABASH means MOST NEARLY to   8. ...
   A. embarrass   B. encourage   C. punish   D. surrender
   E. overthrow
9. TACITURN means MOST NEARLY   9. ...
   A. weak   B. evil   C. tender   D. silent   E. sensitive
10. REMISS means MOST NEARLY   10. ...
   A. memorable   B. neglectful   C. useless   D. prompt   E. exact

---

TEST 6

1. STAGNANT means MOST NEARLY   1. ...
   A. inactive   B. alert   C. selfish   D. difficult   E. scornful
2. MANDATORY means MOST NEARLY   2. ...
   A. instant   B. obligatory   C. evident   D. strategic
   E. unequaled

4

3. INFERNAL means MOST NEARLY
   A. immodest   B. incomplete   C. domestic   D. second-rate
   E. fiendish

3. ...

4. To EXONERATE means MOST NEARLY to
   A. free from blame   B. warn   C. drive out   D. overcharge
   E. plead

4. ...

5. ARBITER means MOST NEARLY
   A. friend   B. judge   C. drug   D. tree surgeon   E. truant

5. ...

6. ENMITY means MOST NEARLY
   A. boredom   B. puzzle   C. offensive language   D. ill will
   E. entanglement

6. ...

7. To DISCRIMINATE means MOST NEARLY to
   A. fail   B. delay   C. accuse   D. distinguish   E. reject

7. ...

8. DERISION means MOST NEARLY
   A. disgust   B. ridicule   C. fear   D. anger   E. heredity

8. ...

9. EXULTANT means MOST NEARLY
   A. essential   B. elated   C. praiseworthy   D. plentiful
   E. high-priced

9. ...

10. OSTENSIBLE means MOST NEARLY
    A. vibrating   B. odd   C. apparent   D. standard   E. ornate

10. ...

TEST 7

1. To ABHOR means MOST NEARLY to
   A. hate   B. admire   C. taste   D. skip   E. resign

1. ...

2. DUTIFUL means MOST NEARLY
   A. lasting   B. sluggish   C. required   D. soothing
   E. obedient

2. ...

3. ZEALOT means MOST NEARLY
   A. breeze   B. enthusiast   C. vault   D. wild animal
   E. musical instrument

3. ...

4. A MAGNANIMOUS attitude is one that is
   A. high-minded   B. faithful   C. concerned   D. individual
   E. small

4. ...

5. To CITE means MOST NEARLY to
   A. protest   B. depart   C. quote   D. agitate   E. perform

5. ...

6. OBLIVION means MOST NEARLY
   A. hindrance   B. accident   C. courtesy   D. forgetfulness
   E. old age

6. ...

7. CARDINAL means MOST NEARLY
   A. independent   B. well-organized   C. subordinate
   D. dignified   E. chief

7. ...

8. To DEPLETE means MOST NEARLY to
   A. restrain   B. corrupt   C. despair   D. exhaust
   E. spread out

8. ...

9. To SUPERSEDE means MOST NEARLY to
   A. retire   B. replace   C. overflow   D. bless   E. oversee

9. ...

10. SPORADIC means MOST NEARLY
    A. bad-tempered   B. infrequent   C. radical   D. reckless
    E. humble

10. ...

5

TEST 8

1. To NEUTRALIZE means MOST NEARLY to
    A. entangle B. strengthen C. counteract D. combat
    E. converse
2. To INSINUATE means MOST NEARLY to
    A. destroy B. hint C. do wrong D. accuse E. release
3. DIMINUTIVE means MOST NEARLY
    A. proud B. slow C. small D. watery E. puzzling
4. PLIGHT means MOST NEARLY
    A. departure B. weight C. conspiracy D. predicament
    E. stamp
5. An ILLICIT relationship is one that is
    A. unlawful B. overpowering C. ill-advised D. small-scale
    E. unreadable
6. A BENIGN manner is one that is
    A. contagious B. fatal C. ignorant D. kindly
    E. decorative
7. REVERIE means MOST NEARLY
    A. abusive language B. love song C. backward step
    D. daydream   E. holy man
8. APPREHENSIVE means MOST NEARLY
    A. quiet B. firm C. curious D. sincere E. fearful
9. To RECOIL means MOST NEARLY to
    A. shrink B. attract C. electrify D. adjust E. fear
10. GUISE means MOST NEARLY
    A. trickery B. request C. innocence D. misdeed
    E. appearance

1. ...
2. ...
3. ...
4. ...
5. ...
6. ...
7. ...
8. ...
9. ...
10. ...

TEST 9

1. To RELINQUISH means MOST NEARLY to
    A. regret B. abandon C. pursue D. secure E. penetrate
2. INJUNCTION means MOST NEARLY
    A. error B. attack C. injustice D. suggestion E. order
3. ADVENT means MOST NEARLY
    A. attachment B. reference C. arrival D. excitement E. vent
4. BICAMERAL means MOST NEARLY
    A. dealing with life forms B. meeting on alternate years
    C. over-sweet D. having two legislative branches
    E. having two meanings
5. A PERVERSE attitude is one that is
    A. contrary B. stingy C. unfortunate D. hereditary
    E. easygoing
6. To THWART means MOST NEARLY to
    A. assist B. whimper C. slice D. escape E. block
7. DEVOID means MOST NEARLY
    A. empty B. illegal C. affectionate D. pious E. annoying
8. A BLAND manner is one that is
    A. gentle B. guilty C. salty D. unfinished E. majestic
9. To OSTRACIZE means MOST NEARLY to
    A. flatter B. scold C. show off D. banish E. vibrate
10. CANDOR means MOST NEARLY
    A. sociability B. outspokenness C. grief D. light
    E. flattery

1. ...
2. ...
3. ...
4. ...
5. ...
6. ...
7. ...
8. ...
9. ...
10. ...

TEST 10

1. ACQUIT means MOST NEARLY   1. ...
   A. increase B. harden C. clear D. sharpen E. sentence
2. DEXTERITY means MOST NEARLY   2. ...
   A. conceit B. skill C. insistence D. embarrassment
   E. guidance
3. ASSIMILATE means MOST NEARLY   3. ...
   A. absorb B. imitate C. maintain D. outrun E. curb
4. DESPONDENCY means MOST NEARLY   4. ...
   A. relief B. gratitude C. dejection D. hatred E.poverty
5. A BUOYANT manner is one that is   5. ...
   A. conceited B. cautioning C. youthful D. musical
   E. cheerful
6. CULINARY means MOST NEARLY   6. ...
   A. having to do with cooking B. pertaining to dressmaking
   C. fond of eating   D. loving money
   E. tending to be secretive
7. CAPRICE means MOST NEARLY   7. ...
   A. wisdom B. ornament C. pillar D. whim E. energy
8. DETERRENT means MOST NEARLY   8. ...
   A. restraining B. cleansing C. deciding D. concluding
   E. crumbling
9. A PUGNACIOUS attitude is one that is   9. ...
   A. sticky B. cowardly C. precise D. vigorous
   E. quarrelsome
10. ABSCOND means MOST NEARLY   10. ...
   A. detest B. reduce C. swallow up D. dismiss E. flee

———

TEST 11

1. DOLDRUMS means MOST NEARLY   1. ...
   A. delirium B. rage C. saturation D. incarceration
   E. listlessness
2. DOUR means MOST NEARLY   2. ...
   A. gloomy B. cowardly C. untidy D. stingy E. doubtful
3. DRAGOON means MOST NEARLY   3. ...
   A. defy B. enlist C. surrender D. lead E. persecute
4. EMPIRICAL means MOST NEARLY   4. ...
   A. experiential B. undeniable C. melancholy D. territorial
   E. traditional
5. ENCOMIUM means MOST NEARLY   5. ...
   A. antidote B. adage C. anteroom D. eulogy E. bombast
6. ENTOMOLOGIST means MOST NEARLY student of   6. ...
   A. insects B. fish C. words D. fossils E. reptiles
7. EPHEMERAL means MOST NEARLY   7. ...
   A. persistent B. useless C. effete D. visionary
   E. short-lived
8. ETIOLOGY means MOST NEARLY   8. ...
   A. epitome B. inertia C. astronomy D. disease E. cause
9. FETISH means MOST NEARLY   9. ...
   A. tuft of hair above horse's hoof B. embryo of an animal
   C. object of excessive devotion   D. spirit of a festival
   E. feast of the Haitians

10. GAMUT means MOST NEARLY   10. ...
    A. gamble B. alphabet C. keys D. chess move E. range

TEST 12

1. HALLOW means MOST NEARLY   1. ...
   A. shout aloud B. make sacred C. haunt D. reveal
   E. hole out
2. HEGEMONY means MOST NEARLY   2. ...
   A. flight B. restraint C. nationalism D. autonomy
   E. leadership
3. HERMETIC means MOST NEARLY   3. ...
   A. air-tight B. protruding C. sequestered D. briskly
   E. ascetic
4. IBID means MOST NEARLY   4. ...
   A. that is B. as an example C. the same D. see above
   E. and so forth
5. IMPUGN means MOST NEARLY   5. ...
   A. enhance B. attribute C. assail D. compromise E. defend
6. INCIPIENT means MOST NEARLY   6. ...
   A. tasteless B. annoying C. unyielding D. ultimate
   E. commencing
7. INEXORABLE means MOST NEARLY   7. ...
   A. hateful B. conciliatory C. unresponsive D. relentless
   E. pliant
8. INTREPID means MOST NEARLY   8. ...
   A. awesome B. bellicose C. undisciplined D. courageous
   E. pacific
9. INVECTIVE means MOST NEARLY   9. ...
   A. self study B. geometrical analysis C. verbal abuse
   D. hard-won victory   E. indecision
10. INVEIGLED means MOST NEARLY   10. ...
    A. ensnared B. terrified C. coerced D. corrupted
    E. incarcerated

TEST 13

1. ITERANT means MOST NEARLY   1. ...
   A. distant B. repeating C. directed D. wandering
   E. errant
2. LAMPOON means MOST NEARLY   2. ...
   A. magazine B. satire C. clown D. lament E. shade
3. LAPIDARY means MOST NEARLY one who   3. ...
   A. collects butterflies B. breaks up large estates
   C. indulges the senses   D. judges the quality of beverages
   E. cuts precious stones
4. MERETRICIOUS means MOST NEARLY   4. ...
   A. according to the metric system B. deserving
   C. scholarly D. indigent E. tawdry
5. MITIGATE means MOST NEARLY   5. ...
   A. exonerate B. handicap C. aggravate D. appease
   E. defile

6. MORES means MOST NEARLY   6. ...
   A. beginnings B. conglomerations C. curses D. mutations
   E. customs
7. NOSTRUM means MOST NEARLY   7. ...
   A. ocean sea B. paternity C. remedy D. pungency E. family
8. OBJURGATE means MOST NEARLY   8. ...
   A. chide B. sacrifice C. oppose D. purge E. repeat
9. OSSIFY means MOST NEARLY   9. ...
   A. vacillate B. harden C. categorize D. tipple E. abstain
10. PARLOUS means MOST NEARLY   10. ...
   A. wise B. bargaining C. talkative D. dangerous
   E. partial

TEST 14

1. ADVENTITIOUS means MOST NEARLY   1. ...
   A. opportunistic B. daring C. helpful D. deceptive
   E. extrinsic
2. AMBIVALENT means MOST NEARLY   2. ...
   A. helpful in walking B. equally skillful with both hands
   C. simultaneously hating and loving D. ambiguous in origin
   E. equivalent
3. AMORPHOUS means MOST NEARLY   3. ...
   A. inelegant B. clamorous C. quiescent D. ardent
   E. formless
4. ANATHEMA means MOST NEARLY   4. ...
   A. despair B. benevolence C. disputation D. anomaly E. curse
5. APIARY means MOST NEARLY   5. ...
   A. bee house B. pear-shaped figure C. main-traveled road
   D. monkey cage   E. bird house
6. APOCRYPHAL means MOST NEARLY of   6. ...
   A. scholarly pursuits   B. sacred origin
   C. ancient beginnings   D. ecclesiastical power
   E. doubtful authenticity
7. APOSTASY means MOST NEARLY   7. ...
   A. confirmation B. defection C. supposition
   D. canonization E. deification
8. ASCETIC means MOST NEARLY   8. ...
   A. exclusive B. sharp C. fragrant D. austere E. authentic
9. BADINAGE means MOST NEARLY   9. ...
   A. indifference B. song C. banter D. mucilage E. autarchy
10. BOGGLE means MOST NEARLY   10. ...
   A. dampen B. hesitate C. undermine D. disarrange E. haggle

---

TEST 15

1. BUCOLIC means MOST NEARLY   1. ...
   A. rustic B. flatulent C. angry D. loud E. bureaucratic
2. CAESURA means MOST NEARLY   2. ...
   A. genesis B. referring to Caesar C. tyranny D. domain
   E. break
3. CAREEN means MOST NEARLY   3. ...
   A. lurch B. wail C. pour D. contain E. corrode

9

4. CARET means MOST NEARLY   4. ...
   A. measure of weight   B. sign of omission
   C. technique in ballet   D. growth of root
   E. notice for caution
5. CARIES means MOST NEARLY   5. ...
   A. treatment B. convalescent C. decay D. chemicals E. roots
6. CASUIST means MOST NEARLY   6. ...
   A. sophistical reasoner B. careless worker
   C. innocent victim D. habitual late-comer E. frenzied lawyer
7. CHIMERICAL means MOST NEARLY   7. ...
   A. scientific B. debasing C. well-ordered D. maniacal
   E. fanciful
8. CLABBER means MOST NEARLY   8. ...
   A. gossip B. climb C. crop D. entwine E. curdle
9. COMME IL FAUT means MOST NEARLY   9. ...
   A. unnecessary B. erroneous C. proper D. mixed
   E. illegal
10. CRYPTIC means MOST NEARLY   10. ...
   A. succinct B. astringent C. death-like D. crotchety
   E. occult

TEST 16

1. CYNOSURE means MOST NEARLY   1. ...
   A. act of completion B. occupation of ease
   C. attitude of doubt D. center of attraction
   E. cynical statement
2. DEBENTURE means MOST NEARLY   2. ...
   A. written acknowledgment of debt
   B. sale of preferred stock
   C. illegal sale of securities
   D. dividend on stocks or bonds
   E. disclaimer in a prospectus
3. DEMURRER means MOST NEARLY   3. ...
   A. promotion B. objection C. interrogation D. retainer
   E. demerit
4. DERELICTION means MOST NEARLY   4. ...
   A. general decline B. damaging criticism C. probable cause
   D. abandoned vessel   E. failure in duty
5. DESCRIED means MOST NEARLY   5. ...
   A. delimned B. defined C. rejected D. erred E. discerned
6. DESIDERATUM means MOST NEARLY   6. ...
   A. final outcome B. hearty approval C. last remnant
   D. desired object E. prescribed treatment
7. DISCRETE means MOST NEARLY   7. ...
   A. separate B. reserved C. foresighted D. unbounded
   E. tactful
8. DISINGENUOUS means MOST NEARLY   8. ...
   A. unsophisticated B. skillful C. apathetic D. naive
   E. insincere
9. DISSIDENT means MOST NEARLY   9. ...
   A. malodorous B. amoral C. discordant D. unfeeling
   E. divisive
10. EGREGIOUS means MOST NEARLY   10. ...
   A. debased B. inconsequential C. incorrigible
   D. egotistical E. prominent

TEST 17

1. EMPATHY means MOST NEARLY   1. ...
    A. comatose condition   B. sympathetic understanding
    C. depressed feeling   D. political subdivision
    E. patriotic devotion
2. ESOTERIC means MOST NEARLY   2. ...
    A. abstruse B. intestinal C. lively D. joining E. essential
3. ESPERANTO means MOST NEARLY   3. ...
    A. fabled country   B. artificial language
    C. European peace manifesto D. place of abandoned hope
    E. pertaining to the Elysian Fields
4. EUPHEMISM means MOST NEARLY   4. ...
    A. pleasant sight   B. right direction
    C. verbal platitude   D. buoyant feeling
    E. inoffensive expression
5. FINICAL means MOST NEARLY   5. ...
    A. blundering B. fastidious C. conclusive D. maniacal
    E. extravagant
6. GUERDON means MOST NEARLY   6. ...
    A. debacle B. shield C. fruit D. obstacle E. recompense
7. GYVES means MOST NEARLY   7. ...
    A. gallows B. chains C. barbs D. vegetables E. jives
8. HEDONIST means MOST NEARLY   8. ...
    A. reviler B. recluse C. pleasure-seeker D. savage E. hermit
9. HIATUS means MOST NEARLY   9. ...
    A. flower B. gap C. mistake D. digression E. hearsay
10. IMBROGLIO means MOST NEARLY   10. ...
    A. secluded dwelling   B. impassioned plea
    C. rampant destruction   D. petit point
    E. complicated situation

TEST 18

1. IMPALPABLE means MOST NEARLY not   1. ...
    A. truthful B. concrete C. throbbing D. deviating
    E. suggestive
2. IMPECUNIOUS means MOST NEARLY   2. ...
    A. poor B. wayward C. troublesome D. inordinate E. ingenuous
3. IMPORTUNATE means MOST NEARLY   3. ...
    A. critical B. empty-handed C. disastrous D. pusillanimous
    E. pressing
4. IMPRIMIS means MOST NEARLY   4. ...
    A. church dignitary B. sanction C. manuscript D. sacred song
    E. in the first place
5. INURED means MOST NEARLY   5. ...
    A. belligerent B. hardened C. apprehensive D. irreverent
    E. injured
6. INVIDIOUS means MOST NEARLY   6. ...
    A. obscure B. unconquerable C. offensive D. niggardly
    E. invariable
7. JOCOSE means MOST NEARLY   7. ...
    A. intemperate B. contemptuous C. morose D. nugatory
    E. facetious

8. LACHRYMOSE means MOST NEARLY   8. ...
   A. milky B. disdainful C. comic D. tearful E. comatose
9. LISSOME means MOST NEARLY   9. ...
   A. nimble B. comely C. laughable D. lackadaisical
   E. aggressive
10. MERCURIAL means MOST NEARLY   10. ...
    A. thermal B. coy C. volatile D. ponderous E. unchangeable

KEYS (CORRECT ANSWERS)

TEST 1		TEST 4		TEST 7		TEST 10		TEST 13		TEST 16	
1.	D	1.	C	1.	A	1.	C	1.	B	1.	D
2.	C	2.	D	2.	E	2.	B	2.	B	2.	A
3.	A	3.	B	3.	B	3.	A	3.	E	3.	B
4.	C	4.	C	4.	A	4.	C	4.	E	4.	E
5.	C	5.	D	5.	C	5.	E	5.	D	5.	E
6.	C	6.	E	6.	D	6.	A	6.	E	6.	D
7.	A	7.	B	7.	E	7.	D	7.	C	7.	A
8.	E	8.	B	8.	D	8.	A	8.	A	8.	E
9.	B	9.	A	9.	B	9.	E	9.	B	9.	C
10.	C	10.	E	10.	B	10.	E	10.	D	10.	E

TEST 2		TEST 5		TEST 8		TEST 11		TEST 14		TEST 17	
1.	A	1.	C	1.	C	1.	E	1.	E	1.	B
2.	B	2.	B	2.	B	2.	A	2.	C	2.	A
3.	C	3.	C	3.	C	3.	E	3.	E	3.	B
4.	B	4.	D	4.	D	4.	A	4.	E	4.	E
5.	A	5.	E	5.	A	5.	D	5.	A	5.	B
6.	C	6.	D	6.	D	6.	A	6.	E	6.	E
7.	E	7.	A	7.	D	7.	E	7.	B	7.	B
8.	B	8.	A	8.	E	8.	E	8.	D	8.	C
9.	A	9.	D	9.	A	9.	C	9.	C	9.	B
10.	D	10.	B	10.	E	10.	E	10.	B	10.	E

TEST 3		TEST 6		TEST 9		TEST 12		TEST 15		TEST 18	
1.	A	1.	A	1.	B	1.	B	1.	A	1.	B
2.	A	2.	B	2.	E	2.	E	2.	E	2.	A
3.	B	3.	E	3.	C	3.	A	3.	A	3.	E
4.	E	4.	A	4.	D	4.	C	4.	B	4.	E
5.	D	5.	B	5.	A	5.	C	5.	C	5.	B
6.	D	6.	D	6.	E	6.	E	6.	A	6.	C
7.	C	7.	D	7.	A	7.	D	7.	E	7.	E
8.	A	8.	B	8.	A	8.	D	8.	E	8.	D
9.	A	9.	B	9.	D	9.	C	9.	C	9.	A
10.	D	10.	C	10.	B	10.	A	10.	E	10.	C

SENTENCE COMPLETION

EXAMINATION SECTION

TEST 1

DIRECTIONS: Each question in this part consists of a sentence in which one word is missing; a blank line indicates where the word has been removed from the sentence. Beneath each sentence are five words, one of which is the missing word. You are to select the number of the missing word by deciding which one of the five words BEST fits in with the meaning of the sentence. *PRINT THE LETTER OF THE CORRECT ANSWER IN THE SPACE AT THE RIGHT.*

1. Although they had little interest in the game they were playing, rather than be _____, they played it through to the end.
   A. inactive   B. inimical   C. busy
   D. complacent   E. vapid

   1.____

2. That he was unworried and at peace with the world could be, perhaps, observed from his ____ brow.
   A. unwrinkled   B. wrinkled   C. furrowed
   D. twisted   E. askew

   2.____

3. Among the hundreds of workers in the assembly plant of the factory, one was ____ because of his skill and speed.
   A. steadfast   B. condemned   C. consistent
   D. outstanding   E. eager

   3.____

4. The story of the invention of many of our best known machines is a consistent one: they are the result of a long series of experiments by many people; thus, the Wright Brothers in 1903 ____ the airplane rather than invented it.
   A. popularized   B. regulated   C. perfected
   D. contrived   E. developed

   4.____

5. As soon as the former political exile returned to his native country, he looked up old supporters, particularly those whom he knew to be ____ and whose help he might need.
   A. potent   B. pusillanimous C. attentive
   D. free   E. retired

   5.____

6. A recent study of the New Deal shows that no other man than the President could have brought together so many ____ interests and combined them into so effective a political organization.
   A. secret   B. interior   C. predatory
   D. harmonious   E. conflicting

   6.____

2

7. A study of tides presents an interesting ____ in that, while the forces that set them in motion are universal in application, presumably affecting all parts of our world without distinction, the action of tides in particular areas is completely local in nature.
   A. phenomenon   B. maneuver   C. paradox
   D. quality   E. spontaneity

7.__

8. Many of the facts that are found in the ancient archives constitute ____ that help shed light upon human activities in the past.
   A. facts   B. reminders   C. particles
   D. sources   E. indications

8.__

9. It is a regrettable fact that in a caste society which deems manual toil a mark of ____, rarely does the laborer improve his social position or gain political power.
   A. inferiority   B. consolation   C. fortitude
   D. hardship   E. brilliance

9.__

10. As a generalization, one can correctly say that crises in history are caused by the re-opening of questions which have been safely ____ for long periods of time.
    A. debated   B. joined   C. recondite
    D. settled   E. unanswered

10.__

TEST 2

1. We can see in retrospect that the high hopes for lasting peace conceived at Versailles in 1919 were ____.
   A. ingenuous   B. transient   C. nostalgic
   D. ingenious   E. species

1.__

2. One of the constructive effects of Nazism was the passage by the U.N. of a resolution to combat ____.
   A. armaments   B. nationalism   C. colonialism
   D. genocide   E. geriatrics

2.__

3. In our prisons, the role of ____ often gains for certain inmates a powerful position among their fellow prisoners.
   A. informer   B. clerk   C. warden
   D. trusty   E. turnkey

3.__

4. It is the ____ liar, experienced in the ways of the world, who finally trips upon some incongruous detail.
   A. consummate   B. incorrigible   C. congenital
   D. flagrant   E. contemptible

4.__

5. Anyone who is called a misogynist can hardly be expected to look upon women with ____ contemptuous eyes.
   A. more than   B. nothing less than C. decidedly
   D. other than   E. always

5.__

6. Demagogues such as Hitler and Mussolini aroused the masses by appealing to their ____ rather than to their intellect.
   A. emotions   B. reason   C. nationalism
   D. conquests   E. duty
   6.___

7. He was in great demand as an entertainer for his ____ abilities: he could sing, dance, tell a joke, or relate a story with equally great skill and facility.
   A. versatile   B. logical   C. culinary
   D. histrionic   E. creative
   7.___

8. The wise politician is aware that, next to knowing when to seize an opportunity, it is also important to know when to ____ an advantage.
   A. develop B. seek   C. revise   D. proclaim E. forego
   8.___

9. Books on psychology inform us that the best way to break a bad habit is to ____ a new habit in its place.
   A. expel   B. substitute   C. conceal
   D. curtail   E. supplant
   9.___

10. The author who uses one word where another uses a whole paragraph, should be considered a ____ writer.
   A. successful   B. grandiloquent   C. succinct
   D. prolix   E. experienced
   10.___

TEST 3

1. The prime minister, fleeing from the rebels who had seized the government, sought ____ in the church.
   A. revenge   B. mercy   C. relief
   D. salvation   E. sanctuary
   1.___

2. It does not take us long to conclude that it is foolish to fight the ____, and that it is far wiser to accept it.
   A. inevitable   B. inconsequential C. impossible
   D. choice   E. invasion
   2.___

3. ____ is usually defined as an excessively high rate of interest.
   A. Injustice   B. Perjury   C. Exorbitant
   D. Embezzlement   E. Usury
   3.___

4. "I ask you, gentlemen of the jury, to find this man guilty since I have ____ the charges brought against him."
   A. documented   B. questioned   C. revised
   D. selected   E. confused
   4.___

5. Although the critic was a close friend of the producer, he told him that he could not ____ his play.
   A. condemn   B. prefer   C. congratulate
   D. endorse   E. revile
   5.___

6. Knowledge of human nature and motivation is an important _____ in all areas of endeavor.   6._____
   A. object   B. incentive   C. opportunity
   D. asset   E. goal

7. Numbered among the audience were kings, princes, dukes,   7._____
   and even a maharajah, all attempting to _____ one another
   in the glitter of their habiliments and the number of
   their escorts.
   A. supersede   B. outdo   C. guide
   D. vanquish   E. equal

8. There seems to be a widespread feeling that peoples who   8._____
   are located below us in respect to latitude are _____ also
   in respect to intellect and ability.
   A. superior   B. melodramatic   C. inferior
   D. ulterior   E. contemptible

9. This should be considered a(n) _____ rather than the usual   9._____
   occurrence.
   A. coincidence   B. specialty   C. development
   D. outgrowth   E. mirage

10. Those who were considered states' rights aherents in the   10._____
    early part of our history espoused the diminution of the
    powers of the national government because they had always
    been _____ of these powers.
    A. solicitous   B. advocates   C. apprehensive
    D. mindful   E. respectful

TEST 4

1. The life of the mining camps as portrayed by Bret Harte -   1._____
   boisterous, material, brawling - was in direct _____ to
   the contemporary Eastern world of conventional morals and
   staid deportment depicted by other men of letters.
   A. model   B. parallel   C. antithesis
   D. relationship   E. response

2. The agreements were to remain in force for three years   2._____
   and were subject to automatic _____ unless terminated by
   the parties concerned on one month's notice.
   A. renewal   B. abrogation   C. amendment
   D. confiscation   E. option

3. In a democracy, people are recognized for what they do   3._____
   rather than for their _____.
   A. alacrity   B. ability   C. reputation
   D. skill   E. pedigree

4. Although he had often loudly proclaimed his _____ concern-   4._____
   ing world affairs, he actually read widely and was usually
   the best informed person in his circle.
   A. weariness   B. complacency   C. condolence
   D. indifference   E. worry

5. This student holds the ____ record of being the sole failure in his class.   5.___
   A. flagrant   B. unhappy   C. egregious
   D. dubious   E. unusual

6. She became enamored ____ the acrobat when she witnessed his act.   6.___
   A. of   B. with   C. for   D. by   E. about

7. This will ____ all previous wills.   7.___
   A. abrogates   B. denies   C. supersedes
   D. prevents   E. continues

8. In the recent terrible Chicago ____, over ninety children were found dead as a result of the fire.   8.___
   A. hurricane   B. destruction   C. panic
   D. holocaust   E. accident

9. I can ascribe no better reason why he shunned society than that he was a ____.   9.___
   A. mentor   B. Centaur   C. aristocrat
   D. misanthrope   E. failure

10. One who attempts to learn all the known facts before he comes to a conclusion may most aptly be described as a ____.   10.___
   A. realist   B. philosopher   C. cynic
   D. pessimist   E. skeptic

TEST 5

1. The judge exercised commendable ____ in dismissing the charge against the prisoner. In spite of the clamor that surrounded the trial, and the heinousness of the offense, the judge could not be swayed to overlook the lack of facts in the case.   1.___
   A. avidity   B. meticulousness   C. clemency
   D. balance   E. querulousness

2. The pianist played the concerto ____, displaying such facility and skill as has rarely been matched in this old auditorium.   2.___
   A. strenuously   B. deftly   C. passionately
   D. casually   E. spiritedly

3. The Tanglewood Symphony Orchestra holds its outdoor concerts far from city turmoil in a ____, bucolic setting.   3.___
   A. spectacular   B. atavistic   C. serene
   D. chaotic   E. catholic

4. Honest satire gives true joy to the thinking man. Thus, the satirist is most ____ when he points out the hypocrisy in human actions.   4.___
   A. elated   B. humiliated   C. ungainly
   D. repressed   E. disdainful

5. She was a(n) ____ who preferred the company of her books 5.__
   to the pleasures of cafe society.
   A. philanthropist   B. stoic   C. exhibitionist
   D. extrovert   E. introvert

6. So many people are so convinced that people are driven by 6.__
   ____ motives that they cannot believe that anybody is
   unselfish!
   A. interior   B. ulterior   C. unworthy
   D. selfish   E. destructive

7. These ____ results were brought about by a chain of 7.__
   fortuitous events.
   A. unfortunate   B. odd   C. harmful
   D. haphazard   E. propitious

8. The bank teller's ____ of the funds was discovered the 8.__
   following month when the auditors examined the books.
   A. embezzlement   B. burglary   C. borrowing
   D. assignment   E. theft

9. The monks gathered in the ____ for their evening meal. 9.__
   A. lounge   B. auditorium   C. refectory
   D. rectory   E. solarium

10. Local officials usually have the responsibility in each 10.__
    area of determining when the need is sufficiently great
    to ____ withdrawals from the community water supply.
    A. encourage   B. justify   C. discontinue
    D. advocate   E. forbid

KEYS (CORRECT ANSWERS)

TEST 1	TEST 2	TEST 3	TEST 4	TEST
1. A	1. A	1. E	1. C	1. I
2. A	2. D	2. A	2. A	2. E
3. D	3. A	3. E	3. E	3. C
4. C	4. A	4. A	4. D	4. A
5. A	5. D	5. D	5. D	5. E
6. E	6. A	6. D	6. A	6. E
7. C	7. A	7. B	7. C	7. I
8. D	8. E	8. C	8. D	8. A
9. A	9. B	9. A	9. D	9. C
10. A	10. C	10. C	10. E	10. E

BASIC FUNDAMENTALS OF ENGLISH EXPRESSION

CONTENTS

———

BASIC FUNDAMENTALS OF ENGLISH EXPRESSION

A. FUNCTIONAL INTRODUCTION TO GRAMMAR
   For examination purposes, there are two clear-cut and yet related divisions in grammar: classification and syntax.
   <u>Classification</u> refers to the required nomenclature for the proper identification and description of the <u>uses</u> of words or groups of words.
   <u>Syntax</u> refers to the relations of words and groups of words with one another in sentences.
   The more usual terms of Classification are the following:

CLASSIFICATION

1. Nominative Absolute
2. Nominative of Direct Address
3. Nominative of Exclamation
4. Predicate Nominative
5. Predicate Adjective
6. Object of a Verb
7. Indirect Object
8. Object of a Preposition
9. Objective Complement
10. Adverbial Objective
11. Retained Object
12. Noun in Apposition
13. Auxiliary Verb
14. Copulative Verb
15. Progressive Forms of the Verb
16. Past Participle
17. Mood
18. Tense
19. Subject - complete subject, including modifiers
20. Predicate - verb and all modifiers and complements
21. Verbals

The more outstanding and the more frequently occurring types of syntactical relationships are defined in the illustrations appearing hereafter.

SYNTAX

I. <u>Uses of the Noun</u>
   A. Nominative Case:
      1. Subject of a verb: MARY bought a hat.
      2. Predicate Nominative: (Double Function)
         a. With a copulative verb: He became PRESIDENT. Is that the SORT of a person you take me for?
         b. With a verb in the passive voice: He was chosen PRESIDENT.
      3. Independent Constructions:
         a. Noun in Apposition with a noun in the nominative case: My sister, CLARA, is going with me.
         b. Nominative Absolute: The TRAIN having stopped, the passengers got out. James stood before me, his HANDS in his pocket
         c. Nominative of Direct Address: MARY, open the door.
         d. Nominative of Exclamation: What a MAN!
   B. Possessive Case:
      1. To show ownership: MARY'S hat is brown.
      2. To indicate the relation of the doer to an act expressed in a particular noun: MARY'S having her homework saved the day. (See Predicate Complement of Copulative Verbal, below)
   C. Objective Case: (Complements)
      1. Object of a
         a. Verb: The child ate the APPLE.
         b. Verbal:
            (1) Infinitive: At times, it's a pleasure to eat an APPLE.
            (2) Participle: Having lost the larger PART of his fortune, my friend found that economy was necessary.
            (3) Participial Noun: Eating an APPLE is a pleasure.

1

    c. Preposition: She gave the book to CLARA.
    d. Cognate Object: He spoke his SPEECH well.
    e. Secondary Object of a Verb or Verbal: He told John the
       ANSWER. He asked John a QUESTION. He paid his workers good
       WAGES. (Differs from the indirect object because the se-
       condary object can be dropped.)
  2. Indirect Object of a
    a. Verb: We gave JOHN our books.
    b. Verbal:
       (1) Infinitive: He asked us to give CATHERINE the money.
       (2) Participle: Giving my FRIEND the money I had borrowed
           I heaved a sigh of relief.
       (3) Participial Noun: Giving PEOPLE money makes most peop
           happier.
  3. Subject of an Infinitive: I expect JOHN to be present. Let
     ME rest!
  4. Objective Complement: (See Predicate Nominative with Passive
     Verb) We elected him PRESIDENT. The Romans called Caesar FRIEN
  5. Retained Object: (See 2a.) John was given our BOOKS.
  6. Adverbial Objective: I wanted to go HOME. The child is three
     YEARS old.
  7. Predicate Complement of Copulative Verbals:
    a. Referring back to the Subject of the Infinitive: I be-
       lieved Allen to be the MAN.
    b. Referring back to the noun modified by a participle:
         Or lonely house,
         Long held the witches' HOME.
    c. Referring back to the Possessive with the Participial
       Noun: There is sense in your hoping to be SECRETARY. I
       was sure of John's being the AGGRESSOR.
  8. Noun in Apposition with a noun in the objective case: I gave
     the song, SOPHISTICATED LADY, to my friend to play.
II. Uses of the Pronoun
  A. Personal Pronouns: Similar to nouns in use, but, in addition,
     they must agree with the antecedent in person, number, and ge
     der.
    1. Nominative Case:
      a. Subject of a verb: SHE bought a hat.
      b. Predicate Nominative with Copulative Verb: It is I
      c. Independent Construction:
         (1) Nominative Absolute: SHE being ill, we decided to go
         (2) Nominative of Direct Address: YOU, will you come!
         (3) Nominative of Exclamation: I! You cannot accuse me!
    2. Possessive Case:
      a. To show ownership: HER hat is brown.
      b. To indicate relation of doer to an act or state expresse
         in a participial noun: HIS having a car saved the day.
    3. Objective Case:
      a. Object of a
         (1) Verb: The child ate IT.
         (2) VERBAL:
             (a) Infinitive: At times it is a pleasure to eat IT.
             (b) Participle: Having lost IT, we hunted for anoth
             (c) Participial Noun: Taking IT in large doses is b
         (3) Preposition: She referred me to HIM for an answer.

2

      b. Indirect Object of a
        (1) Verb: We gave HIM our books.
        (2) Verbal:
            (a) Infinitive: He asked us to give HER the money.
            (b) Participle: Giving HIM the money I had borrowed,
                I heaved a sigh of relief.
            (c) Participial Noun: Giving HIM money made him un-
                happy.
      c. Subject of the Infinitive: I expected HIM to be present.
      d. Retained Object: He was given IT for his own use.
  B. Uses of "it":
    1. Impersonal Pronoun, subject of a verb when no definite subject
      is expressed: IT rains.
    2. Expletive, serving to introduce the verb "is" when the real
      subject is in the Predicate: IT may be true that he did not
      commit the crime.
  C. Compound Personal Pronouns:
    1. Intensively: I, MYSELF, will go.
    2. Reflexively: I have harmed MYSELF. The neighbors left us
      severely to OURSELVES.
  D. Interrogative Pronouns: Similar to personal pronouns in use,
    but, in addition, they assist in asking a question. WHO is that?
    WHOSE is that? WHOM do you expect? WHICH is the better student?
    WHAT is your aim in life? He asked me WHAT I had meant by that
    statement. (Indirect) WHO do you consider is the best agent the
    company has?
  E. Adjective (Demonstrative) Pronouns: Similar to personal pronouns
    in use. THIS is a new hat. THESE are very interesting books. The
    mountains of Colorado are higher than THOSE. I bought ONE, too.
  F. Relative Pronouns: Similar to personal pronouns in use, but, in
    addition, they connect the adjective clauses they introduce with
    the nouns or pronouns modified.
      That is the girl WHO is going with me.
      The men WHOM you see there are marines.
      The men WHOSE lights are lit are seniors.
      Ask her for the book WHICH I recommended.
      Tell her WHAT you have told me. (That which)
      That's WHAT I did it for.
      The book THAT I gave her is lost.
      This is the pillow THAT I asked for.
      Who do you consider is the best agent (THAT) the company has?
        (Elliptical use)
    Adjective clauses are also introduced by relative adverbs:
      There was one time WHEN I almost caught you.
      That is the house WHERE I was born.
  G. Compound relative pronouns:
    I will go with WHOEVER is going my way. (Implies own antece-
    dent: HIM WHO)
III. Uses of the Adjective
  A. Modifier of a noun (pronoun): That was an ORIENTAL rug. This
    dress is plainer than that PRETTY one. I must have the test-tube
    CLEAN. Of dark BROWN gardens and of PEEPING flowers.
  B. Predicate Adjective:
    1. With copulative verb: She was LAZY. This apple is RIPE.
    2. Passive Voice: This man was pronounced GUILTY.
  C. Objective Complement: I called the ship UNSEAWORTHY. I will make
    assurance doubly SURE. She wiped the plate DRY.

IV. Uses of the Adverb

A. Modifier of a verb: She walked RAPIDLY. This matter must be acted UPON.

B. Modifier of a verbal:
1. Infinitive: She attempted to walk RAPIDLY.
2. Participle: Having arrived SILENTLY, she overheard the conversation.
3. Participial Noun: Passing COMMENDABLY is our aim.

C. Modifier of an adjective: The ice was UNUSUALLY smooth this winter.

D. Modifier of another adverb: The wheels revolved VERY swiftly.

E. Modifier of a phrase or clause: He arrived JUST in time. That is EXACTLY what I expected of him.

F. As a relative or conjunctive adverb, introducing a clause and modifying the verb in this clause: I passed the house WHERE he was born. AS he rose from his chair, the audience burst into wild applause.

G. As an interrogative adverb, asking a direct or indirect question and modifying the verb: WHEN did you arrive? Tell us WHY he is always successful.

V. Uses of Verbals: Verbals take adverbial modifiers and complements.

A. The Infinitive.
1. As a noun
   a. Nominative Case:
      (1) Subject of Verb: TO EXIST is a hard job these days.
      (2) Predicate Nominative: Copulative Verb: To work is TO EAT.
      (3) Independent Constructions: Apposition: Our ambition, TO ACT, was never realized.
      (4) Nominative Absolute: To ENJOY ourselves being impossible, we left the theatre.
      (5) Exclamation: TO SOAR! TO SOAR above the earth with wings!
   b. Objective Case:
      (1) Object of a verb: The child asked TO SING. They expect TO TAKE one.
      (2) Object of a verbal: (Infinitive) It is never safe to ask TO GO. (Participle) Having asked TO LEAVE, he refused when the chance came. Bill Brown came asking TO BE ADMITTED to the house. (Participial Noun) Learning TO FLY is amusing.
      (3) Object of a Preposition: There was nothing to do but TO GO.
      (4) Retained Object: He was told TO GO.
      (5) Apposition with noun in objective case: We never realized our ambition, TO ACT.
      (6) Special Use: With an object noun or pronoun as its subject: I wrote for him TO COME. (Such phrases introduced by "for" are used as nouns.) He felt the ground TREMBLE.
2. As an adjective
   a. Modifying a noun: Houses TO RENT are scarce this year.
   b. Predicate Adjective: Our plan seemed TO WORK each day.
3. As an adverb
   a. Modifying a verb: Folks would laugh TO SEE a cindermaid at a court ball.

        b. Modifying an adjective: The army was ready TO MARCH.
        c. Modifying a verbal: (Participle) Having gone out TO SHOP,
           he could not be found. (Participial Noun) Trying TO STUDY
           is impossible.
     4 As part of the complement of a verb or preposition with a
        noun as subject: Let me GO!
     5. As an Independent Expression: TO LIVE! To live in utter for-
        getfulness.
  B. The Participle: The participial form of a verb used as an adjec-
     tive: The men HAVING WORKED steadily, the company decided to
     give them a raise. (Predicate Adjective) He appeared PANTING.
     (Objective Complement) I must have the test-tube CLEANED.
     Special Case: (1) With a noun in the nominative absolute con-
     struction: The day HAVING DAWNED, we started on our trip. (2)
     In rare cases, as an adverb: He ran CRYING down the street.
  C. The Participal Noun: The participial form of a verb used as a
     noun. (Subject) SEEING is believing. (Predicate Nominative)See-
     ing is BELIEVING. (Apposition) The sport, SKATING, is an excit-
     ing one. (Nominative Absolute) SKATING being over, the children
     went home. (With Possessive Pronoun) MARY'S swimming did not
     succeed very well. (Object of verb) I love SKATING. (Object of
     Verbal) He wanted to go SKATING. (Object of a Preposition) The
     pleasure lies in EATING. We went SKATING. (Retained Object) The
     children were given WEAVING to do. (Adverbial Objective) That
     is worth THINKING about. The water was BOILING hot.
VI. Uses of Phrases
  A. As nouns:
     1. The Infinitive Phrase: His aim is TO BE WELL.
     2. Participial Noun Phrase: His only pleasure is BEING WELL.
        MENDING BROKEN CHINA was his occupation.
  B. As adjectives:
     1. Prepositional Phrase:(Modifier of a Noun) The trees OF THE
        FOREST are fading. (Predicate Adjective) The sun is IN ITS
        SPLENDOR.
     2. Infinitive Phrase: (Modifier of a Noun) The house TO BE SOLD
        was burned. (Predicate Adjective) The house was TO BE SOLD.
     3. Participial Phrase: (Modifier of Noun) RUNNING AWAY, he was
        shot.
  C. As adverbs:
     1. Prepositional Phrase: Frank came A-RUNNING. Tom ran crying
        DOWN THE STREET. The room was full OF PEOPLE.
     2. Infinitive Phrase: Folks would laugh TO SEE a cindermaid at
        a ball.
  D. As Independent Elements: It is true, TO BE SURE. It is better,
     IN MY OPINION, to face the situation directly.
VII. Uses of Subordinate Clauses
  A. Noun Clauses: Introduced by subordinating conjunctions such as
     THAT, WHETHER; interrogative pronouns in indirect questions,such
     as WHO, WHICH, WHAT; interrogative adverbs in indirect questions,
     such as WHERE, WHEN, WHY, HOW; all illustrated below.
     1. Subject of a Verb: THAT WE HAVE SURVIVED THE ORDEAL is evident.
     2. Predicate Nominative: The truth is THAT HE FAILED TO PASS.
     3. Noun in Apposition: The fact THAT THE EARTH IS ROUND is never
        disputed.
     4. Object of a Verb or Verbal: Tell me WHERE IS FANCY BRED. I
        wish HE WOULD HELP ME. I begged him to tell me WHAT HE WANTED.
        I asked him just WHAT HE REPORTED.

5. Object of a Preposition: I am going there no matter WHAT YOU SAY. We came to the conclusion from WHAT WE KNOW.
6. Retained Object: He was asked just WHAT HE REPORTED. I was asked WHETHER I ENJOY READING.
7. Special Construction: In apposition with the expletive IT: It is commonly known THAT HE CANNOT BE TRUSTED.

B. Adjective Clauses: Introduced by
relative pronoun, WHO, WHICH, WHAT, THAT;
relative adverb, WHERE, WHEN, AFTER.
1. Modifier of a Noun: Thrice is he armed WHO HATH HIS QUARREL JUST. There is society WHERE NONE INTRUDES. I remember the house WHERE I WAS BORN. Who do you consider is the best agen THE COMPANY HAS?

C. Adverbial Clauses: Introduced by
relative (or conjunctive) adverbs;
subordinating conjunctions such as BECAUSE, IF, SINCE, THOUG
1. Modifier of a Verb, Verbal, Adjective, Adverb: Try AS WE MAY we cannot swim to that rock. I intend to leave WHEN YOU GO. We are glad THAT YOU ARE WITH US. WHERE THE BEE SUCKS, ther suck I.

D. Independent Clause Element: Who DO YOU CONSIDER is the best age the company has? He is, I THINK, able to do the work well.

VIII. **Uses of the Verb**
A. Types of verbs
1. Transitive verbs
   a. These require direct objects to complete the meaning: John ATE the <u>apple.</u> (direct object)
2. Intransitive verbs
   a. These do <u>not</u> require an object to complete the meaning: The boy RAN down the mountain. (Common causes of error ar the misuse of the intransitive verbs RISE, LIE, and SIT and/or the transitive verbs RAISE, LAY, and SET: She LAID on the bed, for She LAY on the bed.
3. Copulative verbs
   a. These verbs, especially forms of the verb TO BE, are used to express simply the relationship between the subject an the predicate (or complement): She LOOKS good; The meat SMELLS bad; I FEEL better. (The most common copulative verbs are: BE, SEEM, PROVE, FEEL, SOUND, LOOK, APPEAR, BECOME, TASTE.)
4. Auxiliary verbs
   a. These verbs assist in forming the voices, modes, and ten-ses of other verbs: She SHOULD go; They HAVE BEEN gone a month; We WERE given the information. (The most common auxiliary verbs are: BE, HAVE, DO, SHALL, WILL, MAY, CAN, MUST, OUGHT, with all their inflectional forms.)

B. Tenses of verbs (Verbs appear in different forms to indicate t time of the action):
1. Present tense: The boy CARRIES the book; She EATS cookies.
2. Past tense: The men COMPLETED the job; We VISITED him at ho
3. Future tense: We WILL DO the job tomorrow; I SHALL GO alone
   a. In speech and in informal writing, WILL and WOULD are no commonly used for all three persons except for the use o SHOULD to express obligation.
   b. In formal writing and careful usage, the following disti tions are observed between SHALL and WILL:

(1) To express simple futurity, use SHALL (or SHOULD) with the first person, and WILL (or WOULD) with the second or third persons: I SHALL be glad to go; They WOULD like to go.

(2) To express determination, intention, etc., use WILL (or WOULD) with the first person, and SHALL (or SHOULD) with the second and third persons: I WILL do it; You SHALL not go; They SHALL not pass.

(3) In questions, use SHALL with the first person: SHALL we see you tonight? SHALL I do it now? With the second person, use the form that is expected in the answer: WILL you lend us the car? (The answer that is expected here is: I WILL or I WILL not.) With the third person, use WILL to express simple futurity: WILL there be someone to meet him at the train?

(4) In indirect discourse, use the auxiliary that would be used if the discourse were direct: The company asked him whether he WOULD pay the bill. (Direct discourse: WILL you pay the bill?) He stated that he WOULD undertake the mission. (Direct discourse: I WILL undertake the mission.) His wife asked him whether he SHOULD be late for supper. (Direct discourse: SHALL you be late for supper?)

4. Present perfect tense: I HAVE BEEN LIVING here for three years.
5. Past perfect tense: He HAD BEEN CONVICTED of a crime many years ago.
6. Future perfect tense: Before you arrive, I SHALL HAVE BAKED the pie.

C. Mood (Mode) (The forms of a verb that indicate the manner of the action):
1. Indicative Mood (used to state a fact or to ask a question): The man FELL; ARE you well?
2. Imperative Mood (used to express a command or an urgent request): DO it at once; ANSWER the telephone.
3. Subjective Mood (used to express a wish, a supposition, a doubt, an exhortation, a concession, a condition contrary to fact):
Wish: If only I WERE able to run faster!
Supposition: They will be married provided their parents CONSENT.
Condition contrary to fact: If you HAD more experience, you would know how to handle the problem.

IX. Special Uses
A. Common Words Used as Different Parts of Speech:
1. But: as relative pronoun: There is none BUT will answer.
as adverb: You are BUT half awake. (only)
as a preposition: Every man BUT him may leave. (except)
I cannot BUT feel cherful.(except to feel)
as a coordinating conjunction: He leaves BUT I stay.
2. Like: (Never used as a conjunction)
as a preposition: He talks LIKE his mother.
as a verb: I LIKE his manner of speech.
3. As: as a relative pronoun: You own the same AS I.
as an adverb: I am AS young as you are.
as a subordinating conjunction: I am as young AS you are.
as a preposition:He has frequently appeared AS Hamlet.
4. Than:as a preposition:He loves money more THAN learning.
as a subordinating conjunction: He knows more THAN I.

7

B. BASIC SYNTAX
(NOTE: Rules are numbered for reference.)

A <u>noun</u> is the name of a person, place, object, or idea.
A <u>pronoun</u> is a word used in place of a noun.
Nouns and pronouns are called <u>substantives.</u>
   1. The subject of a verb is in the <u>nominative</u> case.
    The <u>boy</u> threw the ball.
Transitive verbs express action upon an object or product.
   2. The direct object of a transitive verb is in the <u>objective</u> (<u>accusative</u>) case. <u>Whom</u> shall I fear?
   Intransitive verbs are often followed by substantives which rename their subject. Such complements are called <u>predicate nominatives</u>, <u>predicate nouns,</u> or <u>attribute complements.</u>
   3. A substantive used as <u>attribute complement</u> agrees in case with the subject to which it refers.
    It is <u>I</u>. <u>Whom</u> do you take me to be?
A substantive which helps to complete a verb but renames the object of the verb is called an <u>objective complement</u>.
   4. An <u>objective complement</u> is in the <u>objective</u> case.
    The class elected him <u>president</u>.
   5. The <u>object of a preposition</u> is in the <u>objective case</u>.
    Give it to <u>me</u>. The cat is under the <u>stove</u>.
The receiver of an action may sometimes be thought of as the principal word in an adverbial phrase from which the preposition <u>to</u> or <u>for</u> is omitted. Such a complement is called an <u>indirect object.</u>
   6. An <u>indirect object</u> is in the <u>objective</u> case (dative object).
    Bring <u>me</u> a chair.
<u>Infinitives</u> and <u>participles</u> do not really assert action or being, but they imply it, and in this sense may have subjects.
   Verbs of wishing, desiring, commanding, believing, declaring, perceiving, etc., are likely to be followed by objects which are at the same time <u>subjects of verbals</u>. It is this objective relation which justifies Rule 7.
   7. The subject of a verbal is in the <u>objective case</u>. (Except in independent phrases.)
    She has <u>me</u> to protect her. We thought <u>him</u> to be honest.
   8. Substantives used with verbals in independent phrases are in the <u>nominative case</u>. ("Absolute.")
    His <u>friends</u> advising it, he resigned.
An appositive is a noun or pronoun used as explanatory of or equivalent to another noun or pronoun.
   9. An appositive takes the case of the substantive to which it is attached.
    The book was his, <u>Peter's</u>. (Possessive.)
    'Tis I, Hamlet, the <u>Dane</u>. (Nominative.)
    Give it to me your <u>brother</u>.(Objective.)
   10. A noun or pronoun <u>independent by address</u> is in the <u>nominative</u> case. ("Vocative".)
    "<u>Mens of Athens</u>, _____Him declare I unto you."
    <u>Mr. President</u>, I rise to a point of order.

11. A noun or pronoun used <u>independently with a following adjective, adverb, or phrase</u> may best be regarded as in the objective case, since it is virtually the object in a prepositional phrase from which the preposition is omitted.

<u>Hat in hand</u>, he stood waiting
<u>Beard unkempt</u>, <u>clothes threadbare</u>, he looked down and out.
<u>Fences down</u>, <u>weeds everywhere</u>, the place was desolate.

12. Nouns or pronouns showing ownership are in the <u>possessive</u> case.

<u>John's</u> farm; <u>your</u> shoes.

13. When an inanimate thing is personified, the <u>gender</u> of its noun or pronoun is determied by custom.

<u>She's</u> a good old boat! (Feminine.)
The <u>sun</u> is hiding <u>his</u> head. (Masculine.)

14. <u>Collective nouns are plural</u> when their units act separately as individuals; <u>singular</u> when the units act together as one. <u>Plural titles</u> are in this sense <u>singular</u> nouns.

The class has had its picture taken. (All together.)
The class have had their pictures taken. (Each person by himself.)
"The Newcomes" is by Thackeray.

15. <u>Nouns used adverbially</u> to measure time or distance are in the <u>objective case</u>. (<u>Adverbial objective</u>.)

We walked an <u>hour</u>, travelled four <u>miles</u>.

16. A <u>substantive</u> used as an exclamation is commonly held to be nominative. But if the exclamation repeats an idea already used, it will take the case of the term repeated.

We shall be rich. <u>We</u>! think of that!
"We'll make you do <u>it</u>!" <u>Me</u>! I guess not!

17. A <u>pronoun</u> must agree with its antecedent in <u>number</u>, <u>gender</u>, and <u>person</u>. Collective nouns take singular pronouns when the units act separately

The Ship of State has refused to obey <u>her</u> rudder.
<u>That</u> is <u>he whom</u> you seek. (All three are in 3rd Person, Masculine Gender, Singular Number.)
The <u>case</u> of a pronoun does not depend upon its antecedent, but upon its use in the sentence.
A verb is a word which asserts. (Tells something of its subject.)

18. A verb agrees with its subject in person and number.

I <u>am</u>; You <u>are</u>; He <u>is</u>; She <u>goes</u>; They <u>go</u> .

19. A compound subject with <u>and</u> takes a singular verb if the idea of the combined subject is of <u>one</u> thing; if the compound subject is made of parts acting separately, the verb is <u>plural</u>.

Roosevelt and Wilson <u>were</u> of opposing parties.
The sum and substance of the matter <u>is</u> this.

20. A <u>distributive</u> subject with <u>each</u>, <u>every</u>, <u>everyone</u>, <u>either</u>, <u>neither</u>, etc., requires a verb in the <u>singular</u>; a disjunctive subject with <u>either-or</u>, <u>neither-nor</u>, takes a verb in the <u>singular</u> if the substantives are singular.

<u>Either</u> the book or the teacher <u>is</u> wrong.
<u>Each</u> of us must use his own judgment.

21. <u>Nouns plural in form</u> but singular in meaning commonly take a verb in the <u>singular</u>.

Hydraulics <u>is</u> a practical study nowadays.
Mumps <u>is</u> contagious.
The news <u>is</u> discouraging.

22. When the subject acts upon an object, the verb is in the _active voice_; when the subject is a receiver or product of action, the verb is _passive_.

The hunter _shot_ the door. (Active.)

The deer _was shot_ by the hunter. (Passive.)

23. The _indicative mood_ is used in questions and in simple assertions of fact or matter thought of as possible fact.

Were you there?

You _were_ there.

If you _were_ there, I did not see you. (See subjunctive mood, Rule 24.)

24. The _subjunctive mood_ expresses a wish, or a _condition contrary to fact_.

Would he _were_ here!

If he _were_ here, we would know about it.

(Implying denial. He has not been here.)

25. The _imperative mood_ states a command or request.

Please _go_ at once.

The subject of an imperative verb is _you_ understood; the _you_ is seldom expressed, unless the mood is emphatic.

26. _Infinitives_ may be used as _subject_, _object of verb_, _attribute complement_, _object of preposition_, _appositive_, _adjective modifier_, _adverbial modifier_, or in an _independent phrase_.

For examples, see discussion of _Verbals_ in this section.

27. _Gerunds_ (Verbal nouns in _ing_) have the uses of _nouns_ together with the power of implying action, being or condition.

Examples have been given under _uses_ of Verbals.

28. _Participles_ may be used as _adjectives_, _adverbs_, _subjective complements_, _objective complements_, _following a preposition_, or in _absolute phrases_.

See examples under Verbals.

29. The comparative degree of adjectives and adverbs, not the superlative degree, is used in comparing two persons or things.

He is the _taller_ of the two; in fact, the _tallest_ of the three.

30. A _coordinating conjunction_ connects words, phrases, or clauses of like rank, grammatically independent of each other.

I will come if I can _and_ if the weather is good.

31. A _subordinating conjunction_ joins a dependent clause to a principal one.

Make hay _while_ the sun shines.

32. _Interjections_ commonly have no grammatical relation in the sentence. In certain constructions, however, the interjection seems to have a phrasal modifier.

"Ah! for the pirate's dream of fight!"

33. Verbs _become_, _feel_, _look_, _see_, _smell_, _taste_, _sound_, _grow_ may take an _attribute complement_ to describe the subject, or an _adverb_ to modify the assertion of the verb.

He grew _tall_. Poisonous mushrooms taste _good_.

"He looks _well_" may describe his own condition, and so the word _well_ may be a predicate adjective relating to the subject; or the sentence may mean that he _searches thoroughly_, in which sense _well_ is an adverb modifying _looks_.

34. _Assertions of Simple Futurity_ take the form

I, we	shall
You	will
He, they	will

Assertions of Strong Purpose, Promise, Threat, Consent take the
form   I, we   will
           You   shall
           He, they   shall

35. Adjectives should not take the place of adverbs, nor adverbs the place of adjectives.

36. The six tenses of English verbs in the Active Voice, Indicative Mood, are built up from the "principal parts" as follows:

Present Tense, Past Tense, as in Principal Parts, Future Tense, shall or will (Rule 34) with Present Infinitive (less "to").

Present Perfect, have or has, with Past Participle Past Perfect, had, with Past Participle.

Future Perfect, shall or will (Rule 34), with Present Perfect, the "have" form.

37. The six tenses of English verbs in the Passive Voice, Indicative Mood, invariably use the past participle of the given verb, preceded by an appropriate form of the verb "be."

38. Gerunds, being verbal nouns, are modified by adjectives and possessive pronouns.

Now do it without my watching you.

————

C. COMMON ERRORS IN USAGE

(Numbers refer to rules in the preceding section. Correct forms are given first.)

	RULE
This is the better of the two. *NOT* this is the best of the two	(29)
You and I did it. *NOT* you and me did it, *NOR* me and you.	(1)
We boys will be there. *NOT* us boys will be there.	(1)
It was I, she, he, they. *NOT* me, her, him, them.	(3)
We believed it to be her, him, them. *NOT* she, he, they.	(3)
Between you and me. *NOT* between you and I.	(5)
She is taller than I (am). *NOT* she is taller than me.	(1)
It was known to be he. *NOT* him. He agrees with "It."	(3)
We were sure of its being him. (Usage divided.)	(3, 5)
Let everybody bring his own lunch. *NOT* their own.	(14, 17, 24)
We should all bring our lunches. (Action concerted.)	(17)
Every boy and girl should do his best. Their would be incorrect.	
His or her is correct, for formal.	(17)
Each of us has his problems. *NOT* have their.	(20)
The actor whom you saw was Otis Skinner. *NOT* who.	(2)
Whom did you call for? *NOT* who.	(5)
Whom did you select? *NOT* who.	(2)
Who do you suppose it is? Who agrees with it.	(3)
Who do you think I am? *NOT* whom. Agrees with I.	(3)
Whom did you take me to be? Whom agrees with me.	(3)
The tree looks beautiful. *NOT* beautifully.	(33)
The apple tastes good. *NOT* well.	(33)
The tune sounds harsh.	(33)
Roses smell sweet. *NOT* sweetly.	(33)
She looks charming. *NOT* charmingly.	(33)
We shall be drowned if we go there. *NOT* we will be	(34)

I _shall_ be pleased to help you. _NOT_ _will_ be.   (34)
The senate has adjourned. _NOT_ _have_ adjourned.   (14)
There _are_ all sorts of graft in town. _NOT_ there _is_ all sorts.   (18)
Here _are_ wealth and beauty. _NOT_ here _is_. (Unless taken separately.)(18)
Neither of the men _shows_ signs of giving in. _NOT_ neither show.   (18)
In both cases, there _are_ bad birth and misfortune. _NOT_ there is.
    (Unless taken separately.)   (18)
Our class poet _believes_ in symbolism. _NOT_ _believe_.   (18)
He is one of the best actors _that have ever_ been here. _NOT_ _has_. (17,18)
Let _him_ who will, come. _NOT_ let _he_.   (2)
The congregation _were_ free to express their opinions, _OR_ _was_ free   (14)
    to express its opinions.
I _saw_. _NOT_ I _seen_.   (36)
I _did_. _NOT_ I _done_.   (36)
We _have gone_. _NOT_ _have went_.   (36)
We _were_. _NOT_ we _was_.   (18)
You _began_ it. _NOT_ you _begun_ it.   (36)
The wind _blew_. _NOT_ the wind _blowed_.   (36)
The glass is _broken_. _NOT_ _broke_.   (37)
I _caught_, _have caught_. _NOT_ _catched_, _have catched_.   (36)
Have been _chosen_. _NOT_ have been _chose_.   (37)
We _came_ along. _NOT_ we _come_.   (36)
We _have_ come. _NOT_ _have_ came.   (36)
The baby _crept_. _NOT_ _creeped_.   (36)
You've _done_ it. _NOT_ you've _did_ it.   (36)
We _drew_. _NOT_ we _drawed_.   (36)
He _has drunk_ a glassful. _NOT_ _has drank_   (36)
Have _driven_. _NOT_ have _drove_.   (36)
Have _eaten_. _NOT_ have _ate_.   (36)
I _ate_ my dinner. _NOT_ _eat_   (36)
Has _fallen_. _NOT_ has _fell_.   (36)
The boys _fought_. _NOT_ _fit_.   (36)
Has _flown_. _NOT_ has _flew_.   (36)
I've _forgotten_. _NOT_ _forgot_.   (36)
It _grew_. _NOT_ it _growed_.   (36)
You _lie_ low. _NOT_ _lay_ low. (Lie,to recline;lay,to put down.)   (36)
Have _ridden_. _NOT_ have _rode_.   (36)
We _rang_ the bell. _NOT_ we _rung_ it.   (36)
Had _risen_. _NOT_ had _rose_.   (36)
And then I _ran_ away. _NOT_ then I _run_ away.   (36)
We _sang_ a song. _NOT_ we _sung_ it.   (36)
Troubles _sprang_ up. _NOT_ troubles _sprung_ up.   (36)
Somebody has _stolen_ my hat. _NOT_ has _stole_.   (36)
The place _stunk_. _NOT_ _stank_.   (36)
We _swam_ a mile. _NOT_ we _swum_.   (36)
Who's _taken_ my hat? _NOT_ who's _took_?   (36)
Have _torn_. _NOT_ have _tore_.   (36)
Have _written_. _NOT_ have _wrote_.   (36)
Say it _slowly_. _NOT_ _slow_.   (35)
We can do that as _easily_ as you please. _NOT_ as _easy_.   (35)
The horse threw my brother and _me_ out. _NOT_ my brother and _I_.   (2)
We chose the foreman _who_ we thought could handle the men. _NOW_ whom. (1)
I never saw a taller man than _he_. _NOT_ _him_.   (1)
There isn't another girl in town so handsome as _she_. _NOT_ _her_.   (1)
MOSSES FROM AN OLD MANSE _is_ a collection of essays and stories.
    NOT _are_ a collection.   (14)
Now skate without _my_ helping you. _NOT_ _me_ helping.   (38)
We ought to keep still about _his_ being here. _NOT_ _him_ being.   (38)

ANSWER SHEET

PART _____ TITLE OF POSITION _____

(AS GIVEN IN EXAMINATION ANNOUNCEMENT - INCLUDE OPTION, IF ANY)

EXAMINATION _____ DATE _____

(CITY OR TOWN)   (STATE)

RATING

USE THE SPECIAL PENCIL.   MAKE GLOSSY BLACK MARKS.

	A	B	C	D	E			A	B	C	D	E			A	B	C	D	E			A	B	C	D	E			A	B	C	D	E
1							26							51							76							101					
2							27							52							77							102					
3							28							53							78							103					
4							29							54							79							104					
5							30							55							80							105					
6							31							56							81							106					
7							32							57							82							107					
8							33							58							83							108					
9							34							59							84							109					
10							35							60							85							110					

Make only ONE mark for each answer.   Additional and stray marks may be counted as mistakes.   In making corrections, erase errors COMPLETELY.

	A	B	C	D	E			A	B	C	D	E			A	B	C	D	E			A	B	C	D	E			A	B	C	D	E
11							36							61							86							111					
12							37							62							87							112					
13							38							63							88							113					
14							39							64							89							114					
15							40							65							90							115					
16							41							66							91							116					
17							42							67							92							117					
18							43							68							93							118					
19							44							69							94							119					
20							45							70							95							120					
21							46							71							96							121					
22							47							72							97							122					
23							48							73							98							123					
24							49							74							99							124					
25							50							75							100							125					

ANSWER SHEET

TEST NO. _____ PART _____ TITLE OF POSITION _____

PLACE OF EXAMINATION _____ DATE _____

(CITY OR TOWN)   (STATE)

RATING

USE THE SPECIAL PENCIL.   MAKE GLOSSY BLACK MARKS.

	A B C D E		A B C D E		A B C D E		A B C D E		A B C D E
1	:: :: :: :: ::	26	:: :: :: :: ::	51	:: :: :: :: ::	76	:: :: :: :: ::	101	:: :: :: :: ::
2	:: :: :: :: ::	27	:: :: :: :: ::	52	:: :: :: :: ::	77	:: :: :: :: ::	102	:: :: :: :: ::
3	:: :: :: :: ::	28	:: :: :: :: ::	53	:: :: :: :: ::	78	:: :: :: :: ::	103	:: :: :: :: ::
4	:: :: :: :: ::	29	:: :: :: :: ::	54	:: :: :: :: ::	79	:: :: :: :: ::	104	:: :: :: :: ::
5	:: :: :: :: ::	30	:: :: :: :: ::	55	:: :: :: :: ::	80	:: :: :: :: ::	105	:: :: :: :: ::
6	:: :: :: :: ::	31	:: :: :: :: ::	56	:: :: :: :: ::	81	:: :: :: :: ::	106	:: :: :: :: ::
7	:: :: :: :: ::	32	:: :: :: :: ::	57	:: :: :: :: ::	82	:: :: :: :: ::	107	:: :: :: :: ::
8	:: :: :: :: ::	33	:: :: :: :: ::	58	:: :: :: :: ::	83	:: :: :: :: ::	108	:: :: :: :: ::
9	:: :: :: :: ::	34	:: :: :: :: ::	59	:: :: :: :: ::	84	:: :: :: :: ::	109	:: :: :: :: ::
10	:: :: :: :: ::	35	:: :: :: :: ::	60	:: :: :: :: ::	85	:: :: :: :: ::	110	:: :: :: :: ::

Make only ONE mark for each answer.   Additional and stray marks may be
counted as mistakes.   In making corrections, erase errors COMPLETELY.

	A B C D E		A B C D E		A B C D E		A B C D E		A B C D E
11	:: :: :: :: ::	36	:: :: :: :: ::	61	:: :: :: :: ::	86	:: :: :: :: ::	111	:: :: :: :: ::
12	:: :: :: :: ::	37	:: :: :: :: ::	62	:: :: :: :: ::	87	:: :: :: :: ::	112	:: :: :: :: ::
13	:: :: :: :: ::	38	:: :: :: :: ::	63	:: :: :: :: ::	88	:: :: :: :: ::	113	:: :: :: :: ::
14	:: :: :: :: ::	39	:: :: :: :: ::	64	:: :: :: :: ::	89	:: :: :: :: ::	114	:: :: :: :: ::
15	:: :: :: :: ::	40	:: :: :: :: ::	65	:: :: :: :: ::	90	:: :: :: :: ::	115	:: :: :: :: ::
16	:: :: :: :: ::	41	:: :: :: :: ::	66	:: :: :: :: ::	91	:: :: :: :: ::	116	:: :: :: :: ::
17	:: :: :: :: ::	42	:: :: :: :: ::	67	:: :: :: :: ::	92	:: :: :: :: ::	117	:: :: :: :: ::
18	:: :: :: :: ::	43	:: :: :: :: ::	68	:: :: :: :: ::	93	:: :: :: :: ::	118	:: :: :: :: ::
19	:: :: :: :: ::	44	:: :: :: :: ::	69	:: :: :: :: ::	94	:: :: :: :: ::	119	:: :: :: :: ::
20	:: :: :: :: ::	45	:: :: :: :: ::	70	:: :: :: :: ::	95	:: :: :: :: ::	120	:: :: :: :: ::
21	:: :: :: :: ::	46	:: :: :: :: ::	71	:: :: :: :: ::	96	:: :: :: :: ::	121	:: :: :: :: ::
22	:: :: :: :: ::	47	:: :: :: :: ::	72	:: :: :: :: ::	97	:: :: :: :: ::	122	:: :: :: :: ::
23	:: :: :: :: ::	48	:: :: :: :: ::	73	:: :: :: :: ::	98	:: :: :: :: ::	123	:: :: :: :: ::
24	:: :: :: :: ::	49	:: :: :: :: ::	74	:: :: :: :: ::	99	:: :: :: :: ::	124	:: :: :: :: ::
25	:: :: :: :: ::	50	:: :: :: :: ::	75	:: :: :: :: ::	100	:: :: :: :: ::	125	:: :: :: :: ::